Political Theology in the Canadian Context

edited by Benjamin G. Smillie

Published for the Canadian Corporation for Studies in Religion / Corporation Canadienne des Sciences Religieuses by Wilfrid Laurier University Press

Canadian Cataloguing in Publication Data

Main entry under title:
Political theology in the Canadian context

(SR supplements ; 11)
Proceedings of a conference held at the University of Saskatchewan, Saskatoon, March 10-11, 1977.
Includes index.
ISBN 0-919812-16-3

1. Christianity and politics – Canada – Congresses.
2. Religion and politics – Canada – Congresses.
I. Smillie, Benjamin G. (Benjamin Galletly), 1923-
II. Series.

BR115.P7P64 261.7 C82-094587-0

83 84 85 4 3 2

Cover design by Michael Baldwin, MSIAD

Order from:
Wilfrid Laurier University Press
Wilfrid Laurier University
Waterloo, Ontario, Canada N2L 3C5

CONTENTS

LIST OF TABLES

PREFACE

Tommy Douglas tells a revealing story about two questions that have been put to him in his long and colourful life in politics. He reports that when he was first elected to parliament shortly after leaving the ministry of the Baptist Church at Weyburn, Saskatchewan, people would ask him, "Why are you, a minister of the gospel, involved in politics?" Now, after thirty years in politics, he explains that the question has been reversed. It now comes out, "Why do you, a well-known politician, have anything to do with the church?" Certainly in Saskatchewan, a province that has been called the Athens of Canadian politics, the intensity with which political discussion takes place might lead the observer to come to the conclusion that politics has replaced religion.

We hope that the papers and the discussion that grew out of a conference on "Political Theology in the Canadian Context" will show that theology is at its best when it is political, and politics is saved from a secular idolatry when it listens to a theological critique.

1. Why a Conference on Political Theology?

The Planning Committee had three reasons for holding a Conference on "Political Theology in the Canadian Context" on March 10 and 11, 1977, at the University of Saskatchewan in Saskatoon. First, we were given an initial impetus by what the generosity of the Canada Council makes possible when it encourages the holding of "occasional conferences for scholars wishing to exchange experiences, acquaint themselves with the work of colleagues and coordinate their activities in specific areas of study and research."[1] Those of us who teach in universities are only too well aware of the danger of academic scholarship limiting itself to those within its discipline. Consequently, a "Berlin Wall" is erected around areas of specialty, which leads to incestuous discussion, and this is a particular problem in theology. To help widen the discussion, we invited Kai Nielsen from the Philosophy Department at the University of Calgary, Abraham Rotstein from the Department of Political Economy, University

1. Aid to Humanities and Social Societies (Ottawa, 1974), p. 16.

of Toronto, and Yves Vaillancourt from the University of Quebec's Political Science Department.

A second reason the planners of the Conference had for focusing on this subject was that to the best of our knowledge there has never been an opportunity for Canadian scholars to meet on the subject of political theology. There has been a growing interest in this subject in Europe, Latin America and the United States. In Europe, Jurgen Moltmann, Johannes Metz and Dorothee Sölle, following the tradition of Karl Barth and Dietrich Bonhoeffer, have continued the dialogue between theology and politics. In Latin America, with the proliferation of liberation movements, Rubem Alves, until recently from Brazil, Juan Segundo, and Gustavo Guttierez are a few of the theologians who have brought a theological perspective to a new political militancy in the church. In the United States, Rosemary Ruether, John Bennett, and James Cone follow in the steps of Reinhold Niebuhr in their concern for social political ethics. We find in Canada that there has been a singular lack of concern for this cross-disciplinary dialogue in our departments of religious studies and theological colleges. If one examines the journal Studies in Religion/Sciences Religieuses since its first publication in 1971, one finds very few articles or reviews that have any political commentary, and until recently there has been equally scant interest in Canadian topics.

A third reason for the Conference was that besides providing a forum for Canadian theological scholarship, it helped give an opportunity for church workers from the Canadian Catholic and Protestant churches to enter this discussion. One of the new facts of life in Canada is that both the Canadian Council of Churches and the Canadian Catholic Conference have provided leadership in theological/political concerns that affect Canada. Recently, the Canadian churches sent a fact-finding team to Chile to report on General Pinochet's treatment of political prisoners. A church task force monitored the behaviour of the Canadian delegation to the Bucharest Conference on population, the Rome Conference on food, and the UNCTAD IV Conference at Nairobi in Kenya. Church research teams have provided material on the investment of Canadian banks, in the collusion of Canadian multi-nationals like Noranda with other American mining consortiums in Chile, in Falconbridge in South Africa, and on Reed paper in its environmental pollution of Indian land in Northern Ontario. The information that these church workers provide is enormous, and their presence brought a good critique to some of the more esoteric academic discussion at the Conference.

2. Format of the Book

Publishers have good reasons to distrust those who want to turn the proceedings of a conference into a book. We all have a terrible tendency to verbosity in our oral communication; a solid reminder of this fact was the transcripts of the thirteen hours of tapes that resulted from the Conference. But as this exchange between speakers and Conference participants is here reduced to the main points, the subsequent dialogue, we feel, greatly enhances the main papers.

Besides providing more excitement, the often heated discussion recorded in this book offers a good example of a characteristic of political theology where the emphasis, as William Hordern points out in his introductory paper, is on the truth being discovered in the praxis of concrete problems. There was no attempt to engage in a Schleiermacherian enterprise of trying to convince religious, intellectual, or cultured despisers. The nearest thing to an old-fashioned attack on the Judeo-Christian God came from Kai Nielsen's vigorous assault on pietistic religion from the "presumptions of atheism." He uses the methods of philosophical analysis to vanquish protestant evangelical orthodoxy of the Billy Graham variety. He exposes the political imperialism of Nixon, Reagan, Ford, and Carter, which cloaks itself in fundamental religiosity. Readers will have to decide for themselves if the religion Nielsen attacks is more typical of the Canadian scene than the theological position adopted by most of the speakers at the Conference. Nielsen seeks to establish the presumptions of socialism based on "reasonable, factual information." Ben Smillie counters that humanistic socialism cannot appeal to objective facts for its validity. Socialist countries which fit the ideal prototype of socialism are hard to find, and in the last analysis the justification of any political ideology is based on its interpretation of the human condition. The verification principle for an adequate interpretation is not just the freedom it provides, but its bias on the side of the poor.

When readers get into the papers, responses, and discussion, they may very quickly get the impression that the organizers have put together a "socialist conspiracy" under the guise of an open discussion on politics and theology. A charitable, but vigorous protest comes from a delegate who accuses the speakers of identifying Jesus as a socialist. He insists that justice must come through personal Christian faith. He emphasizes that a political ideology such as socialism has a tendency to pass by the beggar on the street in its concern for serving humanity. He also suggests that this strong emphasis on political theology produces a fractious, contentious division which is not in keeping with the spirit of love, so central to the Christian message. The response of Dorothee Sölle would be spoiled by an attempt at precis. Her ability to describe the increasing political consciousness of housewives becomes an excellent travelogue in political awareness. She suggests that the process of increasing radicalization is the same as the Christian doctrine of conversion. In fact, her own biography was to those of us who attended the most moving illustration of how political radicalization and conversion become incarnated in a dynamic Christian. She concludes, "It is precisely the small reformist steps and the ensuing frustrations which kindles revolutionary fire."

The nature of this radicalization in the Canadian political context received considerable debate. Gregory Baum emphasized that to introduce a radical Marxist rhetoric in the Canadian scene was to fail to grasp the nature of the history of socialism in Canada. A counter argument brought forward by Yves Vaillancourt was that Canadian socialism in the Cooperative Commonwealth Federation/New Democratic Party was no more radical than the socialism of the British Labour party, which was completely compromised with capitalism. While most speakers deplored the factionalism of the left, Abraham Rotstein stated the dilemma succinctly when he suggested that there is a type of purism on the left that is thoroughly sectarian. However, any socialist movement must have a strong, political, moral purity if it is going to survive in our Western capitalist society. The acid test for any political movement is how it can retain its integrity on the road to political power.

There is a very interesting analysis of Quebec's history from the perspective of a Marxist class analysis. This discussion presented by Guy Bourgeault and Yves Vaillancourt faces the burning contemporary question: If Quebec separates, will it be just as compromised with American capitalism as English Canada has become? The answer suggested is that the Quebecois must establish their Frenchness first, just as blacks have had to establish their black identity. After that will come the question of whether Christians for

Socialism, along with the other alliances within the Labour Movement and the Parti Quebecois, will be able to move Quebec to the left.

Finally, we present a brilliant essay on political theology by Abraham Rotstein which develops the theme of "Lordship and Bondage in the Writings of Martin Luther, George Hegel and Karl Marx." Rotstein asks, "Is there a common analytic framework which we can find that will permit us to discuss both certain kinds of theology and certain kinds of politics within a common language or common structure?" He finds such a framework in the apocalyptic tradition. A characteristic of this tradition in Western theology and politics is, first, the awareness of domination and oppression. This is Act I. In this tradition, the closing act, Act IV, culminated in a perfect kingdom. The theme that runs throughout the drama is explained through the Hegelian scheme of lordship and bondage.

Patrick Kerans, in response to Abraham Rotstein, appreciates the rhetoric of transfiguration that moves political action from defeat to a vision of a perfect society. He explains that this is a refreshing alternative to our current liberal ideology, which assumes that political interpretations are based on facts and only those facts are selected that fit the liberal paradigm. He points out, however, that apocalyptic visions go wrong because they are lost in ambiguity. They have no blueprint for action, thus leading to aloofness or resignation.

Roger Hutchinson summarizes the Conference by posing four questions: "What is political theology?" "Why remain Christian?" "What is the nature of our bondage?" and "How do we deal with the Canadian context?" Hutchinson's essay provides a well-organized summary of the speakers' positions.

The editor wishes to express his thanks to those who have helped to make this book possible: the focal person, Mrs. Ruth Ulrich, secretary of the School of Religious Studies, who provided organizing skills to a disorganized theologian; Bob Haverluck, who, as critic and wise political theologian, provided sound advice in reading the manuscripts; and Gerry Haverluck, who tactfully suggested syntactical improvements. All of us who took part in the conference are grateful to the President of the University of Saskatchewan, the Canada Council, and the School of Religious Studies whose financial generosity made the conference possible.

B. G. Smillie

December 19, 1977

SECOND PREFACE, 1981

There will be friends who have every reason to say, "I told you so," as they cautioned the editor against the possibility of finding a publisher for a book based on the papers and discussion of a conference. The caution was well grounded because a Canadian university press, after holding the manuscript for more than two years, went against the recommendations of the majority of the readers and turned the manuscript down on the grounds that it was now out of date! However, the good news is that the Publications Committee of the Canadian Corporation for Studies in Religion (CCSR) agreed to publish the book. Some of the dated discussion has been removed. Some of chapter one has been rewritten in the light of new information, but where the data do not provide any significant difference in the Canadian scene, the original data are retained.

Roger Hutchinson has provided a supplemental conclusion in which he changes the focus of his discussion from political theology to political ethics. Is his doing so not an example of the Protestant problem raised by Dorothee Sölle (in this book) of making theology more palatable to secular participants by making it conform to secular concerns? Also, there is a long tradition in Christian ethics which emphasizes that the main premise of Christian ethics is confession of faith in God; from this faith orientation, ethical actions follow. This issue, along with many others, will continue the political theology debate.

In completing this second draft of the book the editor wishes to express his thanks to Dr. Harold Coward of the CCSR Publications Committee for his good advice and to Dr. Roger Hutchinson for adding a new conclusion. The publication of this book has been made possible through financial assistance from the University of Saskatchewan President's fund for publication, the School of Religious Studies at the University, Lutheran Theological Seminary, and St. Andrew's College (both affiliated with the University). I wish to express a personal word of thanks to Professor Faye Kernan, who helped with manuscript revision; to Dr. Charles Johnston, and to Dr. Erwin Buck, who assisted with translation; and to Mrs. Margaret Laing, who typed the manuscript.

April 30, 1981 B. G. Smillie

THE CONTRIBUTORS

Gregory Baum: Professor of Theology, St. Michael's College, University of Toronto.

Guy Bourgeault: Dean of Continuing Education, University of Montreal.

William Hordern: President of Lutheran Theological Seminary, Saskatoon, Sask.

Roger Hutchinson: Professor of Religious Studies, Victoria College, University of Toronto; research work on the Fellowship for a Christian Social Order 1934-1945.

Patrick Kerans: Professor of Social Work, Maritime School of Social Work, Dalhousie University; author of _Sinful Social Structures_.

Kai Nielsen: Professor of Philosophy, University of Calgary.

Abraham Rotstein: Professor of Economics, University of Toronto; Past Editor of _The Canadian Forum_.

Ben Smillie: Professor of Church and Society, St. Andrew's College, Saskatoon, Sask.; Chairperson of the Conference on Political Theology in the Canadian Context.

Dorothee Sölle: University of Cologne; Author of Political Theology; Visiting Professor of Theology at Union Theological Seminary, Columbia University, New York.

Yves Vaillancourt: Professor, Department of Political Science, University of Quebec at Montreal; collaborating with G. Bourgeault in a research project on L'Eglise et Mouvement Ouvrier au Quebec.

PARTICIPANTS IN THE ORIGINAL DISCUSSION

Barbara Bloom: Professor of Education (Institute of Child Guidance and Development), University of Saskatchewan.

John Foster: Research Director, United Church of Canada.

Kas Iwaasa: United Church Minister, Central Church, Calgary, Alberta.

Charles Johnston: Dean and Professor of Church History, St. Andrew's College, Saskatoon, Sask.

Paul Newman: Professor of Systematic Theology, St. Andrew's College, Saskatoon, Sask.

Alan Richards: United Church Minister, Lethbridge, Alberta.

Christine Wilson: 3rd Year Theology Student, Luther Theological Seminary, Saskatoon, Sask.

Vernon Wishart: Garneau United Church, Edmonton, Alberta.

INTRODUCTION: THEOLOGICAL REFLECTIONS ON THE CANADIAN CONTEXT

B. G. Smillie

This introduction draws on those economists, political scientists, and church researchers[1] who, as Abraham Rotstein explains, follow the Western theological apocalyptic tradition, which sees events in history building up to an overwhelming burden of domination and oppression and envisages a perfect community that follows on the passing of the old order. Excluded, therefore, are many Canadian writers who stand in a rational liberal tradition, inasmuch as they are recorders of inevitable market forces or iron laws of political-sociological behaviour.[2]

1. Is Canada a Captive Nation?

Some readers, in protest against the description of Canada as "captive," "oppressed," "dominated," may accuse this viewpoint of a malevolent pessimism. These "sunny-side up" Canadians point to our standard of living, our democratic system of government, our access to justice and freedom in the courts and political structures, and challenge this gloomy interpretation of Canadian bondage. Perhaps the reason for this bias will be understood if the nagging question is posed that is brought to the fore by a broad political spectrum of Canadians: How is it that Canada can appear so rich in comparison with Third World countries and yet be a satellite of the United States? To state the question statistically, the Canadian annual income per capita in 1974 was $5,854 (in U.S. dollars). The American individual income was $5,923. In the same year, on the island of Tonga, in the south Pacific the per capita income was $39.00. In North Yemen in the Middle East it was $85.00.[3] These figures show our relative wealth. But there are other statistics that show our captivity to foreign ownership. While the present federal energy policy is seeking to buy back ownership of our natural resources, until recently our petroleum refining has been 99% American owned. U.S. ownership extends to our oil and gas (74%), the automobile industry(96%), chemical plants (79%) and our rubber industry (98%).[4]

If this statistical information leaves us unimpressed because we live in the relative luxury of a well-to-do industrial society, in Canada our moral sensibilities become jolted when we see the American domination of our foreign policy. This has required our complicity in manufacturing war materials for the Vietnam war under the Defence Sharing Agreement. It compromised our position on the International Control Commission in Indo-China. Apart from a brief period when Howard Green was Minister of External Affairs,[5] our American bias was reflected in our failure to speak against their escalation of the Vietnam war, and made us Washington's agent in the eyes of the world. We have supported the brutal Chile Junta under General Pinochet. At the time of the coup in September 1973, our Ambassador, Andrew Ross, refused to use the Canadian Embassy to give refuge to those who were hunted by the junta. More recently the Canadian-owned mining company, Noranda, in co-operation with a consortium of American mining companies, spear-headed a new copper mining operation in Chile, giving legitimacy and financial support to those who engineered the Chile coup. Canadian banks are part of an international fiscal cartel in the tourist industry in the Carribean and the mining industry in South Africa. Our branch plant status involves us in further international moral compromises when we are unable to stop an American-owned nickel company, Falconbridge, based in Sudbury, from engaging in mining operations in Namibia, a country that is illegally occupied by South Africa. Our most recent questionable moral practice is the continuing sale of CANDU reactors, which from India's example we know can be misused for nuclear weaponry.

There is an increasingly strident opposition to this American domination within Canada. It comes from economists, political scientists, artists, and cultural historians. A fascinating recent study of Canada's culture by Stephen Clarkson imagines the country placed on "the couch of some celestial shrink specializing in the diagnosis of national psychic disorders."[6] Under such psychiatric diagnosis, Clarkson explains, it becomes clear that Canada has developed a case of "arrested maturation" after a long period of "prolonged dependency." We have now reached a "mid-life crisis."[7] Never having consummated a marriage relationship with the United States, we have become a taken-for-granted mistress who keeps her remonstrances about Korea, NATO, and Vietnam to bedroom tiffs. Faltering at the threshold of national maturity, Canada has not managed to take on a normal nation's sense of self-reliance.[8]

Instead of placing Canada on a national psychiatric couch, political theologians stand in the tradition of the biblical prophets who, in the name of a righteous God, call nations to account for their deeds. Micah, addressing Israel as a spokesman for God, says, "What does the Lord require of you, but to do justice, and to love kindness, and to walk humbly with your God."[9] Canada cannot have any moral integrity as long as it lives in economic and political servitude to the neo-colonial imperial power of the United States, but to a great extent Canada's bondage is self-imposed.

To elaborate: Canada lives partly in the same condition as Israel did in biblical times when it considered itself free. Slavery came from the anaesthetising effect of the prosperity of the promised land. This captivity of Canaan, "the land flowing with milk and honey," made Israel the slave of its own appetites. This slavery of obesity in the midst of the land of plenty had a religious reinforcement in Baal worship. The biblical prophets were constantly calling the judgment of God on this apostate nation which, in setting up shrines, went "whoring after the gods of Baal."[10] Baal worship was in fact the worship of nature. More accurately, it was the worship of fecundity and production. It was the Old Testament version of idolizing the Gross National Product.

The New Testament parallel for the Christian community was to become a slave to the sins of the flesh described by Paul in his castigation of the Corinthian church: "When you meet together, it is not the Lord's supper that you eat. For in eating each one goes ahead with his own meal, and one is hungry and another is drunk. What! Do you not have houses to eat and drink in? Or do you despise the church of God, and humiliate those who have nothing?"[11] In drawing a parallel to the Canadian context, the slavery of obesity is reflected in Canada in a liberal possessive individualism. This possessive individualism not only encourages the most crass form of acquisitive prodigality in our life style, but, even more seriously, it exacerbates the class division between the rich and the poor.

2. The Slavery of Egypt and the Slavery of Canaan: A Comparison between Violent and Subtle Bondage.

The Brazilian theologian, Rubem Alves, has developed his theological position from within a country that has lived under the economic neo-colonialism of Latin America. From this context he asks why there is such a pathetic docility amongst poor people in the midst of the outrage of their squalid life. He answers his own question by drawing analogies between Third World oppression and the Israelites living under the Pharaohs in the captivity of Egypt. The story recounted in the Book of Exodus describes how the oppression of a subjugated race was maintained with forced labour camps presided over by "task masters." Even when the oppression increases and they are required to make bricks without straw, even when the Israelite foremen, agents of the Egyptians, are beaten for not getting enough work done, they don't rebel. Instead, they lash out in fury, not at King Pharaoh, but at the charismatic leadership of Moses and Aaron who try to rouse the slaves out of lethargy. The Israelite sub-foremen resent the restlessness Moses and Aaron have provoked: "You have made us offensive in the sight of Pharaoh and his servants, and have put a sword in their hand to kill us."[12]

The call of God to this enslaved people to get out of the security of the "flesh pots of Egypt" and journey to a utopian promised land, a land flowing with milk and honey, was too disturbing. Alves describes the modern version of the Egyptian bondage as more subtle. He shows that we have become conditioned to think of the violence of colonialism as exploitation which produces poverty and underdevelopment. He comments that although this is true, "the most basic form of violence of colonialism is that it defuturizes the nations under its power."[13] Instead of an open future where they can plan their own destinies, they are forced to acquiesce to the economic demands of their masters. In contrast to the earlier colonialism when African, Asian, and Latin American countries were occupied by their masters, he says, "Today the masters are willing to make concessions. They will allow the black man to be 'integrated' and to participate in the good of his master's world."[14] All the crumbs that fall from the rich nations' tables are given on the condition that the slaves remain slaves, that they will not liberate themselves. The development aid projects of western nations give the Third World handouts and technological gadgets, but they refuse to give them freedom. In this subjugation, a strange thing happens; it is almost impossible to find overt violence because total triumph takes the form of total peace. Both master and slave live under the philosophy of law and order; both hate the possibility of an open future as subversive because it questions the established order.

It would be inappropriate to compare the captivity of Canada with the Third World countries of Latin America, Africa, and Asia. Although Canada might be considered underdeveloped in that it is a vast hinterland for the industrial metropol of the United States,

Canada has no violent task masters like those portrayed in the Egyptian bondage; Canada has no secret police arresting, beating, torturing, and killing peasants as agents of landlords, international fruit companies, or repressive racist governments. However, in describing Israel's subservience in Canaan, certain parallels between Israel and Canada become obvious.

To set the stage for this theme, turn to the biblical record and pick up the history of the Israelite people after their escape from Egypt. After the Exodus they became a loose confederacy of twelve tribes. Wandering in the Sinai Desert for forty years, they eventually arrived in the land of Canaan where they quickly developed the outlook that their new-found prosperity had made them masters of their own destiny and they no longer were dependent on God. The book of Deuteronomy, the flower of Israel's writing compiled in the period of theological reformation, looks back on the early days of Canaanite settlement and says, "God having given you great and goodly cities, which you did not build, and houses full of all good things, which you did not fill, and cisterns hewn out, which you did not hew, and vineyard and olive trees, which you did not plant, and when you eat and are full, then take heed lest you forget the Lord, who brought you out of the land of Egypt, out of the house of bondage."[15]

The biblical writers were not attempting to be anti-materialistic when they spoke of the dangers of prosperity. When the prophet Joel wishes to express the dawn of God's perfect kingdom when young men will see visions and old men will dream dreams, he expresses the delight of this kingdom in very material terms--"the threshing floor shall be full of grain, the vats shall overflow with wine and oil . . . you shall eat in plenty and be satisfied, and praise the name of the Lord your God who hast dealt wondrously with you."[16] These promises of the future reinforced God's creative acts at the beginning. The constant refrain in the Genesis Creation stories (Genesis 1 and 2) after every act of creation is, "and God saw that it was good." The problem with the world of nature which Israel encountered when it arrived in Canaan was not that its bounty should not be enjoyed, but that plenty could become a trap.

The worship of nature was very tempting when one considers that the local conventional religion of the country was Baal worship. The most important ingredient of this religion was the struggle between Baal, the god of weather and vegetation, who died in the perennial struggle with Mot (Death), and then rose again. Every year in the cycle , the lush vegetation of winter and early spring brought the celebration of Baal, but the summer and fall brought drought when Mot was in the ascendency after killing Baal. At this time there was the constant fear of famine and death. Worship centred around the basic religious instinct to worship and cajole the God of nature, even to the point of the cruel sacrifice of little children and the development of temple prostitution to reenact the story of fertility. When the prophets bring an indictment against the Israelites for "whoring after the gods of Baal," it is not only in angry protest against the forsaking of Yahweh, but also in abhorrence of a life of apostasy where faith has been reduced to accumulating dividends with the god who is supposed to produce plenty. Willian Graham, a biblical scholar, explains Baal worship thus:

As one looks back over the almost constant economic and political pressures to which Canaan was subjected, one is not surprised to find that its religion was one which focused men's desires on the production and accumulation of material wealth. Almost constantly under the thumb of imperial masters, it was inevitable that its people should seek some measure of security through the creation of surplus.[17]

Worshipping mammon is perhaps one of the most basic religious inclinations that humans have. But the problem with accumulating surplus in Canada is that it involves us in such prodigal expenditure. When we see ourselves (as the biblical prophets did) involved in the sins of the nation, we have to compare the annual income per capita on the Island of Tonga and in North Yemen with that of Canada. Yet in the city of Saskatoon in 1974 we spent (per family) $346.60 on tobacco and alcohol, and $93.00 on cosmetics and toilet accessories.[18] With two cars as the national average per family in 1974, we spent 12% of our income ($1,939.00) on transportation.[19] The terrible wastefulness of our automobile travel is reflected in the fact that automobiles account for half of our energy consumption. Eighty-five percent of all passenger miles travelled in Canada are travelled by the private automobile, yet it is the least efficient. "It achieves on the average 18.6 passenger miles per gallon in contrast to urban buses at 102 and commuter trains at 123 passenger miles per gallon."[20]

But what makes the prodigality of our life style even more offensive is that our relative affluence is bought at the price of the structural inequalities in our society. If we are Indian or Metis, single parents, live in rural areas of Northern Quebec, Northern Ontario, Northern Manitoba, Northern Saskatchewan or Northern British

Columbia, or if we are a family from the Atlantic Provinces, or the head of a family not working, or the head of a family sixty-five years or older, then we are likely to be poor. In The Poverty Wall, Ian Adams claims that if you qualify in any two of these areas, the family is likely to stay poor.[21]

In Paul's letter to the Corinthian church, he faces a church with a bad reputation. There is immorality, compromise with the local cultic religion in eating food offered to idols, vengeance with lawsuits against fellow members of the church, and drunkenness at the Lord's table. But all these sins fade into insignificance in comparison with the sin of "despising the church of God and humiliating those who have nothing."[22] The Corinthian church is singled out in church history as representative of an antinomianism or lawlessness--people who presume on the grace of God by accepting His love and assuming it gives them a passport to salvation. This becomes the New Testament version of the Old Testament Baal worship. It is a worship of the fleshly appetites. Its evil lies not just in the prodigality of obese living, but, more seriously, in the failure to share what one has.

Sharing what one has in Canadian society means more than cutting back in gas consumption and changing personal consumer habits--it means working politically at a fairer tax structure which would give tax relief to the six million poor in Canada and higher graded income tax for the top 20%. (Based on 1965 figures, the lowest 20% share only 6.7% of the national income while the top 20% take nearly 40%.[23]) It also means supporting the cause of particular groups like working women who are poor, often abandoned by husbands to bring up children alone. What these women need is legislation to establish day care centres, a guaranteed minimum income, low-rent housing, enforcement of equal pay statutes, and better protection under the law from the law (particularly from creditors). What these women want is better retraining programmes so they can break out of menial jobs; they particularly want a lift for their kids over the poverty wall.[24]

In contrast to the individualism and acquisitive self-centredness of Baal worship, the Biblical writers state the expectations of Yahweh with emphasis on the indivisible salvation or damnation of all peoples together. They illustrate how one person's sin led to the punishment of the nation. But the writers especially emphasize that after the Israelites arrived in the God-given promised land, one person's prosperity had to be shared by all. In the fiftieth year, the year of Jubilee, all land reverted to the original owner or his heir, back to those who had been dispossessed. In that year, the debtor who had sold himself to a creditor was released. All debts were cancelled, not out of a spirit of egalitarian moral rectitude, but as a reminder of Israel's humble historical roots: "You also were a slave in Egypt."[25]

Another feature of Canaanite Baal worship that should make us ponder when we look at the danger of the slavery of plenty is that Baal worshippers were willing to serve any God so long as he brought them success. One of the worst kings of Judah who ruled in the seventh century B.C. was Manasseh, whose evil reign brought the insidious practice of child sacrifice to placate the gods. In describing his reign, the French Old Testament scholar, Adolphe Lods, says, "For the man of primitive mentality, the best gods are the gods of the conquerors: Manasseh built altars in two courts of the temple of Yahweh to all the host of heaven, that is, to the various divinities of the Assyrian pantheon of which each was then associated with the celestial body."[26]

Possessive individualism is the Baal god whose worship is based on a highly convincing interpretation of nature which has had a powerful hold in the "success" ideology of our North American technological society. An excellent historical exposition of possessive individualism is provided by the Canadian political scientist, C. B. Macpherson. He traces the genesis of this ideology to Thomas Hobbes and John Locke. Both see the basic ingredient in man as his will to power in what they call"man in the state of nature." Hobbes says:

> Nature made man so equal in the faculties of the body and mind, as, that though there be found one man manifestly stronger in the body or of quicker mind than another, yet when all is reckoned together the differences between man and man is not so considerable as the one man can thereupon claim to himself any benefit to which another man may not pretend as well as he . . . from this equality of ability ariseth equality of hope. And therefore, if any two men desire the same thing, which nevertheless they cannot both enjoy, they become enemies and endeavor to destroy or subdue one another.[27]

To check these dangerous possibilities of every man being against every other in this state of nature, anarchy was avoided by a social contract with a sovereign. In this contract, man gave up some of his individual sovereignty to a sovereign. For Hobbes the sovereigns were the Stuart kings; for Locke, the sovereign was the parliament. Locke reinterpreted the right to power as the right to accumulate property. At first it was the right of equal property, but because of the sacredness of the individual in the Hobbes-Locke system, the right to equal property ultimately became the right of the individual to amass unlimited amounts of property. In his context of Britain, Locke's advocacy for the accumulation of property became increasingly impossible as progressively all the land in England was bought up and land for purchase became scarce. This led to the right to amass fortunes in money with the consequent free market economy. The virtue of rags to riches represented in business tycoons like Andrew Carnegie led to the worst excesses of the large money barons of the industrial revolution; amassing money came to be reinterpreted as the unlimited right to desire.

As long as there were new resources in the world to exploit, the right to acquire (with a philosophy of exponential growth) was the current ideology. But today we do not need 20/20 vision to see that the criterion of happiness based on unlimited desire has had a rude shock; the support systems of our planet's ecology call for drastic limits to growth. Macpherson sees the death throes of possessive individualism through the eyes of Third World leaders who will not accept the moral bankruptcy of western capitalism, polluted with an affluence that bores the rich, dissatisfies the middle class, and cannot provide the poor with a proper diet or a livable house.[28] Macpherson's exposé of individualism as a false god observes that both Hobbes and Locke made their descriptions of man in the state of nature so convincing by portraying seventeenth-century man as though he were universal man.[29] The consequence of their assumption, says Macpherson, is that such a philosophy or theology not only fails to see its historical relativism, but it also produces the assumption in the believer of the inevitability of what is happening as a universal truth. This assumption creates an ideology that equates freedom with the freedom to master an existing or resulting problem (even if it means creating a larger problem). This ideology is exemplified in the gas-guzzling air pollution devices on North American cars that have appeared at a time of limited fossil fuels. Furthermore, this ideology also justifies a philosophy of growth, where growth is equated with acquiring and consuming more of the world's limited resources. All of this produces a paralysis of will which assumes that our nature has decreed this outlook as inevitable.

Robert Pursig calls this outlook "value rigidity," living only out of a certain sequence of facts. He gives a striking example of this in what he calls "the South Indian Monkey Trap." The trap consists of a hollowed-out coconut chained to a stake. Inside the coconut is some rice which can be grabbed through a small hole. The hole is big enough to allow the monkey's hand to go in, but too small for his rice-filled fist to come out.[30] The monkey is easily caught by the villagers because he never grasps that freedom is more important than a handful of rice. The trapped monkey is a good symbol for an acquisitive Canadian Society which lives in bondage to its own greed.

But to reduce Canada's problem to nothing more than the universal taint of greed would be to completely miss the point of Canaanite captivity. Similarly, it would be a totally inadequate analysis of Canadian society if we suggested that our Canadian problem could be summarized as North American possessive individualism. A popular solution to possessive individualism is proposed by environmentalists who suggest that all we have to do is to cut back on consumption. This is the sort of gratuitous advice that is seconded by Prime Minister Trudeau, a millionaire of inherited wealth and a personal recipient of a large part of the public purse for salary and groceries. James Laxer and Robert Laxer call this the "frothy" front of environmental faddism designed to keep the public eye on environmental issues rather than the structural evil of Canadian liberal capitalism.[31] The pitfalls of a class-divided nation like Canada can be prophetically clarified by drawing parallels with the Canaanite experience of Israel.

3. The Precariousness of a Small Nation

The conquest of Palestine by the twelve tribes of Israel was motivated by a desire to bring into existence a holy people devoted to the service of Yahweh--a people who would be a "light to the Gentiles" through their moral integrity, "a Holy Nation." The difficult reality of the situation was that what they won in political conquest they lost in being conquered by the culture they sought to replace.

In the story of the bitter struggle between Baalism and Yahwehism for the allegiance of the Hebrew people, Baalism won through the practice of religious syncreticism. For a brief period during the reign of King David this little nation that stood in the pathway between the powerful empires of Egypt, Assyria, and Babylon, was able to hold a certain autonomy. But David's strength was always dependent on his personal popularity. A native of the southern kingdom of Judah, David welded into a federation the ten northern tribes at Hebron.[32] He was astute enough to bind a covenant people together by creating a new capital and a new centre of worship at Jerusalem, a place with no holy or historical allegiance for any one faction.

But the accolades that have been given David by some of the biblical writers have to be set against Yahweh's prophetic messengers, who saw the whole idea of a monarchical political structure as an invitation to oppression. Particularly in the reign of King Solomon ("perhaps the most overrated figure in the Old Testament"[33]), the prophecy of Samuel, who cautioned the people against a monarchy, came true. Samuel warned that a king would make servants of their sons and daughters; he would take a tenth of their fields, vineyards, and olive trees; and he would take their produce.[34] Solomon, the most ostentatious of Israel's kings, made these prophecies come true by epitomizing poor leadership. He encouraged prodigality and luxury. He over-taxed the economic capacity of his people by squandering wealth and manpower. Even his epitaph in history, the temple in Jerusalem, was dependent on Canaanite and Phoenician craftsmanship. The tolls he extracted from the caravans that criss-crossed the country were made possible by the accident of Israel's geography. Norman Gottwald, an Old Testament scholar, explains that the exploitation of King Solomon's mines in the Arabah region was carried on in an intolerable climate by foreign slave labor.[35] The copper produced became a means for acquiring a royal fortune, as it was exchanged for the gold of Ophir.[36] His international commerce was promoted through Phoenician mercantile prowess. Solomon's wisdom was devoted to working out ways of crossing historical tribal boundaries to maximize forced labor and taxes for his profligate living. His weak son, Rehoboam, brought up in the pampered environment of Solomon's court, provoked rebellion by promising worse oppression to the next generation: "My father chastised you with whips but I will chastise you with scorpions."[37] The leadership of Israel continued to deteriorate following internal rebellion and division into the northern kingdom of Israel (the ten northern tribes) and the southern kingdom of Judah.

In an eloquent description of Israel, a country rich in resources but weak in moral fibre, the British Old Testament scholar, E. W. Heaton, says: "Israel lacked a centre and was all excess; it oscillated between extremes of zeal and extremes of apostasy, extremes of wealth and extremes of poverty, extremes of grandeur and extremes of degradation. The northern kingdom exploited its exposure to the outside world, did nothing by halves and everything in a hurry. After a mere two centuries it hastened to extinction."[38]

To conclude that a series of weak kings were the only villains in oppressing the nation of Israel would be to miss the important characteristics of Canaanite bondage. Also implicated were the religious leaders who supported the syncretism of Yahweh and Baal worship and stifled any criticism by Yahweh's prophets. A typical example of such leaders was Amaziah, "priest of Bethel." Representing official "peace loving" religion, he became terribly upset with the prophet Amos for criticizing the King's court in its grinding of the poor. The prophetic books of the Old Testament always distinguished between the country's prophets, the "yes men" who were ventriloquists of the royal wishes and the Yahweh prophets who were often the official and unofficial opposition to the kings and their retinue:

Then Amaziah the priest of Bethel sent to Jeroboam, king of Israel, saying, "Amos has conspired against you, in the midst of the house of Israel; the land is not able to bear all his words" . . . . And Amaziah said to Amos, "O seer, go, flee away to the land of Judah, and eat bread there and prophesy there; but never again prophesy at Bethel, for it is the King's sanctuary, and it is the temple of the kingdom."[39]

Perhaps the most powerful group in supporting oppression were the moneyed aristocracy. The prophet Isaiah speaks out against the wealthy in Judah: "The Lord enters into judgment with the elders and princes of his people: it is you who have devoured the vineyards, the spoil of the poor is in your houses. What do you mean by crushing my people by grinding the face of the poor."[40] The wives of the wealthy do not escape judgment either. To the privileged women of Samaria, Amos says: "Hear this word, you cows of Bashan, who are in the mountain of Samaria, who oppress the poor, who crush the needy, who say to their husbands, "Bring that we may drink."[41]

The priveleged intellectuals of both Israel and Judah, like the representatives of official religion, played the role of pacifiers. Isiah attacked the counsellors of Hezekiah who sought to make an alliance with Egypt instead of consulting Yahweh.[42] Heaton, in commenting on the school men who became an influential group in the Canaanite life of both kingdoms, says, "the school-trained professional class, the court prophets and the priests together constituted the three principal orders in society . . . and

Jeremiah's ministry is the story of his struggle with all three."[43]

One other group became the most formidable agent of oppression--the neighboring powerful nations. Hosea, in a marvellous metaphor of national stupidity, says, "Ephraim is like a silly dove, silly and without sense, calling to Egypt, going to Assyria."[44] In fact Israel had a lemming-like attraction to the self-destruction hidden in the seductive voice of Assyria, the nation that became the by-word of occupational cruelty. Judah found it difficult to resist Assyria's war propoganda aimed at the eighth century Jerusalem leaders:

Make your peace with me and come out to me; then every one of you will eat of his own vine, and every one of his own fig tree and every one of you will drink the water of his own cistern; until I come and take you away to a land like your own land, a land of grain and wine, a land of bread and vineyards, a land of olive trees and honey, that you may live and not die.[45]

4. Parallels in the Canadian "Canaanite" Captivity

If an observer sat in the gallery of the United Nations and watched the voting alliances on international issues, two observations would become obvious: Canada has a satellite status to the United States, and, compared with the independence of smaller nations, Canada has a national inferiority complex. For example, Cuba, like Canada, is a large producer of sugar. Cuba, a socialist country, has benefited from the recent international boom in the price of sugar. Canada, with its usual pattern of economic hemorrhage, had its profits syphoned off to the multinational sugar cartel.[46] In oil, a small, relatively poor socialist country like Algeria has benefited from the OPEC oil prices while Canadian oil profits have been syphoned off by the American-owned Canadian oil companies.[47] In the following analysis of Canada's economic situation, we Canadians suffer not only from the economic problems of a capitalist system, but also from a stunted imagination.

5. Canada and U.S.: Who Supports Whom?

One of the distorted beliefs held by Canadians has been the assumption that Canada would not be prosperous today without the investment of American capital. In reality the situation is just the opposite. More and more, Canada is bought up by direct foreign ownership and paid for in Canadian dollars. The Canadian economist Kari Levitt quotes statistics showing that in 1964 only 5% of the funds used to finance Canadian capital came from U.S. funds; 85% of U.S.

ownership was paid for out of Canadian earnings of U.S. subsidiaries in Canada, and Canadian banks have supported the U.S. take-over of Canada by providing another 10% of the money needed for increasing U.S. ownership of Canadian companies.[48]

Not only is it false that Canada needs United States capital to remain economically viable, but closer study reveals that Canada in fact has saved the United States from bankruptcy! With escalating involvement in the Vietnam war, United States international monetary deficits piled up, but rather than increasing taxation, United States administration under Lyndon Johnston and Richard Nixon amassed a larger foreign debt (notably in Western Europe and Japan). In 1960 the U.S. dollar remained tied to gold redeemable at $35.00 per ounce; in that year the United States enjoyed a $5 billion surplus in their overall manufacturing trade. By 1971 they owed $16.4 billion to West Germany and $19 billion to Japan.[49] As the whole western economic monetary system was tied to the U.S. dollar, all currency in the western world was threatened by this large overdraft.

The Nixon administration steadfastly refused to increase taxes to pay for their massive debt. Instead they engineered an international economic Watergate by burglarizing the U.S. dollar holdings of their creditors. The U.S. printed money far in excess of their gold reserves. James and Robert Laxer explain:

> On August 15, 1971, President Nixon announced that the U.S. was going off the gold standard, so that American dollars held by foreigners were no longer redeemable for gold. What Nixon had done was to repudiate a vast debt, making American dollars redeemable only with paper which was also not backed by gold. In effect, the United States had successfully taxed all the other nations in the Western world to pay for American military operations. Other nations had no other choice but to accept this new form of taxation. Had they objected and refused to allow their holdings of U.S. dollars to grow, the whole international monetary system would have collapsed.[50]

The heaviest burden of this financial double-dealing fell on Canada, the United States' largest trading partner. U.S. trade figures quoted by the Laxers from the U.S. Bureau of the Census, 1972, indicate the extent of American trade dependency on Canada. In 1965 the U.S. manufacturing trade surplus with all countries was $6,142 million; out of this total, $2,371 million or 42% was with Canada. By 1971 (the year of economic crisis for the U.S.), the United States had a trade surplus of only $60 million, but its manufacturing surplus with Canada was $2,386 million. In other words, without Canada, the United States would have had a trade deficit of

$2,326 million in their manufacturing trade.[51]

As Canadians comprehend the enormity of this rip-off, they have every right to ask how it is that there isn't some attempt at exposure and retaliation against this fiscal larceny. It is not necessary to look far to find two agents of Canada's subjugation. The first is not uniquely found in Canada, but it proves very effective in helping Canadians accept the inevitability of what happens to them: The ideology of a rational empirical methodology in economics and political science gives itself the status of being value free while in truth it is loaded with bias in the facts it chooses to examine and in what it rules out of court. The parameters of conventional wisdom about political reality are swallowed up in legitimizing the present economic-political process. It is one form of the naturalistic fallacy where the "is" swallows up the "ought." This situation has a humorous side which was suggested by the late Frank Underhill in 1936 when he said that Canadian academic economists are divided into two classes: "There are firstly those who have already served on Royal Commissions; and there are secondly those who are still hoping to do so." The second agent of Canada's docility, linked to the first, is based on the assumption that we are pawns of the economic market place. An example can be taken from the report of the 1970 Task Force on Agriculture. This report has been selected because agricultural products are a major export for Canada, and because the Canadian farmer has lived under the bondage of a cost-price squeeze. Hence, one could hope that the projection of agriculturals by a Task Force formed to find new hope for the farmer might suggest some radical changes. The vocabulary of the Task Force on Agriculture suggests openness to change.[53] The report follows all of the liberal ideological assumptions by stressing that Canada's economy is best served by minimum government interference, alleging that if all groups have equal access to free trade market forces, the situation will lead to harmonious rational conclusions. To quote from the report: "Governments should reduce their direct involvement in agriculture and thereby encourage farmers, farm organizations and agri-business to improve their management and leadership functions and stand more self-sufficiently on their own."[54]

The idea that all those involved in agriculture have an "opportunity to improve their management" and stand on their own feet is ludicrous. The same report documents that the gross sales of

238,000 farmers (or 55% of Canadian farmers in 1966) was $5,000 each. Don Mitchell, quoting from the Financial Post, reports that agri-business in the meat processing industry in the city of Lethbridge alone received welfare grants through the Department of Regional Economic Expansion of over $10 million (1969-73) and in one year (1973) declared annual profits of $38 million.[55] To suggest that all agricultural producers, large agri-business companies and marginal farmers, should have equal freedom to operate in a market economy where all have freedom to improve their management, is like inviting free foxes to move freely among free hens!

Not only does this report seek to legitimize a false freedom, it encourages further economic bondage by advocating a free trade continental market with the United States for livestock, livestock products, feed grains, oil seeds, potatoes and some fruits and vegetables. The National Farmers Union castigates the report for promoting a policy that could lead to the destruction of orderly marketing. In the area of beef production, this continentalist policy would leave Canada as an exporter of a raw resource (beef), but not as a secondary manufacturing centre for processing food. The National Farmers' Union draws the conclusion that this policy would lead to the "continuing subservience to meet United States needs."[56]

In the biblical description of Canaanite captivity, priests and court prophets, like the intellectuals, were identified as agents of oppression because they promoted the peace of the status quo. Similarly, through methods of research academics circumscribe the possibility of Canadians breaking out of their captivity. But like its academics, Canada's modern Amaziahs in its church leadership also carry out the same role.

6. Canadian Church Leaders

The Canadian literary critic Ronald Sutherland expounds an interesting thesis to explain the passivity of Canadians at the time of the War Measures Act in October 1970.[57] He states that the American writer Roger Williams published an article entitled "Strong Arm Rule in Canada" shortly after the Trudeau government had proclaimed the War Measures Act on the pretense of an alleged "apprehended insurrection." Williams observed that both French-speaking and English-speaking Canadians trust their government. He noted that Mayor Jean Drapeau was returned to office with 93% of the vote and that 87% of the Canadians supported the use of the Act. Williams was appalled at this passivity. Pointing to the Republican tradition of American politics reflected in the legacy of Paine, Thoreau and Emerson, he indicated that Americans would have taken to the streets in massive protest at this invasion of civil liberties.

Sutherland explained passivity by expanding on Canadian's theological outlook as deriving from Jansenism (in French Canada) and Calvinism (in English Canada). This parallel theological outlook, which emphasizes the majesty of God and the insignificance of humanity, has produced in Canadians a strong reliance on their church establishment as God's representatives in preserving order and good government. Statements on Quebec by Guy Bourgeault and Yves Vaillancourt (included in this book) set the framework of the Catholic Church's compromise with the English conquerors squarely in the historical context. Although Bourgeault and Vaillancourt do not support the thesis that there is a strong Jansenist influence in Quebec,[58] the influence of Calvinism on Protestant English Canada is very clear.

In Canada, there is a Protestant doctrine of election that has given to the church the right to be the custodian of God's grace; the church in its turn has reinforced the political establishment. This has produced in Canada a religious climate of righteousness through the law and conventional acts of good works. Harold Innis, in a series of essays on Canadian Economic history, draws attention to the conservative political role of the church in Canada. In elaborating on Canada's counter-revolutionary tradition, he explains that the Catholic Church in Quebec was the bastion against the republican influence in the French Revolution and that the Puritan United Empire Loyalists' tradition made the Protestant Church in Upper Canada equally supportive of the state. In reinterpreting historian Gibbon's comments on the role of religion in the Roman Empire, Innis says of Canada: "The various political groups which prevailed in Canada were all considered by the people as equally true, by the philosophers as equally false, and by the church as equally useful."[59]

But in Canada's churches there is also a prophetic tradition that has stood in the lineage of the Yahweh prophets against "wickedness in high places." A recent phenomenon is that research organizations like GATT FLY, the Latin American Working Group, the Churches' Task Force on Corporate Responsibility, and Ten Days for World Development, have carried the mantle of the prophets with official support from both the Canadian Council of Churches and the Canadian Catholic Conference. However, these groups are closeted on the periphery of ecclesiastical influence. Operating on shoe-string budgets, they are a great embarrassment particularly to wealthy laymen and their servile domesticated Levites in wealthy 'Chamber of Commerce' churches.

To fulfil the role of official religion in cultural Christendom, the Canadian church has carefully limited God's activity to the spiritual realm, making only occasional sorties into the terrestrial realm in prayers of intercession to bless "all those who are set in authority over us." Through this political quiescence, the church reinforces the dominant class in the Canadian economic and political establishment.

Richard Allen gives an interesting historical perspective on the political compromises of Protestant Orthodoxy.[60] He reflects on the short period of radical social reform in Canada in the 1920s and 1930s that found its impetus in the Social Gospel. Tracing the demise of the Social Gospel, he explains that the radicals who espoused the cause of labour, particularly after the Winnipeg Strike in 1919, left the church. The Reformists continued to keep the wide social and political concerns of both church and nation within the ministry of the church; the Conservatives took the ecumenical theme of the Social Gospel and made it their major platform in the Church Union Movement of 1925. Allen explains that this Conservative group became the advocate of democracy for Canada and particularly for building the Kingdom of God as an "industrial democracy." With special emphasis on management, they addressed those to whom God has committed the direction of industrial affairs.[61] Highly acceptable to the captains of industry, this version of the Social Gospel recognized that all have sinned and fallen short of the glory of God, but all could do their bit for a better society in the vocation of individual honesty and hard work.

The Protestant Church establishment also found its unifying battle cry for social action around the theme of prohibition and temperance. Allen also summarizes this situation: "A temperance act in the hand was worth two industrial reforms in the bush. . . . The failure of the United Church to take any new initiatives in the first three years of its existence, despite its excuses, suggested that union may have simply placed more power behind relatively ineffectual weaponry and more minds behind ineffective strategic concepts."[62]

Allen's criticism of the church union group of the Social Gospel in the 1920s is further supported in the action of the church in the Depression. Although the church did provide charity relief for the western victims of grinding poverty through quantities of food and clothing, politically it lacked courage.

In 1933 the Fellowship for a Christian Social Order (a Christian Socialist group established in 1931) brought in a resolution at a United Church of Canada conference. One of Canada's leading theologians, Roger Hutchinson, chronicles the dramatic events of the Toronto Conference in 1933 when John Line made the resolution calling for: "The socialization of banks, natural resources, transportation and other services and industries insofar as their operation under the private ownership places undue power over the subsistence of the people in the hands of special groups."[63] Responding, George Pidgeon, First Moderator of the United Church and one who would fit Richard Allen's description of a 'conservative social gospeller', claimed that "such a declaration upon controversial matters was not worthy of a church, that the catholicity of the church was broader than political movements and that it should not allow itself to be publicly interpreted as giving 'apparent support to any political party'."[64] Pidgeon exemplifies reactionary Protestantism in his desire to stand above political parties and simultaneously attacks Winnipeg strikers in 1919, accusing them of spreading Bolshevism among foreigners. In defence of the status quo, Pidgeon referred to this popular uprising, which produced sympathy strikes across Canada, as led by "Ukrainian priests and demogogues."[65] Upon examination of the Canadian Church, it is not surprising that the attempts at radicalism were short-lived in the 1930s and at Pidgeon's plea for ecumenical peace at the expense of political concern became the dominant position of the church.

A more recent example of the Protestant Church's support of the Canadian political establishment was seen in the attack on Rev. Ray Hord, Secretary of Evangelism and Social Service of the United Church of Canada. In May 1967, at the time of the mounting criticism of Canada's complicity in the Vietnam war, Ray Hord told the Ontario Welfare Council that he thought Lester Pearson was a puppy dog on L. B. J.'s leash. A Globe and Mail reporter described the events that followed: "Dr. Ernest Long, Secretary of the United Church General Council, read the quote in the morning paper and immediately telephoned Dr. Wilfred Lockhart, the Moderator at the time, in Winnipeg. Dr. Lockhart sent a telegram to the prime minister to apologize for the 'unworthy and unjustified phrase'."[66] The Pentagon Papers have revealed Ray Hord's accuracy in describing the "puppy dog" role of Canada under Lester Pearson in the Vietnam war. However, there has been no public apology to the memory of the late Ray Hord, either by the chief protagonists of this unjustified action or by the church's present officials.[67]

Hence, both ecclesiastical and academic spokesmen have been Canada's tranquilizing leaders, convincing Canadians of the inevitability of present trends and reinforcing political domination with religious opiates. But it is the Canadian economic leadership that represents the upper echelons of power - a power that is for sale to foreign bidders.

7. Canadian Economic Leadership

In historical perspective, Canada's economic leaders should be seen as elite middlemen, characteristic of the colonial form of capitalism. A merchant capitalism, dependent on continental France for survival, developed in the French period. This 'go-between' capital was bartered in staple products of fur, fish, and timber, and traded for manufactured goods through New France merchants who acted for a larger corporate elite in the French metropol. R. T. Naylor explains that after the conquest in 1760, because the French trade had been controlled by the state, there was no indigenous merchant class left in Quebec.[68] But the British merchants, operating first from New England and later from Upper and Lower Canada, formed a new bourgeois merchant class. Because there was no French capitalist class, there developed in Quebec what Yves Vaillancourt describes as a traditional clerical petite bourgeoisie whose ideology influenced education and the training of all professionals: lawyers, doctors, businessmen, and politicians. At the same time, this group served as an intermediary between the masses and the colonial power.

Examination of Canada's economic leadership shows that Canada, like other capitalist countries, has gone through an evolution in the nature of power. It still has household family names like the Eatons and the Siftons, but, as Wallace Clement explains, although class lines remain hardened, the demarcation of modern power has changed.

In a modern capitalist society, "the exercise of power means access to organization through which power can be realized in liberal democracies. This means control over the decision making power of dominant corporations."[69] In making his analysis of Canadian economic power, Clement observes that it is concentrated in 113 companies. Those in top positions come from one of three groupings: engineers and scientists, lawyers (increasing in numbers), and administrators with a commerce background. As the class structure tightens, the idea of upward mobility in Canada's free society becomes more impossible. Of the 700 most powerful Canadians, 195 replicate their fathers' positions, another 39 reach those levels through marriage, and another 247 through elite connections. Of the top 946 in the elite, only 6 (or 0.6%) are women.[70] Only 12 French Canadians are in top branches of financial institutions; 90% are Anglos. The people in this latter group have a certain incestuousness in that most have attended private schools and English Canadian universities and belong to one of six fashionable private clubs.[71] In Canadian society, Jesus' comment-that it is harder for a camel to go through the eye of a needle than for a rich man to enter the kingdom of heaven-becomes, "It is harder and harder for a poor man to enter the kingdom of riches in Canada." John Porter in his Vertical Mosiac (based on the 1951 census) says that 58 people (7.6%) made it to the top in Canadian society in one generation. But in 1971 there were only 26 (2%) in this group.[72]

The most interesting part of Clement's analysis is his description of Canada's economically powerful act as an agent of Canadian economic bondage. Since 1960, particularly with increasing U.S. domination, there has been an increase in the power of multinationals in Canada. At the top of the economic hierarchy, there are three types of elite:

> First is the indigenous elite; in Canada these are Canadians who work in finance, utilities and transportation corporations, with smaller representation in the manufacturing and resource extraction sectors. Second is a comprador elite, the senior management and directors of dominant foreign-controlled branch plants mainly in manufacturing and resource sectors. This group is subservient to the third group, the parasite elites who control major multinational corporations which dominate important sectors of the Canadian economy through branch plants.[73]

Clement's analysis of Canada's elite is accurate (in spite of the criticism this term has received in analyzing a society[74, 75]).

8. The Indigenous Elite

The indigenous elite is different from the national bourgeoisie of the U.S.A., Britain, France, and Japan. The difference is that the Canadian bourgeoisie restrict their area of power to finance rather than industry. They have a sweetheart contract with foreign international capitalism. One of the best representatives of this group is W. Earl McLaughlin, past president of the Royal Bank of Canada. He epitomizes the mediator in the circulation of money. He has the best of both worlds; his ancestors sold out to General Motors of the U.S. in the early 1900s, and he now has six dominant directorships, plus a directorship in General Motors Corporation (Detroit).[76]

9. The Comprador Elite

The comprador elite are Canadians who became agents of American multinationals. Windfall profits made by the oil companies (by artificially escalating the price of oil in collusion with the OPEC countries, and with the tacit consent of the United States) have given the Canadian compradors in the oil industry an opportunity to serve their foreign masters well. They have been able to convince Canadian politicians that Canada has unlimited reserves of oil. Until June 1973, Canadian official releases suggested that Canada had an unlimited supply of oil and natural gas which would last at least until 2050. By October 1974, the comfortable surplus became a dangerous shortage! The raising of gas prices following this scare has produced massive profits for Canadian subsidiaries of American companies. Imperial Oil increased its profits after taxes from $151 million in 1972 to $290 million in 1974. Profits in the oil industry between 1973 - 1974 were $1 billion more than total exploration.[77] Furthermore, because until recently there has been no pipeline in Canada from the Ottawa valley east, Eastern Canada is dependent on oil imports from the Middle East and Venezuela at considerably higher prices than Canada receives for western oil and gas exported to the United States.[78]

What are Canadian compradors doing about this situation? They object if the Canadian government shows any signs of rectifying this sellout on the grounds that it would be discriminatory against "Canadian" oil companies in the west who have had a long trading relationship with their friendly neighbour in the south. An excellent representative of this comprador elite in Canada is J. A. Armstrong, a native of Dauphin, Manitoba, who is president of Imperial Oil of Canada. According to the Globe and Mail profile of him, he is a man who is confident but restrained, with a corporate image that befits the president of a subsidiary of Standard Oil of New Jersey. Armstrong is in favour of a North American energy resource policy. He feels certain that the United States will need increasing quantities of Canadian oil, but he wants assurance of a Canadian commitment to a continental oil policy so that the industry can begin to formulate long term planning.[79] With the U.S. stranglehold on ownership of Canadian oil at 90%,[80] is it possible for this comprador to envisage with a long term continental policy, a programme that would more readily insure American ownership of Canadian oil resources?[81]

10. The Parasite Elite

A brief by the Canadian Council of Churches (Task Force on the Churches and Corporate Responsibility) to the Royal Commission on Corporate Concentration showed concern over the concentration of economic power "in relatively few, mostly unknown hands obscured by the illusory facade of responsibility to shareholders."[82] The report hints at the hypocrisy of Canada's international reputation if Canada cannot control companies that fly its flag overseas. "In many ways, for example, what Falconbridge does in Namibia is at least as important as how Canada votes on Namibia issues at the United Nations. Yet, because of corporate power and control, concerned Canadians, whether minority shareholders or the public, have very limited channels to influence the policies and decisions of their corporations."[83]

The fear that the Task Force expresses is an ominous reality. Because of the power of the parasitic elite within the United States, Canadian sovereignty over a company like Falconbridge is very hard to establish. The history of Falconbridge is a *cause célèbre* of how a parasitic elite operates in Canada. An outline by John Deverell and the Latin American Working Group shows that the Sudbury area in Canada in the 1940s and 1950s provided 90% of all nickel production in the non-communist world.[84] When nickel was first discovered in the Sudbury basin in the 1880s, Samuel Ritchie and a group of Ohio backers were able to purchase mineral patents to this non-renewable Canadian resource. The terms of sale were: one dollar an acre, no limit on the size of the claim, no taxes on undeveloped land, and no requirement for improvement.[85] By 1886, when controls were tightened, Ritchie controlled most of the accessible ores. He secured contracts with the U.S. navy to re-equip the United States fleet with nickel-steel armour plate. The list of American industrial tycoons who moved into lucrative Canadian nickel mining expanded to include J. P. Morgan, founder of International Nickel Company.

The current controller of Falconbridge is the wealthy family enterprise of Howard B. Keck. This family bought out a British and South African consortium through holdings in the Canadian Bank of Commerce. This illustrates how United States multinationals appear to be transnational while they are, in fact, prudentially national. Through political power of the U.S. they have been able to develop large contracts. The Howard Keck connection to Lyndon Johnson was through the oil magnate Robert Anderson who, as Secretary of the Navy in successive American cabinets, was able to insure navy contracts.

John Connally, appointed to the Falconbridge board in 1973, was one more déjà-vu with political influence.[86] He was the prime engineer of the economic blockage of Chile after the election of Salvadore Allende. Conally, as Secretary of the Treasury, was also a U.S. representative to the World Bank; with this portfolio he was able to strengthen the stranglehold on Chile by withholding credit. While Secretary of the Treasury, he supported setting up the Domestic International Sales Corporation (DISC) in the United States. DISC encouraged American companies with branch plants in Canada to repatriate their operation to the States and to take advantage of an indefinite tax deferral by expanding direct control of their foreign operation from the United States.[87] Although this record should have shown that Connally is an undesirable alien in Canada, Canadian impotence lies partly in Canadians having no say over who Falconbridge appoints to its board of Directors.

Preceding sections have outlined the subservience of Canada's economic leadership and how it perpetuates Canaanite captivity of Canada, but an examination of political leadership is also indicated.

11. Canadian Political Leadership

Canada has not had any political leaders in its history to pick up the mantle of David to help establish its independence. But some historians have tried to cast one or another of Canada's prime ministers as latter day liberators, saving the country from absorption into the United States. Following the Civil War, Sir John A. MacDonald is credited with rescuing Canada from the American "Manifest Destiny" policy. At the time of the Boer War, Sir Wilfrid

Laurier kept Quebec within confederation and so preserved the French (another saving characteristic) from becoming Americanized. John Diefenbaker's prairie populism sought to instill the rationale of identity in "my fellow Canadians" and Lester Pearson, with a Nobel peace prize, became the epitome of the Canadian polished diplomat in back room negotiations for peace in the Middle East. And Pierre Trudeau has been touted as giving a daring style to politics and a new emphasis on equal rights for the French language becomes a subterfuge to avoid having to "bite the bullet" on confronting United States takeover. Closer examination of the nature of Canada's capitalistic society shows that those who control economic power also control politicians. Cy Gonick gives an historical example:

> The board of directors of the Grand Trunk Railway reads like a list of the Fathers of Confederation. A study of the industrial elite at the turn of the century reveals that no less than one third held political office at some time in their careers . . . . This pattern repeats itself through the era of Mackenzie King (advisor to the Rockefellers), C. D. Howe, Louis St. Laurent and the Pearson-Trudeau cabinets of Robert Winters, Mitchell Sharp, James Richardson, et al.[88]

Besides its tie to business, another facet of Canadian political leadership is its close liaison with the university. Although academic researchers (who purport to describe the facts in Royal Commission and Task Force reports) become agents of the inevitability of present conditions, the support that academics give the government is not limited to research. George Grant shows that masters of Canadian companies (like Brazilian Traction) are able to get seats on the Board of Governors of universities because of their economic power.[89] They slide easily from campus to civil service to government. Lester Pearson, Robert Winters, and Mitchell Sharp personify what Grant calls "the ruling class." Pierre Trudeau, a millionaire of inherited wealth, is the most recent version of this academic-to-civil-servant-to-politician route. His political philosophy of functionalism fits in with the rational pragmatic ideology which is a hallmark of our capitalist society. Marcel Rioux, the French Canadian separatist professor of sociology, describes Trudeau's functionalism as the philosophy of the ruling class where the function of every institution is to preserve the status quo and the equilibrium that results from it.[90] It is interesting how this functionalism (which sounds open and non-dogmatic) appeals to the Canadian trait described earlier in this review as a predilection for law and stable government. But Pierre Trudeau is representative of what the Canadian public admires!

The Canadian political scientist Paul Fox commented after Trudeau's election in 1967: "There is nothing more attractive to a . . . Canadian than to be titillated into voting for a radical when deep down they are comforted that he is a conservative."[91] Trudeau will go down in Canadian history with the dubious honour of being the most ruthless queller of civil unrest in Canada. His tactics drew the admiration of Prime Minister Smith of Rhodesia and Spiro Agnew of the United States. He is the first Canadian Prime Minister to defend the shibboleth of a "just society" by evoking the War Measures Act in peacetime. In a speech in the Saskatchewan Legislature opposing the War Measures Act, the late Woodrow Lloyd, premier of the Province of Saskatchewan and stout defender of civil liberties, said, "does democracy defend itself by destroying democracy . . . [it is like asking us] to welcome handcuffs in order to prevent our hands from shaking."[92]

Trudeau's functionalism is also anti-nationalistic. His polemic against Quebec nationalism and separatism has its genesis in his earlier writings. He describes nationalism as an anachronism and hopes that in the future "national sovereignty will recede and with it the need for an emotional justification of nationalism."[93] He sees the glue of nationalism becoming as obsolete as the divine rights of kings. In its place, he would promote functionalism in Canada where the aspirations of different regions of Canada could be traded off in a broker-like fashion within confederation. This anti-nationalism makes Trudeau a complete push-over in dealings with the United States because while he has visions of distant international vistas American nationalism moves ruthlessly into larger takeover of Canada, using the rhetoric of continentalism to gain the upper hand.

It is important not to make Liberals (even though they have been the major agents of continentalism) the only culprits in Canada's sell-out. The Columbia River Treaty, ratified in June 1964, shows how all governments can be involved in a give-away of Canadian resources. The damming and flooding of the interior of British Columbia in the Arrow Lake-Kooteney Columbia Valley area has provided cheap energy for the western seaboard of the United States. It has left Canada as the "Continental Waterboy" described by Douglas Waterfield in his book bearing this title.[94] Waterfield explains how Canada was stampeded into downstream concessions to the United States in return for cash revenue for W. A. C. Bennett's Social Credit government in British Columbia. As a result, valuable agriculture and resort land was flooded. Yet Canada is required to regulate the water system to guarantee that there will be no downstream flooding on the United States side of the rivers! Furthermore, Canada is not allowed to divert any part of the river for commercial purposes, so that the Canadian part of the dam system becomes a vast reservoir for American industry.

In negotiating this treaty, Canada ignored the advice of its most distinguished Canadian civil engineer, General A. G. L. McNaughton, stripping him of the power to negotiate from strength. It was a period of minority federal governments and both conservatives and liberals were interested in picking up British Columbia votes. Nevertheless, on the eve of ratification, McNaughton, with considerable bitterness, drew these conclusions about Canada's politicians: "It is indeed a sorry prospect which lies before us unless Parliament will refuse approval for ratification of this iniquitous Treaty, and unless the country will waken to the menace we face, due to the complacency of [David] Fulton, the vanity, ignorance and carelessness of [John] Diefenbaker and the stupidity of [W. A. C.] Bennett."[95]

The question as to why Canada can appear so rich in comparison with other countries and yet be a satellite of the United States has been dealt with by explaining Canada's satellite status as a form of Canaanite captivity. Canada is a country of well-to-do slaves who live with the stunted imagination of a closed future; her captive condition has been maintained by churches which emphasize the righteousness of conformity to the law, by an economic elite who live off the fat of the land while acting as agents of foreign predators, and by political leadership that serves as waterboy.

12. Canadian Obsession with Consensus

Some readers who agree with the hypothesis that Canadians are dominated by the United States and consequently restricted as a nation in their capacity to make sovereign decisions on political and moral issues may think that the issues have been posed too rigidly in terms of villains and victims. In general, Canadians love consensus and hence may view this analysis as divisive. This class cleavage is warranted for two reasons; First, it is important to counteract the national unity obsession because, as Gad Horowitz explains in his review of John Porter's Vertical Mosaic:

When politics is not based on class but on regional or ethnic divisions, the personal troubles of ordinary people are not readily transformed into issues. If a society's dialogue is unity versus discord rather than "right" versus "left", politics can have no profound meaning for the lives of ordinary people, and they cannot use politics to change the conditions of their lives. The Bilingual and Bicultural Commission will not alter the distribution of values among the classes of Canadian society. It may give the French-speaking Albertans French schools, but it will not affect their powerlessness and insecurity, vis-a-vis the elite which decide for them what the content of their daily lives will be.[96]

Secondly, class analysis is important if Canada is to be addressed in the tradition of the prophets. By confining the biblical story to church reading and private devotion, the hard line it advocates in bringing the wealthy under judgement becomes muted in unctuous piety. Unquestionably Amos would address the wives of Canada's wealthy men as "the cows of Bashan . . . who oppress the poor, who crush the needy"[97] through their ostentatious life style. Isaiah would have called God's judgement on the top executives and directors of Canadian companies who apportion large salaries for themselves and so increase for the poor the cost of basic items like fuel and food. Speaking to the rich of his own day Isaiah says: "The Lord enters into judgement with the elders and princes of his people: "It is you who have devoured the vineyard, the spoil of the poor is in your houses."[98]

Canada will have no conception of a "just society" until it recognizes the extent of the massive structural inequality in its class divisions. When E. M. Bronfman, chairman of the Board of Directors of Seagram's of Canada, could walk away with a salary of $788,974.00 in 1979, an increase of 108% over his 1978 salary, and in the same year the average income of a woman in Canada was $7,070.00, one sees the flagrant inequality in the country.[99] This inequality is an affront not only to our sense of fairness but to those in the Christian community who have visions of the kingdom of God taking shape in our country. This is not an attempt to picture some heavenly utopia but to outline some characteristics of a more human alternative. Canada has had its own prophets and like the Rechabites and the Nazarenes in Israel it has had protest groups whose formation has been shaped by their theological understanding and their insistence on an alternative life-style. The theological ferment taking shape in the churches has the ingredients of a political theology tied to environmental issues. Its political origins lie in the socialist alternative for Canada found in the movement politics of the Agrarian revolt, the British idealism of the Cooperative Commonwealth Federation - New Democratic Party and the Marxist socialism.

13. Agrarian Populism

The agrarian revolt in the prairies questioned the bondage of a closed future for the farmer trapped by rail monopolies and the consequent high transportation costs. The farmer also faced a federal trade policy which provided protection through tariffs for farm machinery companies in central Canada but left an unprotected international market for his grains. He was also victim of a banking system located in central Canada that loaned money at high interest rates and foreclosed on farmers in lean years. Land policy provided Canadian giants like the Canadian Pacific Railway and the Hudson Bay Company with tax-free land but left the farmer burdened with debt.

These grievances were fought by prairie populism, becoming politically visible in the Progressive Party in 1921 and in the anti-party Federation idea of the Cooperative Commonwealth Federation. Prairie populism has left an important inheritance for Canadian socialism because it questioned the party system of parliamentary government which became compromised on its road to political power. Populist emphasis on grass roots politics, where issues are worked out by local groups and political leaders can be recalled if they fail to represent the local political movements' wishes, enhances participatory democracy and saves reform movements from being taken over by power-hungry politicians and bureaucrats. The grey bureaucracy provided by Russian communism shows how centralized monolithic socialism can become as oppressive as the monolithic capitalism it has replaced.

The problem with agrarian populism lay in its issue-oriented platform and its abhorrence of political ideology. The history of left populism in both the United States and Canada has shown that it has had to rely on larger parties to include its own issues in their platforms. Both the Democrats in the U.S. and the Liberals in Canada were happy to swallow the issues that farmers wanted, but the same parties had commitments to other interest groups. These commitments were often diametrically opposed to the progressive ideas of agrarian populism. So the leaders of populist groups were invariably faced with a "Hobson's choice" of limited alternatives when they were trapped in a political system which compromised their political zeal. And yet another weakness in this grass roots politics was that although it produced participatory politics it always stood in danger of becoming factionalized into splinter groups. The parallel to agrarian populism in Israel's history is described in the Book of Judges. The twelve tribes who became a federation when they reached Canaan avoided setting up a king because, as the prophets kept reminding them, a king could develop aspirations to omnipotence that would usurp the position of God. They therefore depended on charismatic judges to lead them in periods of crisis. But the writer of the book saw the danger of this "off-and-on" leadership leading to anarchy. "There was no king in Israel and everyone did that which was right in his own eyes."[100]

In a tribute to Canadian agrarian socialism, Seymour Lipset suggests that it was more radical than the American version. It also provided political continuity because its farm leadership, drawn from the British working class, was ideologically stronger through participation in trade unions and co-operatives in Britain.[101] Did the British socialist influence provide the more radical tradition that Lipset suggests? An answer to this necessitates a review of the contribution of British idealism to Canadian socialism.

14. British Idealism and the C.C.F. - N.D.P. Parties

In a speech to the founding convention of the Cooperative Commonwealth Federation in 1933, J. S. Woodsworth, leader of the C.C.F. and former leader of the Independent Labour Party, outlined his expectations for Canadian socialists:

> We aim to replace the capitalist system with its inherent injustice and inhumanity, by a social order from which domination and exploitation of one class by another will be eliminated; in which economic planning will supersede unregulated private enterprise and competition and in which democratic self-government based upon economic equality will be feasible. This social and economic transformation can be brought about by political action, through the election of the people. We do not believe in change by violence.[102]

What happened to this vision? Certainly, it must be lauded as an important vision. The bondage of Canaan in political terms occurs when people are constantly circumscribed by the inevitability of events. The British socialist tradition constantly reiterated that the human situation is understandable, transformable, and is shaped by its dreams. As early as 1913, Woodsworth then a Methodist minister working for the Department of Temperance of the Methodist and Presbyterian churches, did a municipal survey in the city of Regina. His report captured the idealism of British socialism which combined both the idealism of Hegel and the empiricism of Hume. (This double emphasis was philosophically developed by T. H. Green and Edward Caird).[103] Although in his survey Woodsworth gave details about streets, railways, housing, churches, and slum areas in Regina, he did not provide only analysis. He concludes: "The city like the individual may be the builder of her destiny. She only has to set up an ideal for herself, pass through a period of introspection and self-analysis to discover exactly her present state and the steps that must be taken that she may become the ideal city."[104]

Woodsworth's "ideal city" is reminiscent of the New Jerusalem, the biblical version of the perfect community which has been a fundamental stimulant to the Christian socialist who dreams of the kingdom of his Lord and of his Christ. But the problem with Woodsworth's vision was his over-confidence in scientific progress as the agent of a perfect society. His faith in science is revealed in an article he wrote for the Winnipeg Tribune where he said, "Let the church banish poverty as science does malaria."[105] Using this science-malaria metaphor, Woodsworth recalled that malaria-spreading mosquitoes had brought the French attempt to build the Panama Canal to a standstill. Sanitary officials took preventive action by clearing swamps and making it impossible for the mosquitoes to live. Woodsworth proposed that the swamps of the Wimmipeg slums could be cleaned up with better sanitation and co-operation amongst schools, newspapers, businessmen, labour unions, and government departments.[106] But Woodsworth's type of utopian hope based on scientific progress either leads to romanticism which rules out the regressive effects of technological scientism, or it leads to a political cynicism where dreams are shattered by hard facts.

The British socialist tradition built on idealism did provide an ideological tenacity to the C.C.F. - N.D.P. in periods when they had poor results at elections. In 1935 when a C.C.F. organizer wrote Woodsworth asking if he thought that the C.C.F. would hold the balance of power in the next election, he answered: "I confess that I am tired of the mentality of our people who get discouraged unless they can delude themselves into the belief that we are going to be the government . . . . You will agree with me that we are fighting for a principle, and that we should fight for this principle even if we should go down in defeat."[107]

However, the closer this party has come to power, and when it has achieved power in provincial governments, we find that the ideology of progress becomes rampant. Looking at the development ideology of the N.D.P. Government in Saskatchewan on the mining of uranium and the hazard this creates for the environment, we find there is little to choose between them and the main line parties.

The biblical vision of the hope that lies in a remnant people living to serve and not dependent on overt signs of success could provide a healthy corrective to a socialist party that becomes obsessed with coming to and staying in power regardless of compromises. The remnant idea is expressed both by the prophet Isaiah and the apostle Paul: "there shall come forth a shoot from the stump of Jesse."[108] Jesse, the father of King David, was the establisher of a Royal Tree. His illustrious son had expanded Israel's earthly aspirations, but this royal tree had ended in a dead stump. From this dead stump a new shoot was springing forth. This remnant from the old Davidic kingdom was to live recognizing first that it was under judgement itself, second that it was to "execute justice and righteousness in the land,"[109] and third that it was to provide a new type of hope for the nations-a hope based on a peaceable kingdom of harmony between human beings and nature.

15. Marxist Socialism:

Both the populist tradition of the agrarian revolt and the British Idealism of the Canadian labour movement lacked class analysis and failed to expose the pyramids of power which are perpetuated generation after generation in Canadian society. The discussion on the role of Canadian Marxists, on the other hand, suspicious of all capitalist societies have shown the structural inequality in Canada; they have also exposed the emptiness of phrases about "upward mobility" and "equal opportunity for all." Canadian elites in keeping the country in a subservient state should lead Canadians to ask themselves, "Why have we let it happen?" Karl Marx and Frederick Engel offer light on the Canadian predicament. They point out that in a capitalist society people are conditioned to accept the ideology of the status quo which produces a type of blindness. This ideological bias "makes their circumstances appear upside down as in a camera *obscura*, this phenomenon arises just as much from their historical life process as the inversion of objects on the retina does from their physical life process."[110] The irony of this ideological blindness is that it is most prevalent among the best educated and the most powerful. Marx points out, "The ideas of the ruling class are in every age, the ruling ideas: i.e. the class which is the dominant material force in society is at the same time its dominant intellectual force."[111] How does a privileged class dominate those who suffer under the domination? Marx explains that people become brainwashed by a reality where ruling people have the ruling ideas of the age.[112]

In the ministry of Jesus there is an event that makes an interesting comment on religious ideological blindness. Jesus' disciples, recognizing the familiar Palestinian sight of a blind man, turn his problem into a speculative theological question on the roots of sin. "Who sinned, this man or his parents that he was born blind?"[113] After Jesus heals the blind man, the Pharisees enter another theological discussion on their own 20/20 spiritual vision. Based on their pedigree through Abraham and their scholarship in the Mosaic law, they ask, "Are we also blind?" Jesus gives them an answer that shows how ideology becomes masked as religion. He says, "If you were born blind you would have no guilt, but now that you say, 'we see' your guilt remains." Jesus, in his attack on the Pharisees for imagining they could "see" the world through their smug assumptions of "having Abraham as their father" and being the true inheritors of the law, was attacking people who had the false ideological consciousness of a reality that was circumscribed by the mores of Judaism.

Because religious and political criticism of Canadian society is culturally conditioned, it is important to use a totally antithetical ideological critique to unmask the liberal blindness of Canadians. Marxist socialism in its analysis of society reflects the tradition of the biblical prophets. This is illustrated by Rubem Alves, a Brazilian liberation theologian who uses Marxist analysis in his realism about power. He says: "Power doesn't give up power. Will to power does not become will to liberate."[114] God takes sides with those who fight to break the yoke of the oppressor. As the oppressor is stripped of his power to dominate, so he is humanized just as the slave is humanized by no longer being in a servile state.[115]

The great contribution of Canadian Marxists has been the quality of their analysis of Canadian society. They have been fearless in naming the principalities and powers that have subjugated Canadians. They have been uncompromising in showing the class cleavages in Canadian society. Although Christians for Socialism might be criticized for having a romantic view of the sanctity of labour in bringing the new age, they cannot make this an obstacle to supporting Canadian Marxists. Like Cyrus the Persian king, unconscious of his role in the plan of salvation, Marxists show from their support of the cause of liberation that they are the "Lord's anointed."

NOTES

[1]The editor wishes to express his indebtedness to the following writers: Wallace Clement, John Deverell and the Latin American Working Group, Gatt Fly, Cy Gonick, Gad Horowitz, George Grant, James Laxer, Robert Laxer, Kari Levitt, C. B. Macpherson, Don Mitchell, Norman Penner, John Warnock, and Donald Waterfield. These Canadian analysts write with a clarity and love for their country that makes it possible for a layman in the area of political science and economics to become aware of the nature of the Canadian bondage.

[2]Robert Michels, Political Parties (New York: Dove Publications, 1959), 379-392. Seymour Lipset, Agrarian Socialism (updated edition; New York: Anchor Books, 1968); Leo Zakuta, A Protest Movement Becalmed (Toronto: University of Toronto Press, 1964); Walter Young, The Anatomy of a Party: the National C.C.F. 1932-1961 (Toronto: University of Toronto Press, 1969); B. G. Smillie, "J. S. Woodsworth, Civic Pedagogue, 1875-1942." (dissertation, Columbia University, 1970). 205-12.
Three writers, Lipset, Zakuta, and Young, have provided important historical material on Canadian Socialism and yet have distorted the record in imposing Michels' thesis that socialist parties start as charismatic movements with a high degree of voluntary participation among their members but become imcreasingly dominated by oligarchic bureaucracies as they become more powerful. The underlying assumption that can lead to a form of cynicism is that power corrupts all socialist political movements which start on a crusade of social justice. The thesis only works if you are highly selective in the events you choose to record and you develop a knack of starting and stopping the historical clock to make the events fit the law. Smillie elaborates on this criticism.

[3]Department of Economics and Social Affairs, Statistical Year Book, Twenty Eighth Issue (New York: United Nations, 1976), 690-93.

[4]Gatt Fly, What is the New International Economic Order? (Toronto: Canadian Council of Churches, n.d.), 14.

[5]John W. Warnock, Partner to Behemoth (Toronto: New Press, 1970), 285. George Grant, Lament for a Nation (Toronto/Montreal: McClelland and Stewart, 1965), 28-29. Howard Green, who was Minister of External Affairs in the Diefenbaker government supported the Canadian condemnation of the United States for violating the Geneva Agreement in the International Control Commission report of June 2, 1962. This annoyed the Kennedy administration. Grant recognized a certain innocence in Howard Green's foreign policy because he did not "automatically assume the role of an official of a satellite country." This independent bravery in the hard days of the Cuban crisis brings Grant to say of Green that he deserves the prefix "Right Honorable."

[6]Stephen Clarkson, "National Pathology and Cultural Policy," Canadian Forum 57, 674 (September, 1977), 8-12.

[7]Ibid., 8.

[8]Ibid., 9.

[9]Micah 6:8. All biblical quotations are taken from the Revised Standard Version.

[10]Judges 8:33

[11]I Cor. 11:20-22.

[12]Exodus 5:20.

[13]Rubem Alves, A Theology of Human Hope (Washington: Corpus Books, 1969), 107.

[14]Ibid., 112.

[15]Deut. 6:10-12.

[16]Joel 2:24, 26.

[17]William Creighton Graham, The Prophets and Israel's Culture (Chicago: University of Chicago Press, 1934), 17.

[18]Ministry of Industry Trade and Commerce, Statistics Canada: Urban Expenditure, 1974 (Ottawa: Queen's Printers, 1977), 47-49.

[19]Ministry of Supply and Services Canada, Perspective Canada, English Edition (Ottawa: Queen's Printers, 1977), 181.

[20]Science Council of Canada, Canada as a Conserver Society Report No. 27 (Ottawa: Printing and Publishing Supply and Services, Canada, 1977), 65.

[21]Ian Adams, The Poverty Wall (Toronto/Montreal: McClelland and Stewart, 1970), 19-20.

[22]I Cor. 11:22.

[23]Adams, Poverty Wall, 17.

[24]Ibid., 73.

[25]Leviticus 25:25.

[26]Adolphe Lods, The Prophets and the Rise of Judaism (London: Routedge and Kegan Paul, 1937), 127.

[27]Thomas Hobbes, Leviathan (London: George Routledge, n.d.), 78-79.

[28]C. B. Macpherson, Democratic Theory: Essays in Retrieval (London: Oxford University Press, 1973), 160-161.

[29]C. B. Macpherson, The Political Theory of Possessive Individualism (London: Oxford University Press, 1962), 22-23.

[30]Robert Pursig, Zen and the Art of Motorcycle Maintenance (New York: William Morrow, 1974), 312.

[31] James Laxer and Robert Laxer, The Liberal Idea of Canada (Toronto: Lorimer, 1977), 38.

[32] II Samuel 5:13-18.

[33] Norman Gottwald, A Light to the Nations (New York: Harper, 1959), 202.

[34] I Samuel 8:11-18.

[35] Gottwald, A Light, 203

[36] I Kings 9:26-28, 10:1.

[37] I Kings 12:11.

[38] E. W. Heaton, The Hebrew Kingdoms (London: Oxford University Press, 1968), 3.

[39] Amos 7:10, 11-13.

[40] Isaiah 31:1-3.

[41] Amos 4:1.

[42] Isaiah 31:1-3.

[43] Heaton, Hebrew Kingdoms, 177.

[44] Hosea 7-11.

[45] II Kings 18:31-33.

[46] Gatt Fly, Sugar: Who Pays the Price? (Toronto: 600 Jarvis Street, June, 1975), 20-26.

[47] Gatt Fly, What is the New International Economic Order? (Toronto: 600 Jarvis Street, n.d.), 5.

[48] Kari Levitt, Silent Surrender (Toronto: MacMillan, 1970) 11.

[49] Laxer and Laxer, Liberal Idea, 38.

[50] Ibid., 39.

[51] U.S. Bureau of the Census, Statistical Abstract of the United States, 1972 (Washington, D.C.: Government Printing Office, 1972), 776. Quoted by Laxer and Laxer, Ibid., 40.

[52] Frank H. Underhill, In Search of Canadian Liberalism (Toronto: MacMillan, 1961), 109.

[53] Report of the Task Force on Agriculture, Canadian Agriculture in the Seventies, December, 1969 (Ottawa: Queen's Printers, 1970), 410.

[54] Ibid., 431.

[54] Ibid., 431.

[55] Don Mitchell, The Politics of Food (Toronto: James Lorimer, 1975), 50.

[56] National Farmers' Union, Presentation to the Canadian Agricultural Congress (Ottawa: Nov. 25-27, 1970), 11.

[57] Ronald Sutherland, "Christianity in Canada and the Canadian Mystique." Texts prepared for Conference on the Survival of Canada and the Christian Church, Feb. 23-25, 1973 (Toronto: Ecumenical Centre, 1973), 15-19.

[58] Jean Charles Falardeau, "Social Organization and Culture," in Marcel Riox and Yves Martin (eds.) French Canadian Society 1, Carlton Library Series, (Toronto: McClelland and Stewart, 1964), 347, 349. Falardeau illustrates the Quebec Church's fanatic loyalty to the British crown and anti-French sentiment by citing an event in 1789 when a Te Deum was sung in the Cathedral of Quebec on the occasion of the British victory at Aboukir. He also describes the strong twist in the allegiance of the French Canadian clergy who promoted a new indigenous identity. He says, "whereas in Europe ultramontanism was generally associated with anti-nationalism, French-Canadian ultramontanism was characterized by a fiercely nationalistic attitude."

[59] Harold A. Innis, Essays in Canadian Economic History, ed. Mary Q. Innis (Toronto: University of Toronto Press, 1956), 384.

[60] Richard Allen, The Social Passion: Religion and Social Reform in Canada, 1913-1928 (Toronto: University of Toronto Press, 1971), 261.

[61] Ibid., 144.

[62] Ibid., 273.

[63] Roger Hutchinson, "The Canadian Social Gospel in the Context of Christian Social Ethics," in Richard Allen (ed.), The Social Gospel in Canada (Ottawa: National Museum of Canada, 1975), 296.

[64] Ibid., 297.

[65] Allen, Social Passion, 110.

[66] Martin O'Malley,"'Hail Politics, Power and Protocol' and 'Pity the Protestant, Amen!,'" The Globe Magazine (Toronto: Jan. 9, 1971), 6-7.

[67] Neil Sheehan, The Pentagon Papers, as published by the New York Times (New York/Chicago: Quadrangle Books, 1971), 297-299, 404. A memo dated Aug. 8, 1964, under the joint authorship of the American Ambassador to South Vietnam and General Westmoreland, shows the attitude of the United States military to J. Blair Seaborn, Canadian representative on the International Control Commission. He was expected to carry United States conditions to North Vietnam as the U.S. escalated the bombing of the North. There is also evidence that Seaborn, who as a member of the control Commission was supposed to

take a neutral stance, was an agent of the American war effort providing secret diplomatic dispatches to Washington about North Vietnamese morale.

[68]R. T. Naylor, "The Rise and Fall of the Third Commercial Empire of the St. Lawrence," in Gary Teeple (ed.), Capitalism and the National Question in Canada (Toronto: University of Toronto Press, 1972), 36.

[69]Wallace Clement, The Canadian Corporate Elite (The Carlton Library, 89; Toronto: McClelland and Stewart, 1975), 36.

[70]Ibid., 190-191.

[71]Ibid., 178.

[72]Ibid., 187.

[73]Ibid., 117.

[74]John Hutcheson, "Class and Income Distribution in Canada," in Robert M. Laxer (ed.), Canada Ltd. (Toronto: McClelland and Stewart, 1973), 57-83. We ought to mention that we will use the sociological category, elite, even though it has sometimes been used, as John Hutcheson suggests, to avoid the issues of class. Hutcheson, in his Marxist analysis of Canadian society, faults William Kilbourn and John Porter for their division of society into elites as it suggests that Canada is a country with the opportunity for upward mobility into elite groups. We have already suggested that this upward mobility is an illusion.

[75]T. B. Bottomore, Elites and Society (Hammondsworth: Pelican Books, 1966) 83-87. We support the position of T. B. Bottomore, who also recognizes no upward mobility but insists that the ruling class in a modern society is made up of such an amorphous group of directors, managers, and in the case of Russia, bureaucrats, who have all the power of industrial capitalists. He concludes it is important to reject the idea of the circulation of elites, but retain this category.

[76]Ibid., 356.

[77]Cy Gonick, Inflation and Wage Controls (Winnipeg: Canadian Dimension, 1976), 64-65.

[78]James Laxer, The Energy Poker Game (Toronto/Chicago: New Press, 1970), 29.

[79]Ibid., 12.

[80]James Lorimer, Canada's Oil Monopoly (The story of the $12 Billion Rip-off of Canadian Consumers, Toronto: Lorimer, 1981), 52-54. East of the Ottawa Valley the eastern provinces have been dependent on OPEC imported oil controlled by the "Big Four" American oil companies, Imperial, Gulf, Shell and Texaco. Petro Canada, an oil company owned by the Canadian Government and founded in 1976 acquired Petro Fina in 1981. It has been unable to influence the power of the Big Four because there is a vertical integration

between the Canadian subsidiary and the American parent, rather than an arm's length relationship, because the subsidiary has had to charge a dictated price from the parent which has put the wholesale and retail price of imported oil well above the international price. "The sizeable transfer price premiums paid to the offshore parent multinationals by the Canadian subsidiaries adversely affected the Canadian economy." 338-348, 429-430. In western Canada the Big Four American owned companies have also enjoyed a monopoly position with an economic power to force the smaller companies into line through owning the lion's share of the production of oil. By being able to license the users of the inter-provincial pipeline, they have also controlled the tap for the distribution of Canadian oil to flow east to Ontario. To complete the picture of their total domination, they have also owned the storage and processing of oil through their refineries. This has enabled them to influence the wholesale and retail price of oil through their monopoly position.

[81] James Laxer, "Always look to Imperial," The Big Tough Expensive Job James Laxer and Anne Martin (eds.), (Don Mills: Press Porcépic, 1976), 20. J. A. Armstrong's unquestioning loyalty to his American employer Exxon of New York is reflected in a 1976 interview with Raoul Engel, Global Television reporter. Engel was aware that Armstrong had holdings of $425,000 in Imperial Oil, the Canadian subsidiary of Exxon who owned at that time $1.4 billion in shareholder equity. In attempting to clarify whether or not Imperial Oil was American controlled, Engel asked Armstrong, ". . . if it came down to out and out disagreement to bare knuckles, what then?" Armstrong replied ". . . they could get rid of us. It's that simple."

[82] Task Force on the Churches and Corporate Responsibility, A Submission to the Royal Commission on Corporate Concentration (Feb. 16, 1976), 2-3.

[83] Ibid., 3.

[84] John Deverell and the Latin American Working Group, Falconbridge (Toronto: James Lorimer, 1975), 12.

[85] Ibid., 22.

[86] Ibid., 71.

[87] Ibid., 76.

[88] Gonick, Inflation, 99f.

[89] George Grant, Technology and Empire (Toronto: House of Anansi, 1969), 115.

[90] Marcel Rioux, Quebec in Question (Toronto: Lewis, 1971), 105.

[91] Quoted by Cy Gonick, "A Man to Hold Quebec," The Nation (April 29, 1968), 564.

[92] C. B. Koester (ed.), The Measure of the Man: Selected Speeches of Woodrow Stanley Lloyd (Saskatoon: Western Producer, Prairie Books, 1976), 95-96.

[93]Pierre Elliott Trudeau, Federalism and the French Canadian (Toronto: MacMillan, 1968), 196.

[94]Donald C. Waterfield, Continental Waterboy (Toronto: Clarke Irwin, 1970).

[95]Ibid., 231; A. G. L. McNaughton, letter to Donald C. Waterfield, Dec. 20, 1962.

[96]Gad Horowitz, "Creative Politics, Mosaics and Identity," in James L. Heap (ed.), Everybody's Canada (Toronto: Burns and MacEachern, 1974), 151.

[97]Amos 4:1.

[98]Isaiah 3:14.

[99]Financial Times of Canada (May 26, 1980), 20-21; The Alberta Democrat 7/2, 12.

[100]Judges 17:6.

[101]Seymour Martin Lipset, Agrarian Socialism (Updated Edition; New York: Anchor Books, 1950, 1968), 43.

[102]J. S. Woodsworth, Address to the Regina Convention 1933, "The First Ten Years 1932-1942" (Toronto: Co-operative Commonwealth Federation Seventh National Convention, 1942), 11.

[103]Rudolf Metz, A Hundred Years of British Philosophy (London: George Allen and Unwin, 1938), 286-293. For an elaboration of the philosophical background of J. S. Woodsworth see Smillie, Civic Pedagogue 30-39.

[104]J. S. Woodsworth, "Report of a Preliminary and General Social Survey of Regina," Department of Temperance and Moral Reform of the Methodist Church and the Board of Social Service and Evangelism of the Presbyterian Church (n.p. Sept., 1913), 21.

[105]J. S. Woodsworth, "Let the Church Banish Poverty as Science does Malaria." The Winnipeg Tribune (June 12, 1915); Woodsworth Papers, (Ottawa: Public Archives of Canada), Vol. 30.

[106]Ibid.,

[107]J. S. Woodsworth letter to John Mitchell, May 14, 1935, Woodsworth Papers, (P. A. C.) 3, 849.

[108]Isaiah 11:1; Romans 15:15.

[109]Jeremiah 23:5.

[110]Karl Marx and Fredrick Engel, Excerpts from the German Ideology, Basic Writings on Politics and Philosophy, Lewis S. Feuer (ed.), (New York: Anchor Books, 1959), 247.

[111]Karl Marx, Selected Writings in Sociology and Social Philosophy T. B. Bottomore and Miximilien Rubel (eds.), (Harmondsworth, Middlesex: Penguin Books, 1961), 93.

[112]Ibid.

[113]John 9:2.

[114]Alves, Theology, 122.

[115]Ibid.

2

POLITICAL THEOLOGY

William Hordern

The term "political theology" has a strange ring to most people. It is widely held that religion and politics do not mix or, at least, should not mix. Recently, a Canadian officer of Cargill Grain Company condemned the Canadian churches for "dabbling in politics," and he exhorted them to return to their proper concerns, the inner, personal, spiritual needs of persons. In other words, while it is right and fitting for churches to send gifts of food to the starving, it is none of the churches' business when giant international firms, like Cargill, manipulate the food supply of the world in a way that leads to starvation. The Cargill official had an obvious personal axe to grind, but a lot of people, including many within the churches themselves, would agree that religion is a matter of individual inner spiritual life and should not impinge on the political realm. Hence a political theology is a contradiction in terms.

In the minds of many the term political theology revives memories of those times in history when the church became involved in dubious political activity-giving spiritual support to unsavory governments, making political deals to enhance its own power and prestige in the world, and using the weapons of the state to enforce its views of orthodoxy. In reaction to these dark pages of ecclesiastical history many, both within the church and outside of it, see the separation of the church and state as a major gain for humanity. Political theology, they fear, would reverse democratic gains and return us to the evils of an earlier day.

Or again, politics, by its very nature, calls for commitment to particular causes, the enactment of policies which benefit some and are costly to others. Theology, however, is a universal pursuit in which thinkers try to see reality from God's point of view. It has no place for particularistic concerns or the taking of sides; it speaks equally to and for all people. Politics by its nature must distort all that theology is meant to achieve, and hence again it appears that a political theology is like a square circle, a contradiction in terms.

Despite these considerations, one of the most lively of modern theological movements is known as "political theology." The purpose of this essay is to see how it has come onto the theological scene and something of what it is attempting to do.

One of the remarkable things about political theology is that it is ecumenical. Whereas in the past theological movements normally have been Protestant, Catholic, or Jewish, political theology has important representatives from all of these groups. It is often difficult to find who is responsible for coining a new theological term, but it appears to me that the Roman Catholic theologian, Johannes Metz, was the first to make conscious use of it. Believing that contemporary religion was too much concerned with the private inner life of persons, Metz espoused political theology as a means of the "deprivitization" of religion. But Roman Catholic theologian Joseph Petulla suggests that the Protestant theologian, Karl Barth may "unwittingly" have set the stage for political theology.[1] A recent book from Germany, however, called Karl Barth and Radical Politics, suggests that it may not have been so unwitting on Barth's part.[2]

Karl Barth is the watershed for twentieth century Protestant theology. Whether other theologians have agreed or disagreed with him, they cannot ignore the fact that he has changed the whole context in which modern theology has operated. Karl Barth instigated the movement that overthrew the liberal theology that had dominated Protestant thought in the nineteenth century. Liberalism came close to being an ecumenical theology as parallel ideas appeared in the "modernist" movement of Roman Catholicism around the turn of the century. Modernism appeared to be crushed by Pope Pius X in 1907, but in the wake of Vatican II it appears that modernism may have gone underground rather than disappeared.

There was much that was good about liberal theology. It was determined to bring Christian theology into intimate relationship with the modern world. (Hence the term "modernism"). It accepted the historical criticism of the Scriptures and turned to modern philosophies to undergird theological thinking. It refused to believe that Christians had to sacrifice their intellects in order to retain the faith. Liberal theology emphasized that God is immanent in the world and particularly can be found within the experience of the individual. This meant that liberalism was optimistic about the world and humanity. Believing that God was immanent within the world, it was easy for liberals to espouse the belief in progress that was so popular in the nineteenth century. God, they believed, is working in the world so that it is continually getting to be better and better. Evil is being overcome; humanity is evolving out of its darker ages. This optimism led in a subtle way to blessing the status quo. Inasmuch as progress is inevitably moving ahead under divine direction, the current social situation is the best yet. And so bourgois capitalism appears as the highest state reached by humanity.

Early in the twentieth century in North America, a wing of liberalism developed into the social gospel. Because this movement attacked capitalism, North Americans have tended to overlook the degree to which liberalism was identified with the status quo. Today we are beginning to take a new look at the social gospel, and it appears that it was not the left wing of liberalism but was rather a break from liberalism. In many ways it can be considered the North American equivalent of the Barthian revolt in Europe. But that is a thesis for another paper.

Karl Barth was raised and trained in the reigning liberal theology at the beginning of this century. But when he went to his first parish in Safenwil, Switzerland in 1911, to minister to proletarian people, he became an active member of the socialist movement. When the war came in 1914 Barth became disillusioned with liberal theology because one by one all of his German professors whom he had revered came out in support of the German cause in the war. This revealed to Barth that the liberal theology, with its ligitimate concern to understand and relate to the modern world, had ended up in simply conforming to that world and blessing the status quo.

In 1919 Barth published his epic work, a commentary on the Epistle to the Romans. In it he emphasized the otherness of God. We cannot identify God or his will with the world or human affairs. God stands in judgment over even the best attainments of human beings. God is not known by taking humanity at its best and adding a few superlatives; he is known only in his revelation of himself, particularly in Jesus Christ. Humanity is always involved in the sin of identifying God with their own achievements and aspirations. This is the modern form of idolatry, the worshipping of human institutions and achievements as divine manifestations. But the wholly other God who reveals himself to us cannot be identified with any human movement.

The whole thrust of the Barthian theology was a challenge to the static view of the world that dominated liberal theology. Instead of a smooth progress which meant that the current status quo stood at the apex of human achievements, Barth saw a God who created a crisis by calling us to a radical break with the status quo. As he put it in his Romans, the radical who wants to change things may be wrong, but he has a chance of being right. The conservative who wants to keep things as they are is always wrong.

Because of Barth's emphasis upon the otherness of God, he could not identify God's will with the socialist movement. But Barth did see a real relationship between Christianity and socialism. We cannot identify Christianity with what socialists do, but what Christianity and socialism want are very close. In action socialists are as prone as anyone else to make mistakes or to allow their personal interests to pervert their methods of achieving their goals. The Christian, therefore, must be critical of socialism in action, more critical perhaps than it is of capitalism because the socialists do have the right goals, and hence their failures may threaten the very goals themselves. Both the goals of Christianity and socialism are concerned with the poor and the oppressed and aim to bring social justice for them. Jesus identified himself with the poor and promised them liberation from oppression and a coming kingdom of justice. As Barth put it, "One cannot reach lower down the social scale in the choice of one's associates than Jesus did. To him there was no one underneath who was too low or too bad."[3] This was not a cheap paternalistic attitude. Jesus did not feel sorry for the poor, he pitied the rich as his condemnations of them and woes to them indicate.

Barth was in Germany as a professor when the Nazi regime took over. Barth opposed it and organized the Barmen Declaration of the churches against Nazism. As a result he had to flee from Germany back to his native Switzerland, whence he continued to oppose Nazism until the end of World War Two. Despite all of Barth's political involvement, his followers tended to form what was known as "neo-orthodox theology" which became less and less political. Influenced by existential theology, it tended to return to a preoccupation with the individual person, individual problems, and individual relationships to God.

In the 1960s neo-orthodox theology broke up and a number of theological movements, including the death-of-God theology, rose and fell. Near the end of the decade the theology of hope emerged as the dominant theological position. It too was ecumenical inasmuch as it included Roman Catholic and Jewish thinkers as well as Protestants. The theology of hope, like Barth, was opposed to a static theology that blesses the status quo. It was based upon the concept that God is the God of the future. That is, the biblical God is one who makes and keeps his promises. Hence Christian faith means going forward with hope that the promises of God will be fulfilled. Hope includes both a this-worldly and an other-worldly element. To believe in God and the Risen Christ means to believe that the future is open. God will do that which has not been done before. We cannot predict the future simply upon the basis of the past. Once people said there always has been slavery, therefore, there always will be slavery. But the promises of God for liberation were fulfilled and slavery has nearly disappeared. And so today when people say there always have been wars, there always will be wars; women have always been subordinate to men, they always will be; starvation has always been the lot of many people, it always will be; the theology of hope says that to believe in God is to believe that what has always been will _not_ always be. The biblical God is the one who says that he makes all things new, and to have faith in him is to hope that past evils can be eliminated from the future.

The theology of hope appealed to churches in the Third World and to oppressed groups such as the blacks in the United States. But these groups felt that there were weaknesses in it. Rubem Alves, a South American theologian, picked up the theme of hope but, looking at it from the point of view of his oppressed compatriots, said that it was too Platonic. Its hope was like a Platonic idea which hovers above the reality of the present, calling us forward. The God of the future is so much ahead of us that he is not intimately involved in the history where we now are. Furthermore, the theology of hope rests so firmly upon God's predetermined plan for humanity that it is of no aid to oppressed people who have to plan strategies for overthrowing oppressive governments and social systems.

As a result of the inspiration of hope theology and the criticism of it, there has developed in recent years a theological movement known as "liberation theology." It is noteworthy that it did not arise in the circles from which theological movements normally have come. Heretofore, theological movements have originated in the theological schools of Europe and North America where white middle class male scholars have had a monopoly. Liberation theology has developed in the Third World countries in what were thought of as the "mission fields" of the churches of Europe and North America. Also it has developed among non-white races. In the United States, James Cone and others have developed a Black Theology of Liberation. And a number of women have made important contributions to this theology. In short, liberation theology has been written by people who see the social struggle from the viewpoint of the exploited.

At first sight, it might seem that liberation theology is simply jumping on the bandwagon of a popular theme. We hear much today of liberation movements in Third World countries and we have women's liberation movements, gay liberation and so on. Liberation is in the air. But there is more to it than that. In the New Testament the word "redemption" is widely used. Jesus is often referred to as redeemer and his work is to redeem the people. In an individualistic theological period, the word redemption has taken on other-worldly individualistic connotations. To be redeemed is to have one's ticket for heaven in the hereafter. But if we go back to the environment of the New Testament, we find that the word "redemption" was a widely used term of the time. If a person was in slavery and someone was prepared to pay the redemption price, he or she could be redeemed from slavery and freed. Similarly, if people had been captured in war or by brigands and held for ransom, they could be redeemed from their captivity by someone willing to pay the price. . Seeing what the word redemption meant in the time of the New Testament, it would appear that the best way to translate it into modern language is with the word "liberation." If Jesus came to redeem people, it means that he came to liberate them from the bondage in which they were held.

Liberation theologians see this spelled out for them in the fourth chapter of Luke's Gospel. Jesus has just sensed his call from God, he has been tempted in the wilderness, and now he returns to his new mission. To do so, he reads from the book of Isaiah and, when finished announces that this Scripture is fulfilled in him. The passage reads,

> The Spirit of the Lord is upon me because he has anointed me to preach good news to the poor.
> He has sent me to proclaim release to the captives and recovering of sight to the blind,
> to set at liberty those who are oppressed, to proclaim the acceptable year of the Lord. (Lk. 4:18-19)

Liberation theology points out that the center of Jesus' mission is to bring "good news" to the poor. As we read Luke's Gospel in its entirety, we cannot pretend that this is the "poor in spirit" or some such spiritualized concept. He means the economically and socially poor. And the good news is not pie in the sky but a promise of release from captivity, liberty for those who are oppressed. Finally, when he speaks of the "acceptable year of the Lord," any Jew would immediately know that he was talking about a radical transformation of the social system to bring justice to the poor and oppressed. Jesus interpreted his mission and purpose in terms of liberation for the oppressed groups in society.

It is in this context that we need to see political theology. There is, so far as I can see, no sharp line of demarcation between liberation theology and political theology. It is not surprising that Dorothee Sölle, a leading exponent of political theology, has chosen here to speak on the theme of liberation. One could list several theologians whose work could equally well be described as liberation theology or political theology.

What then do we mean by "political theology?" What is new about it? Certainly it is not new for the church and its theology to be concerned with political affairs. The medieval church was always in politics up to its neck. That often is one of the major criticisms of it. The Reformers, Luther and Calvin, both insisted that the Christian has political duties. The Gospel calls us to love our neighbour, but if that is so, Christians cannot ignore the political realm, because, as Luther and Calvin both saw, political matters have a great deal to do with the welfare of the neighbour we are called to love. In later times churches were active in the political campaign to abolish slavery, active on both sides, I am sorry to say. The social gospel called Christians to be engaged with the political events of their time. In more recent times the churches, particularly the black churches, were active in the battle for racial equality in the United States. Even those Christians who claim that the church should be involved only in saving individuals, have been politically active in issues like prohibition of alcohol, suppression of pornography, control of drug use, and opposition to gambling. This remains a strange inconsistency on the part of those Christians who oppose political activity. The inconsistency is most apparent in time of war. These groups condemn Christians who oppose a war and say that the church should stay out of politics. But the same groups turn around and bless their country's war efforts and pray for victory, ignoring the political implications. Whatever the inconsistencies involved, it is evident that even groups which oppose political action in theory are, in fact, involved in politics at crucial points. And so again, we have to ask, what is new about political theology?

Political theology is more than an application of Christian ethics to political problems. As we have seen, in one way or another, Christians always have done that. However, one element in political theology is a reaction to the tendency of theology in the last century to be so concerned with individuals that it has lost any political concern. Conservative theologies have emphasized that the task of the church is to save souls. Sometimes they piously affirm that the only way to change society is to first change individuals. Liberal theologies, on the other hand, have found their own way, particularly in existentialist forms, to concentrate upon individual concerns. And so Johannes Metz says that a first task of political theology is to "deprivatize" theology and to turn its gaze to the socio-political nature of our problems. Political theology is attempting to restore theological concern for political questions but that does not get to the heart of its nature.

A most important element in political theology is its affirmation that, in fact, all theology is done from a socio-political perspective. This is a claim that startles and disturbs most theologians. Traditionally theology has worked with the presuppositions of Greek and Germanic philosophy which affirm that thought is to seek universal truths that apply equally to all people. Theology must attempt to see all of reality from the perspective of God himself. There was no room in such theology for a particularist view from one limited human perspective. What theology is to get is pure doctrine, divine truths that stand above the changing vicissitudes of human history.

The liberation theologies challenged this view of theology. They claimed that divine truth, like all other truth, has to be understood from particular points of view, from the view of classes, or racial, sexual, and age groups. This way of thinking, these theologies affirmed, is closer to the Hebraic way of thinking in which the Bible was written. The biblical God is not pictured as addressing a message to whom it may concern, but he chooses a particular people and in their lives, in their historical development, he makes himself known. Similarly today, says a liberation theologian like James Cone, we have to write theology from out of our experience. And so he develops a black theology. The experience of the black people in the United States enables them to understand the Bible in a way that white Christians cannot. The black people have been slaves; they have been discriminated against; they have been dehumanized and exploited. And as they read the Bible, it becomes clear to them that its God is the God of the oppressed. He is the God who delivered his people from slavery in Egypt, the God whose prophets condemned the rich and powerful for grinding the faces of the poor in the dust, the God whose Son came proclaiming that he brought good news for the poor and deliverance for captives. White theologians, drawn from the middle class of a racist society, cannot help but distort the biblical message, says Cone.

Political theology has carried this thrust of liberation theology even further. It has analyzed the way in which all theology reflects a class bias. Theologians who had thought that they were seeking the truth, the whole truth, and nothing but the truth, are revealed as speaking the truth from the perspective of a white, male, middle class. Thus, for example, Dorothee Sölle takes the statement of Rudolf Bultmann which says, "The meaning of history always lies in the present."[4] Then she puts the question, "Whose interest is served by always perceiving the meaning of history in the present? To which class do those persons belong who talk that way?" It is obvious, she notes, that the wretched of the earth, some two thirds of the world's people, cannot think that way. It may appear that Bultmann has arrived at his conclusion by an objective evaluation of philosophical and theological ideas. But in fact he is presenting a viewpoint which arises from his own social class to justify the status quo. He bypasses the concern to find the meaning of history in a better society to be built in the future.

From such analyses, it becomes evident to students of political theology that we have to examine the political context of theological statements to find their meaning. The nature of the political society determines what questions are asked by theologians, what concerns seem imperative. At the beginning of the nineteenth century, the great liberal theologian Schleiermacher was concerned because Christianity was repudiated or ignored by most of the intelligentsia of his time. He wrote a famous book called _Lectures on Religion to its Cultured_

Despisers. Ever since then, theology has been preoccupied with an apologetic to the intellectual elite. The political situation of theologians dictated that this was the social group that was most crucial. On the other hand, when the liberationist political theologian, Gustavo Gutierrez, was asked why Latin American liberation theology was so deeply engaged with Marx, he replied, "Because the people use him."[5] Here, the concerns and questions for theology do not come from the questions of the intelligentsia, but from the struggle of the poor to find justice.

Once political theology has revealed the class-interest of all theology, it hopes to free theology so that a conscious choice can be made as to which class will provide the perspective from which to view the world. And here it is obvious that loyalty to the biblical faith means that theology must be written from the perspective of the poor, the oppressed, the wretched of the earth. As Frederick Herzog puts it, "Theology that does not take the world's poor into account from the word 'go' isn't Christian theology."[6] Theology written from the viewpoint of the poor and oppressed is unusual in the history of the church, but it is not without precedent. And so political theologians are interested to look through history and re-examine some of those who have done their theology in the context of the poor. Names like Joachim of Flores, Savanarola, John Hus, Thomas Muentzer, the social gospel, and Dietrich Bonhoeffer have been suggested as forerunners of political theology.

A second major aspect of political theology is its concept of praxis. I am not quite sure why a theology, dedicated to speaking from the perspective of the poor and oppressed, should show such a fondness for a technical term that would baffle the poor. I do not think that I shall lose much if I translate it into "practice." This concern is also a reaction to a set of presuppositions inherited by theology from Greek philosophy. That philosophy viewed theory as prior to and superior to practice. In pure thought we come the closest to truth and reality; when theory is put into practice it is always distorted and made less pure. This Greek point of view still is with us in the academic view that pure science is a nobler and more worthy pursuit than that of the technician who puts the findings of pure science into practice. In theological seminaries it results in the attitude which views the brighter students as likely candidates for a Ph.D. and ultimately a teaching post. As for the rest, it is said, often with condescension, "They will make good pastors."

Political theology says that this dichotomy of theory first and practice second is all wrong. Theory and practice must be continually interrelated. Obviously the thought of Marx has influenced political theology here. Marx, in a famous statement, said that it had always been supposed that the task of philosophy is to interpret the world, but he was concerned to change the world. However, Frederick Herzog insists that this is the biblical framework also. In the New Testament, there first came practice--the acts of God, the life of Jesus, his identification with the poor, his feeding of the hungry and healing of the sick. Only later came the theory to interpret all of this.

For the political theologian, practice is the ever-necessary test of any theory. Dorothee Sölle quotes Jesus' statement, "Not every one who says unto me, 'Lord, Lord,' shall enter the kingdom of heaven, but he who does the will of my father who is in heaven." (Matt. 7:21) She goes on to affirm that "Lord, Lord" talk is a very good way of avoiding the will of God and asks if this is not the case with most theology. She finds that existentialist theology was correct in asserting that the truth of theological statements can be known only in the living of life. Religious knowledge is not a matter of theory in the head, but of commitment, decision, and life. But political theology sees, as existentialists did not, that life is inevitably lived in a political context. The political order may provide a society in which it is virtually impossible for individuals to live in a liberated way. "There are situations that systematically destroy the mother-child relationship; there are ways of organizing labour that define the relation of the strong to the weak on a Darwinian model."[7] Hence Christian practice must be such that it strives to change such social patterns. She thus affirms,

> Truth as it is meant here cannot tolerate abstraction, naked theory, pure doctrine or the abrupt, unexpected, and therefore dogmatic kerygma. The truth of Christ exists only as concrete realization, which means: the verification principle of every theological statement is the praxis that it enables for the future. Theological statements contain as much truth as they deliver practically in transforming reality.[8]

Gutierrez, in the same vein, argues that bourgeois theology, with its claim to be universal, will regard any new theology that comes along as a "toy" to play with and ultimately to incorporate into its universal system. In other words, a toy is to be played with in the intellectual games of the theologians who score debating points against each other. But liberation theology is playing for keeps. In identifying with the quest of the poor for justice, it does not count victory by debating points won against an opponent but by victories for justice in the political arena.

It is important to see that political theology is not calling for a mindless activism. It is not opposed to theory per se, it is simply committed to the view that theory must be put into practice and tested by the results that it can bring about. It aims to bring about a living interaction of deed and thought, in which each is influenced and transformed by the other.

In the concern to bring theory and practice together, political theology needs a methodology for analyzing the political scene. At this point political theologies take differing paths. A considerable number of political theologians have turned to Karl Marx for methodology to analyze society, finding a number of features in Marx that are parallel to the Bible. Interestingly enough, it would seem that perhaps more Roman Catholic theologians than Protestants find Marx helpful at this point. Thus Joseph Petulla calls his book Christian Political Theology: A Marxian Guide, and Jose Miranda has written a book with the title Marx and The Bible. On the other hand, Herzog, a Protestant American, grants that Gutierrez is right to use Marx in South America because the people use Marx, but finds that "We can't say anything similar about the North American poor." Herzog is therefore more inclined to use a biblical than a Marxian methodology. However, political theologians are usually careful to see that they do not become the prisoners of any particular method of analysis. As Joseph Petulla puts it, "Political theology assumes that no single model of reality or mode of analysis provides a total explanation of social praxis."[9]

At this point the question may be raised as to why the term theology is kept. If a Marxian analysis of society is used, and the aim is to be active in the political sphere, why not call it a new form of politics. Or again, we might say that political theology has simply turned more traditional church positions on their head. Since the time of Constantine most theologians have blessed the status quo and exalted tradition. Other theologians have pointed out that there was idolatry involved in so simply baptizing the status quo with the authority of God. But is not the new political theology guilty of the same idolatry? Instead of blessing the status quo, it is blessing socialist or other radical movements, and instead of exalting tradition, it is exalting the future. But it still comes out as the mirror image of the traditional position that it rejects.

Political theologians have been aware of these dangers. They insist that the adjective "political" does not mean that theology should be replaced by political science. They do not claim to present a concrete political program. They do not affirm that there are specifically Christian solutions to world problems so that theologians might come up with brighter political methods than atheists. Political theology is concerned to sensitize the Church to recognizing the socio-political aspect of life. For better or for worse, we must see that the Christian life is continually coloured by its socio-political arena.

Dorothee Sölle says that political theology is not a political program but a "theological hermeneutic."[10] A hermeneutic is a method or principle of interpretation which one uses in exegeting a document such as the Scripture. Existential theology used the hermeneutical principle of the individual's questions about the self, how a person could achieve authentic living. With this hermeneutic, a person naturally goes to Scripture to get answers to questions such as, "Who am I?," "What must I do to be saved?," "How can I live the abundant (or authentic or meaningful) life?". Obviously, the hermeneutical principles with which a person approaches Scripture will determine to a great extent what Scripture can say to that person.

Political theology, says Sölle, begins with the hermeneutical principle that asks how authentic life can be achieved for all persons. This does not abandon the concern of the individual, but it recognizes that individual concerns can only be answered within a social context because no one can be saved alone. The Scripture is thus searched to find the light that it throws upon the common socio-political life of people.

When the Scripture is approached with this hermeneutical principle, it becomes evident that it is speaking to many things that were overlooked by an existentialist or individualistic hermeneutic. An individualistic hermeneutic leads to the assumption that society can only be changed by first changing individuals. This results in the kind of pious statement which says that if Christians would just live their faith more earnestly, there would be no hunger in the world today, or, if there were more Christians there would be no starvation. Such pious moralisms, of course, are irrelevant to the issues at stake. They have no political implications or fruits. They assume that good will, if we had enough of it, would in and of itself solve all social problems. It entirely overlooks what Paul called the principalities and powers in high places against which he fought (Ephesians 6:12). That is, it overlooks the machinations such as the international agro-business corporations that manipulate the distribution of food for profit, not to relieve hunger, and which cannot be overcome by good will. As a result, it is manifestly evident that Christians who affirm that we have to change individuals to change society, do not get converts who tackle the socio-political problems that curse millions today. Having started with an individualistic question to Scripture, an individualistic answer is found which does not motivate the convert to change society.

On the other hand, a political hermeneutic finds the Bible speaking to social problems from the beginning. Individualistic theology tends to see sin, for example, as a problem of the individual. Sin occurs where the individual makes his or her choice against the will of God. Sin is present, therefore, only in actions arising from out of individual choice. Isaiah, in a well known passage where he confronts the transcendent majesty of God, cries out, "Woe is me, for I am a man of unclean lips . . . ." Individualistic theology understands that. When I stand before God, I am acutely aware of my personal sins. But Isaiah did not stop there, he went on to say, "And I dwell among a people of unclean lips." (Isaiah 6:5). Individualistic interpretations have never understood that. Is not the problem that _I_ am a sinner? What does it matter to me that my neighbours also sin? In fact, is it not something of a relief to know that I dwell among a people of unclean lips because, after all, what I am doing cannot be so bad if everyone is doing it. But a political hermeneutic recognizes what Isaiah is talking about; he is referring to the fact that simply by living in a society one participates in the social sin of that society.

Dorothee Sölle says that the most decisive division between theological generations and camps is that between those who see and those who do not see the political interpretation of sin.[11] Individualistic theology says that political theology does not take sin seriously because it believes that changing social conditions can remove sin. Political theology, however, insists that there is a much more profound seriousness about sin where there is a hope that we can change the social conditions which alienate and destroy human persons.

As an illustration of what political theology means by the political nature of sin, I would use a situation that occurred during the Civil War in the United States. In the rich Shenandoah Valley, there were a large number of farmers who were Christian pacifists. They refused to be conscripted into the Confederate armies. In the last year of the war, General Grant sent Sheridan into the Shenandoah Valley with orders to destroy all productivity. "When you are finished," he was told, "See to it that if a crow wants to fly over the region, it will have to carry its own provisions." As the pacifist farmers watched the army destroying their crops, burning their barns and slaughtering their livestock, they felt that they were suffering as innocent bystanders. They had refused to be involved in the war or its ways; they had gone on minding their their own business. And now the war had unjustly encroached upon their peaceful lives. But what Grant saw was that so long as the Confederate army could be supplied by the Shenandoah Valley, the war could go on indefinitely. In fact, the peaceful Christians of the Valley were a most vital cog in the Confederate war machine.

This is a good illustration of the political nature of sin as seen by political theology. The pacifist farmers had made no individual choice to be involved in the war, but simply by living, working, and selling in their society, they were participating in the sin of war. And so today political theology says we must see the sin that is involved when we participate in our society. We may have the best will in the world towards the Indians and yet our economic purchases are helping to inflict mercury poisoning on the Indians of the Kenora region. Christians send missionaries to countries to convert the natives but have no twinge of conscience at buying the exports of those countries at a price which condemns the people they want to convert to a life of poverty and degradation. Political theology's interpretation of the Scripture leads it to see that we cannot simply repent of our individual sins and change our individual ways. True repentance must face up to these political sins and strive to remove them as well.

This, then, in brief outline, and without any attempt at evaluation, is political theology. The topic of this conference is Political Theology and the Canadian Context. I think that you can see why the latter half of the topic is included. By its very nature political theology forces us to look at our own context. Political theology is not addressed to whom it may concern, it is addressed to specific situations. Long ago, Walter Rauschenbusch, the great exponent of the social gospel, complained that traditional theology so emphasized the doctrine of original sin that Christians were led to feel that any sins which they had added later could not be very serious because they paled to insignificance by comparison to the original sin with which we are all saddled. Such views of original sin are addressed to all in general and hence say very little to anyone in particular. Political theology forces us to examine our own situation and our own contributions to the sinful state.

Political theology in the Canadian context cannot mean simply what it means elsewhere. Our problems are not the same as those of others. Canadians are always tempted to get upset about the black problem in the United States because we have nothing quite analogous to it. Political theology, taken seriously, will force us to look at the problem of our own Indians, Metis, and Eskimos instead of thanking God we don't treat the blacks like they do in the United States or South Africa. It will force us to view within a Christian context the fact of our division into English and French speaking components. It will mean that we cannot be preoccupied with the temptations to pride of a powerful nation like the United States but must analyze the temptations that come from being a relatively powerless land.

But it is not just in analyzing the problems that the Canadian context must be taken into account. We have to find the answers that can be put into practice here. For example, I do not believe that a Canadian political theology could draw as heavily on Marxism as the political theologies of other lands. Canada has a strong socialist tradition but it has owed very little to Marx. It has drawn upon the British Fabians, and, perhaps most important of all, it grew out of the Christian Social Gospel. In the Canadian context, we have to ask what that means for political theology.

Generally, Canada has imported its theology. In large part this is evident in that the theological teachers and leaders either came from other countries or were trained in other countries. But that is not the real nub of the problem. Even those who were born, raised and trained here in Canada, were still trained in theologies that were imported. The Canadian church has not really found a Canadian identity. One of the values in looking at political theology is that it may force us to rethink our Christian faith in a Canadian context.

NOTES

[1]Joseph Petulla, Christian Political Theology: A Marxian Guide (Maryknoll, N.Y.: Orbis Books, 1972), 231-32.

[2]See George Hunsinger (ed.), Karl Barth and Radical Politics (Philadelphia: Westminster Press, 1976).

[3]Ibid., 24.

[4]Dorothee Sölle, Political Theology (Philadelphia: Fortress Press, 1974), 48-49.

[5]Frederick Herzog, "Birth Pangs: Liberation Theology in North America," The Christian Century (Dec. 15, 1976), 1123.

[6]Ibid., 1124.

[7]Sölle, Political Theology, 61.

[8]Ibid., 76.

[9]Petulla, Christian Political Theology, 29.

[10]Sölle, Political Theology, 59.

[11]Ibid., 83.

3

POLITICS AND THEOLOGY: DO WE NEED A POLITICAL THEOLOGY

Kai Nielsen

1

I shall begin by trying to give some reasonable construal of what political theology might come to. Traditionally, and somewhat ethnocentrically, theology is taken to be that discipline which more or less systematically examines the nature and attributes of God, his relation to creatures (human and otherwise), and to the rest of the universe. Political theology concerns itself with the political and broadly social aspects of this. Theology, as the editors of New Theology 6 tell us, "exists--to help people interpret, to inspire them, and to judge their aspirations and methods."[1] It of course unavoidably does this in a determinate community and against a specific cultural background. So while inspirational talents are supposedly required, critical talents are as well, for questions of truth and moral appositeness are also at issue.

It is just here where I have a considerable block. As an atheist and socialist, I do not think we need or indeed should have a theology, let alone a political theology. I see no need to rework, or refashion, or develop Christian or Jewish doctrine to capture the insights of the socialist tradition and yet at the same time to transcend them. And, while I realize there are many--though still not nearly enough--courageous and progressive Catholics, I find the idea, recently vetted, of "Catholic Marxists" alternatively amusing and saddening. I could, or course, following Husserl's methodological advice, bracket such central beliefs of mine and ask, hypothetically, suppose Christianity were true and suppose we were Christians, what then should we do as political Christians and what are the socio-political implications of our Christian eschatology? Shall we follow in the footsteps of Luther or Calvin or alternatively of their great but neglected contemporary, Thomas Müntzer, or shall we take some quite different road? But it is more fitting that people who actually believe in such things carry out that exercise. I can be more useful and most faithful to my own intent if I take another tack, namely that of arguing that we do not need and indeed should not have a political theology at all or any sort of Christian or Jewish

Weltanschauung.

I shall at first proceed indirectly by commenting on the religious scene as I see it today. In doing this, I shall try to show what this means politically and humanly. I shall then proceed to indicate how reflection on that and on our actual situation justifies making the twin presumptions of atheism and socialism. In doing this, I shall *try* to show that such presumptions are not, as they might at first appear to be, presumptuous, and I shall show that such presumptions are not assumptions, are defeasible and can thus be defeated. Moreover one might, as does Antony Flew, make one without making the other. It would, however, hardly be in place for me in this context to trot out once again a new defense of atheism or of socialism.[2] What I shall do instead is to trot out minimal defenses, sufficient, I believe, to give some credence to the presumptions of atheism and socialism and then try to show how those who would supplement this with a political theology are doing something that (a) is unnecessary, and (b) is undesirable.

2

I shall first say something about the mushrooming of religiosity in North America and its relationship to and effect on our political consciousness. It comes as a shock, something straining our incredulity as intellectuals, to see the facts about religiosity in North America--a religiosity out of control by European standards. Statistical sampling reveals that 87% of the people in Canada profess belief in God and the United States has the astounding total of 94%.[3] And the dominant religion, at least on the Protestant side, but it affects many Catholics as well, is not a religion deeply influenced by Harvey Cox or the Bishop of Woolich but a fundamentalistic Evangelical Protestantism essentially inspired by Billy Graham types. This Evangelical Protestantism is very distant from the view of the world of religious intelligentsia. In an age in which biblical scholarship is highly developed and tolerably sophisticated, the religion of the man on the street is biblical literalism. The editors of *New Theology Today*, a yearly scholarly review of theological literature, writing in 1968, find, in spite of surface differences, *Honest to God*, *The Secular Meaning of the Gospel*, and *The Secular City*, to be books which belong "to a single movement or mood or style."[4] What they are referring to is a common picture of the world which depicts most people in Western technological society--including most Christians--as having "moved into a post religious era," where their lives are to be characterized as having a pragmatic empirical temper.[5]

The picture we get is that of a thoroughly secularized human being, in the more fortunate cases in control of himself and functioning as a reform minded productive urban animal, who does not go in much for metaphysics, or the myth of ideology, let alone the occult. New Theology's editors see this theological posture as decisively influencing the religious situation both in North America and the world. Moreover they do not see the conservative evangelical Christians as a powerful cultural force against this secularized, de-mythologized, and sometimes even Godless Christianity; for them the strong oppositional forces are the theologies of hope such as we find in the work of Jürgen Moltmann or Wolfhart Pannenberg, where, going beyond the secularized Christianity of say Van Buren or Tillich, we get a futuristic humanism influenced by Bloch and the Frankfurt School Neo-Marxists. We get here, if we take this as providing the core of contemporary theological debate, something which is staggeringly at a distance from where, in North America at least, most plain religious folk are at. The cultural space between the intelligentsia and the non-intelligentsia is very great indeed. And this gap is not narrowed very much even when we think of such comparatively conservative theologians, Anglo-Catholic and Protestant, as E. L. Mascall and Gordon Kaufman. The world that these academic theologians live in and the world of those concerned Christians who urge America to wake up before God destroys it like he destroyed Sodom and Babylon could hardly be more complete. Indeed when I read something like David Wilkerson's Racing Toward Judgment, I feel like an anthropologist studying Dobuans who have discovered some device which enables them to write. This stands in radical contrast to the writings of such sensitive and reflective philosophical critics of the cultural scene as Alastair MacIntyre or Max Horkheimer. In the work of such critics--critics who are not insensitive to the historical importance of Judaism and Christianity--one gets the sense that one is already living in a post-Christian Age.[6] Still there are all those Neanderthal Evangelicals out there who are branching into a cultural analogue of an evolutionary cul du sac. Yet they are the overwhelming mass of the people.

Faced with these cultural facts, it is difficult not to feel very disheartened. The great mass of us are not only very much in need of a political education, we are as well very much in need of some kind of reflective understanding of ourselves and our world. We are, as Freud put it, in need of being soberly educated. And it is both important and sobering to remember that men such as Carter, Nixon, Ford, and Reagan, men who are (or were) key members of a class who will have important effects on the lives of vast numbers of human beings, are or at least pretend to be just such primitive, tribalized christians.

There are many reasons why such religiosity is alive and well and living in North America.[7] I want to fasten on but one cluster of factors which I believe is very important and is, as well, important to the topic of political theology. What I refer to in cultures such as ours is what appears to be a growing conviction that progressive political endeavours are doomed to defeat and a consequent despairing sense of powerlessness.[8] Both among intelligentsia, a very pervasive conviction has arisen to the effect that in our society we have lost the capacity to shape our collective destinies, to control our lives together as social beings or even, in any proper sense, to understand them so that we can see where we are going and so that we can try to forge a rational and human society where human beings can flourish. More and more--in Horkheimer's apt phrase--our societies appear to be administered societies in which we have a sense that our collective lives are out of control, propelled by complex forces whose workings we only very dimly understand. And with this there is fear, or at least a kind of inchoate anxiety, about the future. We may have passed the point of no return where for us it may very well be all down hill. Many have come to believe that there is no reasonable hope for redirecting our collective lives in a more humane direction either by revolution or by piecemeal social engineering. Our everyday lives are largely constituted by drab, often meaningless routines, rounded off with a drink and a round with the tube; and, given conventional wisdom, our futures, barring some not unlikely major catastrophe (including the possibility of another great war), are <u>at best</u> a somewhat more comfortable version of the present.

In such a situation it is surely understandable that there is a "widespread yearning to be relieved of the anxieties and despair of our time, and to find shelter in simple belief and strong conviction."[9]

Moreover, the type of religion that flows forth in response is an inward turning type of religion, though it also often confusedly mixes together patriotism and simple religious faith. So, while remaining inward turning and passive before political power, such a religiosity, conveniently for the ruling class, combines that pervasiveness with (a) the mindless belief that their well-being in the world is a special favour of God, and (b) a moral majority ideology that good public policies and practices will only come from 'twice born', simple, direct, and thoroughly honest people cleansed in spirit and in the flesh.

This religiosity both is and is not political. It is political in the sense that, particularly in the United States, these evangelicals tend to look on themselves as the truest Americans, follow Dulles in favouring sermons on the cold war, go in for a virulent anti-communism, regard themselves as a chosen people with a mission in life, confuse the Christian faith with the American flag, and "condone social exploitation as a necessary price of 'economic freedom'."[10] But it is profoundly apolitical in its pietistic emphasis on personal salvation through a personal experience of Christ. In short, as one commentator has well put it, "the evangelic value of religion for these people is found in the therapeutic--God makes you feel better. Extreme moments of recommitment are likely to appear as a pill for depression."[11] Jesus, in short, is a kind of super-psychiatrist. One's own consciousness is expanded and the sense of inner emptiness and despair relieved. As Christopher Lasch has argued well, contemporary evangelicals, unlike some of their historically important antecedents, are in reality on a quest for the therapeutic; they lack genuinely eschatological conceptions or a conception of salvation, where, with unavoidable socio-political implications, one speaks of a new man and a new age.[12] Rather here the political vision, where it exists at all, is backward looking to an allegedly simpler and more virtuous age--another mythical Golden Age. Salvation comes to attaining personal well-being, health, and psychic security. There is no call for a new life for humankind with a deep and well-thought-through subordination of one's personal quest for liberation to the needs and interests of others.

The paucity of the 'vision of salvation,' or, if one can so dignify it, 'the political theology,' of such a religious grouping comes out dramatically in a full-page ad run by one such group in the Sunday New York Times of November 7, 1976. It is evidently a well financed group for such an advertisement costs around twenty or thirty thousand dollars. We are told that it is "An Urgent Message to the President and People of the United States" and we are warned of black days ahead. The message comes out loud and clear:

> God is going to judge America for its blatant sins. His upraised fist is poised, ready to destroy pride and the self-proclaimed greatness of a corrupted nation. This nation will soon stagger like a drunkard with judgment falling upon us in a series of "black days." The holocausts that wiped out the decadent societies of Nineveh, Sodom, and Babylon loom straight ahead for America.
>
> The Commander of the armies of Heaven will shake this nation like a tent in a storm. Awesome earthquakes will devastate many of our cities with death and destruction such as this nation has never before witnessed. America is not immune to God's judgment. He is no respector of persons. If America continues committing the sins of Sodom, America must be judged as Sodom was.[13]

If we do not turn away from our sins, the statement continues, God will turn His wrath upon us and bring upon us devastation and calamity. God, we are told, is "giving America its final 'goodness' call"; the party is over . . .," and "it's time to get our houses in order." "Born-again Christians," we are further told, "are intensely patriotic and it is their love for America that prompts them to warn all who will listen." But what is it for us, according to such evangelicals, to get our houses in order and to escape the wrath of God? It is for the nation to return to God via "a revolution of morals." But this is no Nietzschean or anarchist transvaluation of values. It is rather a return to the tried and the true, a return to a simple morality of personal integrity, upright living, honesty, directness, and decency with "wholesome sexual values." It is a puritan morality that demands that we rout the evils of a Godless age. We live, it stresses, in an age when "Morals are melting like snow." To revitalize morality, for morality to become a pervasive force again, we must come to hate as God hates all this crime, violence, and ridicule of puritan standards. We live, we are further told, in a sick age in which "Sadomasochists, filled with aggression and hostility, now go about our American streets searching for victims. Uncaged rapists prey upon this society, molesting the innocent and the nation is stricken with a porno plague." It is this sort of thing we must rout, and we must also end the cult of violence in the mass-media and the influence of ungodly agnostics in the classroom and in the councils of government. We must, in fact, repent our sins and return to Christ by avoiding these ways before God rains down destruction on us.

The part about the social role and freedoms of the ungodly agnostics apart, the evils pointed to in this call for a 'revolution of morals' are genuine evils or (as in the case of pornography) ills in our society. But that these ills should be singled out as major and overriding ills--the ills that account for the emptiness and senselessness of our lives and the poverty of our expectations and our hopes--rather than as ills which are, in considerable measure at least, symptomatic of other very different and much more deeply embedded ills, reveals a considerable poverty in moral imagination. In this fundamentalist clarion call to awaken America we get the above stress along with a complete ignoring of the evils and ills flowing from militarism, the arms race, multinational corporations, stagnation, the inability of people to find work, and the debasing and dehumanizing quality of much of our work. It is silent--and this document is not atypical--about the exploitation of people, the rape of the Third World, racism, vast wealth in the midst of poverty (often extreme, crippling poverty), deep and persistent inequalities in all kinds of life expectations, sexism and the deterioration of face-to-face human relations. It worries about pornography without ever worrying about sexist attitudes and the treatment of women as sex objects, which in part anyway, generates the social relations that trigger and sustain an interest in pornography. It worries about crime in the streets and the pushing of drugs while turning a blind eye to the deeper moral problems which provide the environment for crime and the need for drugs. There is in this puritanical fundamentalist demand to put our houses in order not the slightest conception of a truly human society in which human beings could live together in solidarity, love, and happiness, and where a sensitive and perspicuous conception of equality and respect would provide the grounds for making social justice a reality.

There is in their vision nothing but the most negative and impoverished conception of a good society. It is hardly the basis on which to build a political theology, or if we do root a political theology in such a cluster of conceptions, it will not, as in T. S. Eliot's view of life, be just a conservative political theology, but a positively reactionary one which will hardly provide a heart in a heartless world, but will express in all its rigidity and talk of destruction, and in the blind eye it turns to human exploitation and the degradation of some men by other men, a remarkable coldness and hardness of heart.

If this is to be our vision of Christ and a salvation in Christ, who needs it? It has nothing of the millenarian future that made some forms of Christianity deeply compelling to a hard-pressed and hapless people. No matter how much they were rooted in illusion, these millenarian conceptions held out a hope for a human future, gave us the ideal of a heart in a heartless world. We have instead, with these contemporary evangelicals, a religion which in effect, if not always in intention, is through and through reactionary, which massively supports the basic structures of economic and political power, and which not infrequently supports the most reactionary elements in the power elite of the capitalist system.

This fundamentalism is a form of Christianity which is as alien to most Christian intelligentsia as it is to me, but it is the dominant religion of North America. Billy Graham is the second most admired man in America and he has been the unofficial chaplain of the White House. And this very neanderthal religion, with its attendant neanderthal political theology ('political ideology' would be a better term), is the religion of Carter, Ford and Reagan.

The theologians Martin Marty and Dean Peerman, remarking on the theological picture and how they expect it to unfold, dismiss conservative political theology and, after trying to keep in balance the diverging trends, confidently remark: "Do not look for a new political conservatism in post-secular theology."[14] Well, highbrow theology is one thing, and the theology and religious forms of life that deeply affect the great masses of the people is another.

There are, I should add, more respectable conservative traditions of political theology than the one I have discussed. There are those theologians who will not blink at the fact that while we live in a world of reasonable abundance, many are hungry, and that while the powerful among us have an incredible technological mastery, it has not been employed to humanize life for the masses but has frequently been employed as a tool of destruction, suppression, and exploitation. These theologians will, like any reflective and humane person, be saddened by such news, but they will believe (a) that, given man's sinful human nature, such things are unavoidable, (b) Christianity will compromise itself if it meddles in politics, and (c) that the need for order is so important, given the corrupt and often vicious little animal that man is, that if Christianity must involve itself in politics it should do so on the side of tradition and established order. Such theologians might well echo Goethe's "Better injustice than disorder."

All the quite varied groups of theologians represented in New Theology No. 6 are antagonists to such a conservative theological posture as well as (of course) to the reactionary position that I have taken some pains to characterize. But the first major point I want to make is that the non-reactionary theology, while influential in the academy, is, if we look at the actual present life of Christianity, very much a minority phenomenon.

In drawing attention to this reactionary ideological role of Christianity, I am not giving to understand that this attests to the moral insensitivity or moral callousness of the Canadian or American people or anything silly like that. Such unhistorical moralizing or moral argument is itself ridiculous. What I am saying is that from quite understandable motives the mass of Christians in North America have been encultured and indeed indoctrinated into a form of moral ideology that reflects a very deeply embedded 'false consciousness' about their situation.

Such religion, or (as it is better called) such religiosity, is mere ideology rooted in the material conditions of our social life. There is, for most people in North America, a deterioration of their social life. Life is becoming more of a struggle, more like a state of nature, at the same time as it is becoming more and more administered. Life in Tokyo, Sao Paulo, or New York, for instance, becomes more and more a pollution-backdropped rat-race while individuals face more and more controls and an ever narrower margin of autonomy. And even for those--and they are by no means most--who have a measure of affluence, that affluence is surrounded by a very uncertain future indeed. No one knows what kind of a life we are going to have twenty-five years from now. And into the life we do have, in spite of its cult of personal relationships, we find a super-abundance of envy and attempts at domination and subtle forms of exploitation. We are terrified of aging and of death and have a very pervasive sense of inner emptiness and loneliness and a sense that we do not control our lives or even understand how we would order and direct them if only we could. We have no sense of the future and little satisfaction in the present, and as a lonely crowd we feel that our lives lack authenticity without even more than the vaguest understanding of what it would be like to escape inauthenticity. All political and social commitments are suspect as ideologies, and the sane and cultivated voices among us seem to have little to offer us save, à la Schopenhauer, resignation and irony.

In such a situation it is small wonder that we should, grasping at straws, grasp at a religious way out, particularly when it is put in therapeutic terms. Given our sense of political powerlessness, given the idiocy and pointlessness of so much of our lives--that is the idiocy and pointlessness of many of the jobs people have and of much of our popular culture--and given the increasing "war of all against all" that is the reality of our social existence, and which is at least seemingly beyond human rationalization, it is understandable that there should be such an extensive yearning to be relieved of one's anxieties and fears for the future and to be done with one's stumbling, inchoate efforts to make sense of the incredible tangle of modern life and to find shelter in a simple and familiar faith. But, understandable or not, such a response is an ideological response --an ostrich-like response--that reveals massive self-deception and false consciousness.

Karl Marx and Friedrich Engels both stressed that religious beliefs characteristically serve the dominant class interests of the society in which they have their life. Such beliefs promote a false consciousness which disguises for religious people the actual structure and mode of functioning of the society in which they live. Religious functions on the one hand as a useful control mechanism for the ruling classes by supporting the existing social order through giving to understand that the social order is sanctioned by some divine authority, but on the other hand it also functions, in Marx's famous phrase, as "the opiate of the people." The oppressed and the exploited are consoled and reconciled to their lot by offering them in heaven what they have been denied on earth and by diverting their attention from real ills and a genuine critique of society to concerns about one's own sins and inadequacies and to a concern with the heavenly city of God's reign. There have been, and indeed still are, courageous Christians such as Dietrich Bonhoeffer, Father Berrigan, and today in South Africa, Beyers Naude, who have struggled against the oppressive existing social order, but massively and not surprisingly the Christian churches have been on the side of the dominant ruling interests and have functioned to reconcile people, against their own interests, to such a class rule. They have repeatedly offered them illusory hopes in such a way as to stem revolt and, wherever possible, to batten down the struggled for human liberation.

The exceptions and the existence of theologies of hope should not blind us to the fact that religion in general and Christianity in particular have repeatedly taught suffering, degraded and exploited human beings to accept their fate as being--mysterious though it be--a part of God's Providential Order. And such conceptions, as Feuerbach shows, help them to turn their very real human hopes, aspirations, and expectations into unreal ones. Our task is not collectively to struggle to achieve another better world; instead we are to learn 'to die to the world' and to earthly aspirations and to regard all such worldly aspirations as fundamentally illusory. That we should, as the cliche goes, overcome in this '*spiritual sense*' is the essential thing. Brechtian concerns with 'this life' as the centre of one's endeavours are, they tell us, a mark of shallowness.

It is indeed true that not all Christianity has been so oriented, but the mainstream has surely had that thrust. There are certainly theologians who would accept much of what I have said and who would respond by remarking that when one clearly thinks through 'the essence of Christianity' or what it is, given a reflective conception of Christ, to be a Christian, Christianity cannot continue to be what it has massively been. It cannot continue, given such a conception, to be a repressive force but must become a liberating force. To be a genuine Christian in Christendom one must be committed to an emancipatory *praxis*, which very well may be in some circumstances genuinely revolutionary; someone, so the account goes, who is truly committed to Christ will be committed to a genuine eschatology with humanistic socio-political implications. A Marxist humanism and a Christian humanism will converge.

We have here, with such a suggestion of a 'liberation theology,' I suspect, a *persuasive* definition of 'Christianity', but, leaving that aside, my response is the following. Even if the very idea of Christianity so commits one, if one were a genuine Christian, it does not follow that one must or even should be a Christian to be so committed, and such definitional or conceptual manoeuvers do nothing to alter the social fact that historically speaking Christianity has been massively on the side of a repressive status quo. In present day South Africa, to illustrate, a few very courageous Christians--those connected with the Christian Institute for instance--have fought intrepidly against their brutalitarian regime, but as a knowledge of the bruderbund and a few days listening to radio South Africa will verify, the church and state work hand in glove to strengthen and rationalize the oppression and exploitation.[15]

It may be despair (to use Kierkegaard's foreshortening of my above discussion) that triggers and sustains religion. But it may be that this driving of a reflective and sensitive person to despair is not rooted in our common tragic human condition, but in certain alterable social conditions. Alternatively, it may be, even if this despair is an unalterable fact of human existence, that a religious response is not the most adequate response or the most human response to it. Camus' response or Bertrand Russell's may be a more adequate one than Kierkegaard's. This last point involves what I shall call the presumption of atheism and the former (though indirectly) the presumption of socialism. Like all presumptions, these presumptions are defeasible--can be defeated--but if the arguments I shall give in the next section are near to their mark, the burden of proof would shift to the Christian or Jewish theologian to defeat them and to show that a political theology is possible and that it is desirable. I shall argue that human beings need not despair without a belief in God. Moreover, even if our prospects are far harsher than I believe them to be, and we have no rational hope, in Brecht's phrase, of building securely the "foundations of human happiness," this need not and indeed should not drive us to God.

3

The form of atheism, the presumption of which I will be defending, is the minimal negative form of atheism somewhat similarly defended by Antony Flew.[16] To be such an atheist one needs not assert the non-existence or even the probable non-existence of God. One, to be such an atheist, only needs not be a theist. The obvious question is whether one is as justified, as Flew thinks one is, in starting there. That is to say, is it fair to say that the onus of proof is on the believer-the Christian, Moslem, or Jew--to show why one should be a theist and to "first . . . introduce and to defend his proposed concept of God; and, second to provide sufficient reason for believing that this concept of his does have an application?"[17] I think that it is. The Christian or Jew, reacting against this, will, relevantly here, appeal to consensus. Christians and Jews vastly outnumber sceptics. But if we look at the matter cross-culturally, Christian belief will begin to look like one bit of tribal folklore among others when it is set alongside the vast array of diverse and often radically conflicting or at least incommensurate cosmological beliefs of the various cultures of the world. In such a tower of Babel, with all those incommensurate putative revelations going, how can it be anything else but arrogance or cultural ignorance to claim that Christianity is the Way and the Truth--the one genuine form of revelation or even, if one is rather more pluralistic, the most ultimate and final revelation or even an ultimate form of revealed truth? Given all those diverse beliefs--*Weltanschauungen*--why single out Christianity, or Judaism, or Islam? Minimally, given that not inconsiderable diversity, how can we be justified in starting with anything other than a presumption of the negative form of atheism just mentioned, i.e. non-atheism?

That a culture in which Christianity is embedded conquered most of the world and subdued and often destroyed many of the other cultures and now is numerically very extensive only shows that it was a very powerful material and scientific culture; it does nothing to establish that its religious culture or moral culture is superior; it only shows that it rode in on the coat-tails of such a dominant material culture.

If alternatively I am told that cultural relativism does not entail any form of normative, including a religiously normative, relativism or scepticism, I can readily agree that there is no such entailment but still perfectly consistently, and without giving an inch, remark that, in the face of that diversity of religious *Weltanschauungen*, at bottom not really saying anything like the same thing, the burden of proof is on the Christian to show why one should opt for God.[18] And that, of course, is my presumption of atheism. Given all this diversity, it appears at least to be hubristic, and a little bit irrational to boot, to commit oneself to Christ and believe in God or for that matter in any of the various divinities or transcendental conceptions. One, if one does that, is just arbitrarily committing oneself to one of those religions rather than another, and those religions are very diverse.

The presumption of atheism seems more and more modest and less and less presumptuous if, in addition to the above considerations, we keep firmly before our minds the problematical nature of these religious conceptions and the fact that their central doctrinal beliefs appear at least to be perfectly groundless.[19] (It is the groundlessness together with the vast diversity of belief which most forcefully poses problems for the proud claims of Christianity and Judaism.) It is very unclear whether we understand what we are talking about when we speak of God and the soul. We can paraphrase 'God' and 'soul' in terms of various descriptions but they (e.g. 'the infinite individual transcendent to the universe' and 'a simple immaterial substance') are at least as opaque as the terms they paraphrase. We haven't any idea for any of these very central conceptions of Judaism or Christianity what it would be like to use them in sentences which could be used to make assertions which we had grounds for believing to be either true or false. We have no evidence, and actually we have no understanding of where to look for evidence or even an understanding of what we would take as evidence sufficient to establish even the probable truth of such religious claims.[20]

Even if in fact my claim is, as I do not think it is, too strong and we do have some conception of what would count as evidence for our religious claims, we still in fact do not have such evidence.[21] So, given the radical diversity of religious beliefs as between the cultures of the world, the problematic nature of the conceptions built into these beliefs--conceptions where their very intelligibility and coherence is in question--and given the complete lack of evidence for the truth of these religious beliefs, the presumption of atheism appears at least to be quite justified.[22]

At this point many Jews and Christians are likely to respond, in effect attempting to defeat the presumption of atheism, that, scandal to the intellect or not, and no matter how things stand cognitively or evidentially with Judaism or Christianity, if morality is not to be a shambles and life is to make any sense at all, one must make the leap of faith. It indeed may be like whistling in the dark when we do not know the tune, but only self-deception can shield us from a recognition that without God life is meaningless and morality groundless and moral endeavour pointless.

Perhaps I am self-deceived, or effectively indoctrinated by others, but I do not believe that any of this is true and I have on several occasions tried to show why my belief is justified.[23] I shall be brief now. It is indeed true that moral perplexity runs deep, and moral ambivalence and anguish should be extensive. A recognition of this should be common ground between morally sensitive believers and sceptics. But there is no need to have the religious commitments of Christianity or its sister religions or any religious commitment at all to make sense of morality. Torturing human beings is vile; exploiting and degrading human beings is thoroughly evil; cruelty to human beings and animals is morally unacceptable; and treating one's promises lightly or being careless about the truth is wrong. If we know anything to be wrong we know these things to be wrong, and they would be wrong and be just as wrong in a Godless world as in a world with God.

There is indeed a philosophical problem about how we know these things to be wrong, but this is as much a problem for the believer as for the sceptic. I would say that for anyone--for believer and sceptic alike--if he or she has an understanding of the concept of morality, has an understanding of what it is to take the moral point of view, he or she will, *eo ipso*, understand that it is wrong to harm others, that promises are to be kept, and the truth is to be told. This does not mean that he or she will be committed to the belief that a lie *never* can rightly be told, that a promise *never* can be broken, or that a human being in *no circumstance* can rightly be harmed. But if there is no understanding that such acts always require very special justification and that the presumption of morality is always against them, then there is no understanding of the concept of morality. But this understanding is not intrinsically or logically bound up with knowing God or knowing about God or the taking of a religious point of view.

It might be responded that such an understanding does imply a knowledge of the reality of God because we *only* know these things to be wrong because God wills it, and they are only wrong because God prohibits it. Leaving aside sceptical questions about how we can know or whether we can know, and what God does or does not will, the old question arises whether something is good simply because God wills it or does God will it because it is good? What is plain--leaving aside for a moment--is that something is not good simply because it is will or commanded; indeed it is not even morally a good thing to do simply because it is will or commanded by an omnipotently powerful being unless we want to reduce morality to power worship, as has one well known but (on this issue) rather confused philosopher.[24] But might--naked power--doesn't make right. And there is no implication that it will become right even when conjoined with faultless intelligence. There can be--and indeed are--thoroughly ruthless, exploitative, manipulative people who are very intelligent indeed. Neither omnipotence nor omniscience imply goodness.

However, it is still not implausible to say that it is _God's_ willing it which makes all the difference, for God after all is the supreme, perfect good. But I in turn ask, _how_ do we know that or _do_ we know that? If we say we know it through studying the Scriptures and through the example of Jesus, then it is only in virtue of our own quite independent moral understanding of the goodness of his behaviour and the behaviour of the characters in the Bible that we come to recognize this. Moral understanding is not grounded in a belief in God; just the reverse is the case: an understanding of the religious _significance_ of Jesus and the Scriptures presupposes a moral understanding.

If, alternatively, we claim that we do not come to understand that God is the supreme and perfect good in that way but claim that it is a necessary truth--a proposition, like 'Puppies are young dogs,' which is true by definition--then we still should ask: how do we understand that putatively necessary proposition? But again we should recognize that it is only by having an understanding of what goodness is that we come to have some glimmering of the more complex and extremely perplexing notions of supreme goodness or perfect goodness. The crucial thing to see is that there are things which we can recognize on reflection to be wrong, God or no God, and that we can be far more confident that we are right in claiming that they are wrong than we can be in claiming any knowledge of God or God's order.

Finally, someone might say that since God is the cause of everything there could be no goodness or anything else if there were no God. But this confuses _causes_ and _reasons_, confuses questions about causally bringing something into existence or sustaining its existence and justifying its existence. If there is the God of the

Jews and the Christians everything causally depends on Him, but still even if there were no God who made the world, it would still be wrong to torture children, and even if there were no people to be kind, it would be timelessly true that human kindness would be a good thing and that the goodness of human kindness does not become good or cease to be good because of God's fiat or anyone else's.

In terms of its fundamental rationale, morality is utterly independent of belief in God. To make sense of our lives as moral beings there is no need to make what may be an intellectually stultifying blind leap of religious faith. Such a moral understanding, as well as a capacity for moral response and action, is available to us even if we are human beings who are utterly without religious faith.

Furthermore, it does not follow that our lives are pointless, empty or meaningless if there is no God, that we are somehow, by that very fact (if it is a fact), condemned to an Oblomov-like, senseless existence. There is no reason why we must despair if God is dead. If there is no God, it is indeed true that we are not blessed with the questionable blessing of being made for a purpose; furthermore, if there is neither God nor _Logos_, there is no purpose to life, no plan for the universe or providential ordering of things in accordance with which we must live our lives. Yet from the fact, if it is a fact, that there is no purpose to life or no purposes for which we are made, it does not at all follow that there are no purposes _in_ life that are worth achieving, doing, or having, so that life in reality must be just one damn thing after another that finally senselessly terminates in death.[25] 'Purpose of life' is ambiguous: in talking of it we can on the one hand be talking of 'a purpose to life' or 'purposes for which we are made' or on the other we can be talking of 'purposes in life' in the sense of plans we form, ends we seek, etc. that result from our deliberate and intentional acts and our desires, including our reflective desires. The former require something like a God or a _Logos_, but the latter most certainly do not. Yet it is only the latter that are plainly necessary to make life meaningful in the sense that there are in our lives and our environment things worthwhile doing, having, or experiencing, things that bring joy, understanding, exhilaration, or contentment to ourselves or to others. That we will not have these things forever does not make them worthless any more than the inevitability of death and the probability of decay robs them, or our lives generally, of sense. In a Godless world our lives are not robbed of meaning.

4

It might be responded that I do not have Part 1 and Part 3 of this essay in tandem. By that I mean that at least apparently against the thrust of the previous section, in Part 2, somewhat in the spirit of Horkheimer, I caught something of the human need which used to be satisfied by such cultural phenomena as Judaism or Christianity. Human beings do not only need to be able to face death and to recognize that there are some things worth having of doing even if they have no cosmological significance, they also yearn for and need some conception of a collective life, some conception of a good social order--something more than what we have by small extrapolations from what we have now--and they need, as well, some reasonable hope that such an order can come into being. And this yearning is not at all diminished if they recognize, *contra* Tolstoy and Pascal, that not all activity is pointless and that life is not meaningless even if these needs cannot be met. What I show in Part 2, against the spirit of Part 3, is something of the extent of our cultural pessimism about such a wholistic rationalizing and humanizing of life. We have come to have a deep sense of our powerlessness, and we have an awareness of the failure of the political. We have--or more accurately at least people in North America and Western Europe have--a sense that we cannot control or significantly direct our collective destinites, and some of us feel that we do not even understand what is happening to us and what even in theory would be the desirable solution to or resolution of our predicament.

What religion has done for us, no matter with what mythology, is to rationalize life to give us a sense, as medieval men had or indeed as even the characters of *Maria Chapdelaine* had, of a stable world with accepted and rationalized, i.e. justified, expectations, and a definite ordering of life.[26] Where the Christian order was confidently dominant, there was no generally felt failure of the political: the future was marked out, our stations and duties known, and the sense of hopelessness and inner emptiness was not widespread but only a characteristic of a few cultural eccentrics.[27] Part 2 brings out something of that, but Part 3, with its rationalistic arguments for the presumption of atheism, even if well taken, does not touch these considerations and some might even feel that a thorough thinking through of their implications might defeat that presumption.

Some remarks of Max Horkheimer's in his Critique of Instrumental Reason will perhaps make more evident what I want to say. Horkheimer relates a certain story of the way philosophy has developed and its relation to religion and theology. Philosophers of what he calls 'the great tradition'--the overwhelmingly dominant tradition from Plato to Hegel--tried in various ways, in competition with religious Weltschauungen, to provide "a philosophical justification of the world."[28] It is difficult, especially briefly, to provide any very precise characterization of what this comes to. It would be to give us a world view which could withstand rigorous critical inspection and would in some way or other answer to the sort of malaise which in its contemporary forms, in bourgeois countries at least, frequently leads particularly but not exclusively in the uneducated to the rather bizarre forms of religiosity I have described, and with many of the intelligentsia who cannot swallow such blatant mythology, to resignation, distancing and irony. It would be, if such a world view were possible, a world view which would provide some rationally justified knowledge (grounded belief) of who we are, how we got here, where we can go, and where most likely we are going. It would undermine relativism and scepticism and give us an Archimedian point with which to assess social institutions and indeed whole societies and ways of living.

However, with the development of modern thought since Hegel, there has not only been an increasing disenchantment with religion but there has also been a disenchantment with the belief that there can be, let alone is, anything like a philosophical justification of the world. (Richard Rorty's Philosophy and the Mirror of Nature and Stanley Cavell's, The Claim of Reason subtly capture what is involved here.) To a philosophically educated modern consciousness, such a belief--the standard commitment of the great tradition--has seemed increasingly remote and ideological. Even Schopenhauer, Hegel's contemporary, thought such a task misconceived. Similarly, the dominant philosophical developments in the English and Scandinavian-speaking worlds--movements Horkheimer thinks of as supplanting philosophy--believe that such an enterprise is a hopeless house of cards reflecting little more than a cluster of conceptual confusions. In such quarters interest in the traditional philosophers remain, but it is an interest in their particular philosophical (i.e. conceptual) claims.

The truth is that a reflective person who naively turns to philosophy without much prior understanding of what has been going on will find his expectations unmet. Graduate students in philosophy, and even advanced majors, have been professionally processed so that at least most of the time they no longer have such expectations. (Again Richard Rorty's Philosophy and the Mirror of Nature will help make them conscious that they have been so processed.)

I should not be misunderstood: this is not an unwitting change or a conspiracy among the analytic philosophers. There are reasons for it which are not just causes. That is to say, they are genuine reasons. (I do not say that the reasons are sufficient to make the case but they are plainly relevant reasons.) Still, for anyone who will reflect, there should be at least a sense of loss here. Yet the fact remains that such an expectation--felt by a reflective person who naively (i.e. uninformedly) turns to philosophy--will quite self-consciously not be met by the best developments in contemporary Anglo-American philosophy. Such an approach will either try piecemeal to dispel certain very fundamental conceptual confusions or it will, emulating science, give us a hopefully very rigorous account of such topics as reference, meaning, truth, mind, matter, and reality (e.g. Hilary Putnam's Mind Language and Reality), but it will not--quite definitely not--try to articulate a conception of a way of life or provide an Archimedean point for assessing societies. To read the best practitioners of such analytical ways of going about things, Ryle, Austin, Davidson, Dummett, and Putnam (to take outstanding examples) is to be introduced to very exciting and exacting minds indeed, but they do not, except indirectly, meet the great Weltanschauung problems that triggered interest in philosophy in the first place and set the great tradition in competition with religious Weltanschauungen. And, as important as it is, John Rawls' masterful A Theory of Justice will not do so either. While addressing itself to fundamental questions in substantive social philosophy, it quite deliberately provides no basis at all for assessing the relative merits of socialism and capitalism. That is, Rawl's account of the justice of social institutions, aiming to give us an Archimedean point for their assessment, quite intentionally affords us not even the nucleus of a basis for coming to grips with the most fundamental human issue of social justice of our time.[29]

We--or at least many of us--want an overall view of the world which would, in some measure, provide both a critical and an emancipatory vantage point and which, in some general way, would guide our reflective practice. We could, using it, rationalize and humanize politics and sensibly order our collective lives. But neither philosophy, science, nor any other 'discipline' will do anything like that at all. It is widely believed that with the death of the great tradition, the end of ideology, and with what Horkheimer, toward the end of his life, thought of as the dissolution of Marxism, no such hope is reasonable. Thus, it is understandable, if perhaps over-dramatic, that Horkheimer should speak in this context of "the abandonment of mankind."[30]

If we reflect on this, we could well understand how some people--indeed reflective, tough-minded people--could come to accept Flew's points about Pascal's and Tolstoy's confusions about making sense of one's life and, á la Horkheimer, could also come to see the importance of Schopenhauer's posture about 'freedom from illusions' while still finding Flew's updated Humean posture, even when supplemented by Horkheimer's Schopenhauer, not enough.[31] Surely it is a mistake to say that there is nothing worthwhile having, avoiding, or protecting, and that all purposes are absurd and utterly pointless. And it is not true that if God is dead nothing matters. But there is in our collective lives much absurdity and emptiness, much pointless and destructive activity, and we do not have--or at least do not seem to have--much power to halt it, or much understanding of what kind of society we should seek to bring into being, or even how we should go about resolving that question, or, even if we were clear about that, about how we should go about bringing that society into being. The suspicion is very deep that all such talk is 'merely ideology'--hot air for the weekend supplements. It is small wonder that so many people feel abandoned and feel a very pervasive anxiety and, in spite of the intellectual impediments to religion, turn to the Luddite faiths that offer a simple solution to the problems of life.

So one could see how at least with one's feet one could defeat the presumption of atheism. The presumption, taken by itself, as Antony Flew, Paul Edwards, or Sidney Hook would take it, is vulnerable to the considerations I have trotted out. Such a presumption will not adequately meet our needs without either some more general positive world view, speaking to what Habermas calls our emancipatory interests, or without a thorough and conclusive showing that the world is impossible.[32]

Horkheimer is no more about to take a Kierkegaardian leap of faith than is Flew, Edwards, or Hook, but he sees very clearly, as did Schopenhauer, both the strengths and the weaknesses of enlightenment rationalism.[33] However, it is not only religion and philosophy which have set out a general view of life with normative implications. Now we need to examine the presumption of socialism and see if it, together with the presumption of atheism, can rightly escape defeat and can block the necessity or the desirability of articulating a political theology.

5

Marxism in its many varieties, including the Neo-Marxism or critical theory of the Frankfurt School, while denying it is philosophy or simply philosophy or, of course, political theology, does attempt to do something of what the great tradition in philosophy attempted and what political theology does. However, it aspires to do so on a much more realistic and on a much more rational basis than has either philosophy or theology. (We should not forget that Marx and Engels remark in their German Ideology "Philosophy and the study of the actual world have the same relation to one another as masturbation and sexual love."[34]) However, while it is now true that Marx and Marxism are treated more seriously in bourgeois societies than they have been for a long time, it is still perfectly evident and quite proper that there should be a very considerable scepticism about them. This is no more the place for a full-scale discussion of Marxism or, what is not identical to it, socialism, than it is for a full-scale discussion of atheism. I shall, except incidentally, not discuss Marxism, but I shall, appealing principally to some not very controversial facts and to some rather untendentious moral considerations, try to make a case for the presumption of socialism and then, particularly with the relevance of political theology in mind, examine some of the major considerations that might be thought to defeat the presumption of socialism and incline one toward a political theology.

What I want to show in support of the presumption of socialism is that capitalism in countries such as our own and in times such as ours is both an immoral socio-economic system, and for most people, even in North America and Western Europe, it is, in a quite non-moral sense of 'irrational,' irrational to support capitalism.[35] My intent should not be misunderstood. I do not believe for a moment that moral and social criticism or indeed any rational arguments will suffice to end capitalism and establish socialism. It that is thought to be the role of moral critique here, it deserves the derision that Marx heaped on it. But that is not my intent. I am rather concerned to argue that such considerations, along with a reasonable amount of factual information, are sufficient to establish the presumption of socialism among our reflective and informed commitments, where the 'our' ranges over people like you and me who have the good fortune to be in the position where we can, and frequently do, engage in usually somewhat informed public discussion over such large-scale matters.[36]

I first need, so we have some sense of what we are talking about, to characterize 'capitalism' and 'socialism,' and then I shall turn to my arguments for the latter's presumption. Capitalism is a socio-economic order distinguished by the private ownership and control of the means of production vested in a minority class called 'the capitalist class', by basically a market system which determines the incomes and distribution of output arising from its productive activity, and by a cluster of distinctive social relations characterized by a culture containing an ideology of acquisitiveness and possessive individualism with its dominant drive for wealth and for individuals--only contingently and selfishly in collaboration--seeking to maximize their own individual expectable utilities. Socialism by contrast is a socio-economic order distinguished by the social ownership and control of the means of production and exchange, initially by the working class (the vast mass of people) and eventually by (in a classless society) humankind as a whole; by a genuine workers' control of their own productive activities; and by social relations in which there is extensive political freedom and decentralization of control of production.[37]

These are obviously ideal types for there are plainly examples of both capitalism and socialism which do not satisfy these conditions. Indeed in the case of socialism it is doubtful whether all these conditions are satisfied anywhere, though perhaps Chile under the Allende government was slowly but genuinely moving in that direction. However, to afford us an ideal characterization of what these two socio-economic orders could be best understood as representing, the above characterizations, within certain limits of vagueness are at least roughly what we need.

I want now to argue why, if we reflect carefully on the matter and take note of certain facts, we should conclude that capitalism is immoral. Our ears, particularly the ears of academics and intellectuals (most particularly philosophers), have been conditioned to resist and indeed usually to turn off at such remarks. I feel this myself. I only ask you to try for a moment to bracket that preconception and to attend to the argument and then ask yourselves whether my claim cannot fairly be made and if I am close to the mark about the facts in the case. (I further think, no matter what position you take about the relation of the 'is' to the 'ought,' that it should not affect your appraisal of what I say below. After all, even the most severe autonomist admits that questions concerning what the facts are are not irrelevant to moral claims.)

Capitalism, I argue, is an immoral socio-economic system because it is an exploitative, repressive, aggressive, destructive, inegalitarian, dehumanizing, imperialistic socio-economic system, which, with its acquisitiveness and possessive individualism, makes selfishness into a virtue, necessitates alienated labour, alienated consumption, alienated social relations, and is inextricably committed to production for profit rather than, except incidentally, to production which would satisfy the real needs of human beings.

In certain circumstances certain inequalities may be justified or at least excusable inequalities, but many of the inequalities prevalent under capitalism have no such justification or excuse. They are grossly unfair and unjust without even the simulacrum of a justification or excuse. The United States, the lynchpin power in the capitalist social system, has as the historian Gabriel Kolko put it, "a grossly inequitable distribution of wealth and income that has not been altered in any essential manner in this century."[38] In capitalist societies we have millionaires, multi-millionaires, centimillionaires, and billionaires, while even in the advanced industrial countries, to say nothing about the much worse conditions in South America, Africa, and the Indian sub-continent, literally millions of people subsist in a state of poverty that dehumanizes them and sometimes even brings them close to starvation. In the United States approximately 1% of the people own about 80% of all publicly held corporate stock. Within that group of people are found the top managers and controllers of American society. Even here the situation may be worse than the statistic indicates, for in addition there are in the United States many more stocks held in foundations and trusts with the final control of these foundations and trusts resting in this miniscule but extremely powerful ruling class. In a nation of over two hundred million about two hundred thousand households own most of the nations corporate wealth and 85% of the households in the United States own no corporate wealth at all. (So much for people's capitalism!)

In Canada 90% of the people own no stocks or enterprises at all, and the top 1% of all income earners in Canada in 1968 held 42% of all Canadian stocks. (We must remember that this is only part of the story in Canada for our economy is preponderantly [75%] owned by foreign capitalists.) The United Kingdom in spite of the power of the labour party and a number of labour governments is not very different in this respect from Canada or the United States. It still remained the case in 1968 that "two per cent of the British people still own 55% of all private wealth. Ten percent own 80%. When income from property is added to earnings, the top 1 percent of the British people receive about as much income as the bottom 30 percent put together."[39]

Finally, even in Sweden after 40 years of Social Democratic rule, only recently ended, during which time Sweden has become one of the most affluent countries in the world, it is still the case that there are, even with their model welfare system, widespread inequalities and that the structure of their monoply capitalism has not been weakened the least bit. Perhaps it has even been strengthened. In Sweden the upper 10% receives 27% of all income and the ownership of Sweden's corporate wealth is as concentrated as in any other capitalist country in the world. Fifteen well-known families are the dominant powers in Sweden, and of these fifteen families, five control the Swedish economy through corporate ownership with combined links to the insurance companies and three key banks. Indeed one family, the Wallenbergs, control one-third of Sweden's export economy and one-third of its financial markets.[40]

In short, we can accurately say of all the modern capitalist countries that corporate wealth is,in an almost unbelievable concentration,in the hands of a miniscule percentage of people.

This has not altered significantly over decades and--not surprisingly--the wealth has remained for the most part in the hands of the same families as inherited wealth. Popular mythology to the contrary notwithstanding, there is little upward mobility from the various strata in the working class to the ruling capitalist class, or even to the lower strata of the managerial elite who are the well protected servants of the ruling class.[41] Moreover, this gross inequality--or even anything approximating it--has no functional justification or rationale at all. There are no good grounds for claiming that all of us will be a little better off if we will continue to opt for that system with these inequalities rather than a socialist alternative without such vast inequalities. Rather the actual situation is just one of plain greed and the exploitation of one group of people by another, with a disproportionately large amount of the goods, powers, amenities and benefits of life going to very few people while the vast majority of people do not get such amenities, powers, or benefits and have very little control over their own lives. There are, of course, the upper strata of the working class, the class who work for a wage and own little or nothing of the means of production, such as the middle-managers, non-self-employed professional people, and the like, who often tend in their action, commitments, and attitudes to be clearly for the capitalist system. For the most part they (at present at any rate) identify with the capitalist class and get some not inconsiderable trickle-down benefits from it. It has been estimated that together with self-employed businessmen self-employed professionals, and people who live in a modest way off the earnings of their securities, they constitute at most about 20% of the population while the capitalist class constitutes between 0.5% and 2% of the population. The rest of the people--the vast majority of the people--are exploited by the system, and it is not in their objective interests to see the capitalist system continue.

So our first and very fundamental reason for judging the capitalist system to be immoral is that it is a grossly inegalitarian system maintaining a class divided social order where a few rich and powerful exploit--live off--the productive labour of people who without capital must sell their labour to them to survive. Such exploitation and such inequalities are plainly unjust. They do not--when such considerations are vividly kept in view--square with the reflective and considered judgments and moral sensibilities of informed and rational persons who have a reasonably developed sense of justice.

Capitalism is also immoral because it is essentially, and not just accidentally, dehumanizing. Under it men will--indeed must--engage in alienated labour for it is a system that insures alienated labour, as I shall show below. The rationale for industry and for work under capitalism is to make a profit. The name of the game is capital accumulation for the maximization of profit and power for the capitalist ruling class (some 0.5% to 2% of the people). Production in fact is primarily for profit and only incidentally to satisfy the real needs of human beings. Most people under such a system must simply sell their labour to survive; they do not work for the intrinsic desirability of the work itself or for its extrinsic desirability in the producing of things of value to human beings. They work for a wage, often with thorough boredom and sometimes with the sense that it is 'the curse of Adam', hoping understandably enough, given the nature of their work, to get it over with as quickly as possible so that they can pursue their 'real life' apart from their work. They often, given the demands of the system under which they work, must deliberately produce shoddy goods with a built in obsolescence; they must also produce goods for which there is no rational need. They must do these things to make a wage in order to live and in order that their families may live. Yet even if they clearly see from everyone's point of view, other than the capitalist's, the senselessness of their work, they will also recognize that in that system they have little or no say concerning what is produced and how much of it is produced. The senseless work must go on if that is what their masters ordain.

Under socialism the name of the game would not be production for profit but for human use and to meet human needs; in addition, if it were a genuine form of socialism and not--as it is in the Soviet Union--a form of state socialism or statism, there would be workers' control as well as social ownership of the means of production.[42] Indeed it would be more accurate to say that without workers' control there will be no genuine social control of the means of production. Where these several conditions are not being met--as they are not in Canada and the other capitalist countries--work for the vast majority of people is alienated and often dehumanizing labour sometimes with little rational or human point other than to create profit for the capitalist class who exploit them.

6

If, taking the ideal types of both capitalism and socialism, capitalism both morally and rationally gets such bad marks, and socialism with its commitments to democracy, equality, and a commitment to production to meet human needs, comes off so much better, then it would seem the presumption of socialism is justified. But it is just these things that I have tried to establish in the previous section. If I am near to my mark, it would appear at least to be the case that the presumption of socialism is justified.

If both the presumption of atheism and the presumption of socialism are justified, then we have a minimal world view that, at least until a sustained and thoroughly convincing counter-argument is forthcoming, is rationally justified and provides an attractive Archimedean point and an overall guide such that people, in Horkheimer's vivid phrase, would not be abandoned to the social world in which one could have no rational hopes for a truly human society and could not escape alienation.

However, as we have seen, presumptions are defeasible and it is surely the case that many would rush in to try to defeat the presumption of socialism. Even if it were in the range of my competencies, I could not here even begin to say--indeed even acknowledge--all the things that need to be said or all the challenges that can be reasonably make. But I shall make something of a start with some of the more pressing ones.

Some, perhaps many, will say that I am on cloud cuckoo, for in Europe and North America at least, the achievement of socialism is plainly impossible and, since 'ought implies can', it is pointless to talk of the desirability of socialism. Others will say that, whatever might be said about the comparative desirability of the ideal types, given the societies which are actually called socialist, they hardly provide models of more humane, more truly human, and more democratic societies, than do such at least relatively progressive capitalist societies as Sweden, Norway, or Canada.[44] These two challenges to the presumption of socialism are not as distinct as they may at first seem, and they both plainly merit careful consideration.

I shall consider the second challenge first. There are no good reasons, in societies such as ours with long traditions of parliamentary democracy and at least a nominal respect for human rights, to believe that socialists arising out of such a milieu would not be thorough democrats and would not be more like Luxembourg than like Lenin.[45] Moreover the very historical circumstances including the level of cultural and economic development, are such that there is no good reason to believe that anything like the questionable sides vis-à-vis democracy that seem at least to have obtained in the Russian or even the Chinese or Cuban situation need be repeated. Recall that Allende, even under extreme provocation, did not abrogate such traditional bourgeois liberties. And, if socialism were to come to the advanced industrial bourgeois democracies, there is no good reason to think that it would follow a Russian model where the conditions of life were so radically different from those which obtain in the bourgeois democracies. Capitalist countries (Denmark, the United States, South Africa, and Brazil) are also very different politically and, to put it modestly, differ considerably in their respect for democratic liberties. But where, as in my own non-eccentric characterization of socialism, democracy is built into the very concept of socialism, why think these liberties will be abused and that all or even most emergent socialist societies in advanced industrial states with bourgeois democracies in the saddle as prior societal forms will turn into deformations of their ideals and all take a Russian-like road or even a Chinese-like road? Why should we, whatever political judgments we make about the various--and very different--extent socialist societies, assume that new ones emerging in very different conditions will all take the same road or will tend to develop like the extant socialist societies? All capitalist societies have not taken the same road. Both Denmark and South Africa are thoroughly capitalist societies, but they are in important political and social respects radically different societies. The spectre of the Russian bear should not frighten us away from the presumption of socialism.

Arguments about this second challenge naturally lead us back to the first challenge, a challenge we have yet to consider. The first challenge could be expanded, given the above argument concerning the second challenge, into the claim that in any society, human nature being what it is, socialism must suffer deformation in short order. A new ruling class or at least a new ruling elite will inevitably emerge undermining the drive for human equality, for democracy, and for workers' control; in short social forces will inevitably emerge which will undermine socialism. Given this as at least a very real possibility, if not an established inevitability, why rock the boat and provoke all the fears and uncertainties that may come with revolution or with radical transformation?

Most certainly the critic making the challenge could continue: capitalist societies are unjust and exploitative, and in certain though not all ways their democracies (where they even have formal ones) are of a questionable character, but with them--that is in those bourgeois societies which have democracies--we at least have, with a slowly rising standard of living and stability, something which is familiar and provides some assurance about the future. Only desperate human beings, more deeply exploited and alienated than we are, will reasonably take the high risk strategy of opting for socialism. It is unreasonable to expect socialism to be on the agenda where the working class is hardly even conscious of itself as a class. But we can only defend the presumption of socialism where socialism is a possibility (i.e. a reasonable probability). But it is quixotic and utterly unrealistic to think that it is.

The most concessive and the weakest reply that could be make to that challenge is to reply that even if there is in such societies no prospect of socialism, it still, like a perfect vacuum or perfect competition, could be taken as an ideal, a benchmark, to orient the progressive development of societies. I do not think such a defense should be so readily rejected out of hand as both parties to the dispute are likely to be inclined to do. Yet it still is a more extreme fall-back position than defenders of the presumption of socialism usually take or indeed should take.

A more straightforward and less concessive reply is to deny that we can be anything like so certain that socialism is not on the agenda. The capitalist consciousness industry, to use Enzenberger's fine conception, would like us to believe that in countries such as Canada socialism is not on the agenda.[46] But we must go carefully here. First, as Chomsky has plausibly argued, we do not have the scientific ability--and perhaps never will--to make such vast and such long-range social predictions.[47] Nobody really knows what kind of world we will live in twenty-five years from now. For all we know, or even have good reason to believe, it could very well be a quite different world than most of us at present expect. It is probably simply a lack of imagination and reflection that makes us expect it will be pretty much an enlarged and perhaps worsened version of the social world we know. Against socialists it is fair enough to argue that no one has a good capitalist breakdown theory and to remind them that capitalism has been very adaptable and very resilient indeed. But the other side of that coin is that we do not know that it will continue to be indefinitely adaptable. We unfortunately do not know whose side history is on; we cannot predict when and how capitalism will collapse, though it is surely reasonable to believe that no particular socio-economic formation will last forever. Keynesian and Neo-Keynesian conceptions seem to be in deep trouble, and things have repeatedly happened in our societies which were not at all foreseen. There *may* indeed, à la Charles Taylor, be good theoretical reasons why this must be so, but be that as it may, the crucial thing is that we are really in no position to be so sure that socialism, in a decade or so, is not a reasonable possibility first in Western Europe, starting in the South, and then in North America.[48]

I am not asserting that anyone can cogently claim that 'history is on their side,' but I am asserting that it cannot be justifiably claimed that we have sufficiently good reasons to believe that we will go on to just more of the same or move, as some futurists and cultural pessimists would like us to believe, into a kind of totalitarian administered society--a fascism with a modern techno-cratic look. The latter is an anxiety that the culture industry or consciousness industry would plainly like to instill; it is a brake on those no longer enamoured of bourgeois ideology, a hidden persuader which helps keep them passive, in effect operating on the maxim: 'Hold on, hold on to nurse for fear of finding something worse.' The sober view of the matter is that we do not know what the future will bring, but looking at France, Italy, and the rest of Southern Europe, from Greece to Portugal, as far as educated guesses are concerned, the prospects for some form of socialism being down the road a bit are not so utterly dim.

What we cannot reasonably do is rule out such a possibility and employ the 'ought implies can' maxim. Moreover, given our lack of knowledge here, we can have no good grounds, if something like the critique of capitalism I have given is well taken, for saying that defenses and professions of socialism by intellectuals are wildly quixotic and thus (sic!) indefensible. Furthermore, we know from many of the great bourgeois thinkers (Locke, Rousseau, and Kant, for example) that, in advance of what the conventional wisdom of their time sanctioned, they set out certain conceptions about desirable social relations which indeed their theorizing helped make a social reality. Why the same cannot obtain for socialist ideals in our own time escapes me. It is surely in the interests of the capitalist class to make socialism seem an impossibility. But this very fact should make us doubly cautious of those who would challenge the presumption of socialism on the grounds that socialism is either impossible or at least highly unlikely. There are enough real ways in which we are powerless without enhancing our sense of being powerless by verbal legerdemain.

There is a lot more to be said pro and contra about these and other challenges to the presumption of socialism, but there is no space left to consider them here. What I think I have done is to give some sense of how the argumentative terrain runs and some sense of how a defense of the presumption of socialism might reasonably proceed. If such a case has been made, and if my earlier arguments for the presumption of atheism are well taken, then we are in a very strong position to claim that a political theology is not needed. There is no good reason to think it is desirable and it may not even be a coherent possibility. In atheistic socialism, of which Marxism is historically the most important variety, we have the kind of view of the world we need, giving people a guiding framework and a genuine sense of their nonabandonment.

I want to make one final observation. I suppose that many, for good reasons or bad, will reject the presumption of socialism. I would say to those who do so, you should still keep firmly before your minds that this rejection, even if justified, will not justify your developing or adopting a political theology, for the presumption of atheism can stand on its own. Without the presumption of socialism, a presumption of atheism may drive one, as it did Horkheimer in the last years of his life, to a profound cultural pessimism in which Schopenhauer replaces Marx as providing the deepest insights concerning our troubled times.[49] Horkheimer managed this quite consistently without reverting to a religious world view. We might go this way in the face of a rejection of the framework and indeed even the core ideals and expectations of socialism or, alternatively, we might turn, as does Flew, to an essentially Humean rationalistic-empiricism to underpin our presumption and subsequent defense of atheism. Or finally, in what I think is a deeper and more adequate response to the claims of both theology and the great tradition than we find in either Horkheimer or Flew, we might go in a radically different direction by adopting thorough relativism about _Weltbilder_ and thus also of _Weltanschauungen_ that we find in Wittgenstein's _On Certainty_.[50] To recognize the extent and the unavoidability of groundless belief is to be aware of the shallowness and inadequacy of Flew's rationalism which would, as he puts it, throughout cleave "to the Agnostic Principle, that we ought always to proportion our belief to the evidence."[51] The arguments of _On Certainty_ shatter such rationalism, but they do not undermine the presumption of atheism. On the contrary, such a thorough going relativism supports it in a much stronger way by giving far fewer hostages to tendentious epistemological and methodological theses than does Flew's rather brittle Humean rationalism. But if we move in any of these basic directions, whether we, à la Horkheimer, follow Schopenhauer, à la Flew, follow Hume, or go the profoundly original and challenging direction of the late Wittgenstein, we will have no reason for having a political theology but have instead a powerful battery of arguments for rejecting the very idea of such a thing as an idea rooted in illusion.

NOTES

A version of this paper was presented to the conference "Political Theology in the Canadian Context" at the University of Saskatchewan, March 10, 1977.

[1]Martin E. Marty and Dean G. Peerman, "Theology and Revolution," New Theology 6 (London: Collier-Macmillan Ltd., 1969), 9.

[2]I have done the former most succinctly in my "In Defense of Atheism" and "Religion and Commitment," both reprinted in Norbert O. Schedler (ed.), Philosophy of Religion: Contemporary Perspectives (New York: Macmillan Publishing Co., Inc., 1974); the latter occurs succinctly in my "A Defense of Radicalism," Question (January, 1974). That people who make the presumption of atheism do not always make the presumption of socialism is clearly evidenced in Flew's response in the same issue.

[3]The results of a recent Gallup poll. See the discussion of this by numerous authors, including Sidney Hook, Antony Flew, Arthur Danto, Walter Kaufmann, and myself, in the symposiom "The Resurgence of Fundamentalism," The Humanist 36 (January/February 1977), (March/April 1977), (May/June 1977).

[4]Martin E. Marty and Dean G. Peerman, "Theology and Revolution."

[5]Ibid.

[6]Alasdair MacIntyre, Marxism and Christianity (London: Gerald Duchworth, 1969), and Alasdair MacIntyre, "The Debate about God, Victorian Relevance and Contemporary Irrelevance," in Alasdair MacIntyre and Paul Ricoeur, The Religious Significance of Atheism (New York: Columbia University Press, 1969), and Max Horkheimer, Critique of Instrumental Reason, trans. by Matthew J. O'Connell and others (New York: Seabury Press, 1974).

[7]See the discussions mentioned in footnote 3 as well as John H. Schaar "Getting Religion," New York Review of Books (October 23, 1976); Christopher Lasch, "Narcissistic America," and Elizabeth Hardwick, "Piety and Politics," both in New York Review of Books (August 5, 1976).

[8]John H. Schaar, "Getting Religion," Christopher Lasch, "Narcissistic America," and Kai Nielsen, "Religiosity and Powerlessness." The Humanist 36, 3. (May/June 1977), 46-48.

[9]Schaar, "Getting Religion," 16.

[10]Lasch, "Narcissistic America," 20.

[11]Hardwick, "Piety and Politics," 22.

[12]Lasch, "Narcissistic America," 12.

[13]See the full page advertisement "America is Racing Toward Judgment," The New York Times (November 7, 1976), 5. For a significant sociological background note concerning such religions see Kenneth Briggs, "New Spiritual Organizations Considered Likely to Last," The New York Times (June 22, 1977), 13.

[14]Marty and Peerman, "Theology and Revolution," 12.

[15]The various publications of the Christian Institute of South Africa are of interest here and in particular the essays by Beyers Naudé. See as well The Trial of Beyers Naudé, edited by the International Commission of Jurists, Geneva (London: Search Press, 1975). More abstractly and philosophically note the essays by D. C. S. Oosthuizen, The Ethics of Illegal Action (Johannesburg: Raven Press, 1973).

[16]Antony Flew, The Presumption of Atheism (New York: Barnes & Noble, 1976), and see my "The Burden of Proof: A Critical Notice of The Presumption of Atheism," Religious Studies Review (1977).

[17]Flew, Presumptions of Atheism, 15.

[18]Kai Nielsen, Contemporary Critiques of Religion (New York: Herder and Herder, 1971), chapter 5.

[19]The works I have in mind are D. Z. Phillips, The Concept of Prayer (London: Routledge and Kegan Paul, 1970); Faith and Philosophical Inquiry (London: Routledge and Kegan Paul, 1970); and Paul L. Holmer "Wittgenstein and Theology" in Dallas M. High (ed.), New Essays on Religious Language (New York: Oxford University Press, 1973), chapter 2.

[20]See my Contemporary Critiques of Religion, Sceptism; see Terence Penelhum, Problems of Religious Knowledge (London: Macmillan Press, 1971); and Terence Penelhum, Religion and Rationality (New York: Random House, 1971).

[21]The two books by Penelhum cited in the previous footnote are important in this context.

[22]Contrast Antony Flew, Presumption of Atheism, and D. Z. Phillips, Religion Without Explanation (Oxford: Basil Blackwell, 1975).

[23]Nielsen, Ethics Without God (London: Pemberton Books, 1973); "Linguistic Philosophy and 'The meaning of Life'" in E. D. Klemke (ed.), The Meanings of Life (New York: Oxford University Press, 1981); and "Linguistic Philosophy and Beliefs" in Philosophy Today No. 2, Jerry H. Gill (ed.), (New York: Macmillan, 1969).

[24]Peter Geach, God and the Soul (London: Routledge & Kegan Paul, 1969), chapter 9.

[25]Kurt Baier, "The Meaning of Life" in Peter Angeles (ed.), Critiques of God (Buffalo, New York: Prometheus Books, 1976); chapters 2 and 3 in my Ethics Without God and my articles cited in footnote 23.

[26]Louis Hemon, Maria Chapdelaine (Montreal: Le Febvre, 1916).

[27]Nielsen, "Religiosity and Powerlessless," The Humanist, 37,3 (May/June 1977), 46-48; and references in footnote 7.

[28]Horkheimer, Critique, 78

[29]Nielsen, "On Philosophic Method," International Philosophical Quarterly, 16,3, (September, 1976).

[30]Horkheimer, Critique, 80 and 82; Douglas Kellner, "The Frankfurt School Revisited," The New German Critique, 4 (Winter, 1975), 131-153.

[31]See my discussion of Flew cited in footnote 16.

[32]Nielsen, "Can There Be an Emancipatory Rationality?", Critica, 8, 24 (December, 1976); and "Rationality, Needs and Politics," Cultural Hermeneutics 4 (1977).

[33]Nielsen, "The Burden of Proof," Religious Studies Review (1977).

[34]Karl Marx, The German Ideology (London: 1965), 255.

[35]I use 'rational' here in the quite restricted non-moral sense employed by such philosophers as Rawls, or Brandt, and by most bourgeois economists. I do not think that this is an adequate conception of rationality. But I agree with David Gauthier that it is a distinctive conception of rationality which is a key ideological conception in our society and that it distorts our understanding of ourselves and our world. David Gauthier, "The Social Contract as Ideology," Philosophy and Public Affairs 6, 2 (Winter, 1977), 130-164. See Nielsen, "Principles of Rationality," Philosophical Papers, 3, 2 (October, 1974), 55-89; and Mary Gibson, "Rationality," Philosophy and Public Affairs, 6, 31 (Spring, 1977), 193-225.

[36]Nielsen, "Class Conflict, Marxism and the Good-Reasons Approach," Social Praxis, 2 (1974), 89-112.

[37]Robert L. Heilbroner has pointed out that in actual practice--ideal types aside--there are different socialisms. There are, as he points out, "at least two, and possibly three" distinct social orders which rest on the public ownership of the means of production. First, there is the 'industrial socialism' of the Societ Union and its allies. This 'socialism' has, according to Heilbroner, "two salient features: an industrial apparatus closely resembling that of capitalism, both in structure and in outlook and a highly centralized,

bureaucratic, and repressive, social and political 'superstructure'." We have, secondly, the 'non-industrialized socialism' of the underdeveloped world where "political centralization and social repression exist, but not the framework of industrialism . . . ." Thirdly, there is a socialism, closer to our ideal type, which combines a high degree of industrialism and a social ownership of the means of production with political freedom and decentralized control. When I argue for socialism it is for this third type of socialism. See Robert L. Heilbroner, "The Human Prospect," The New York Review of Books, 20, 21 and 22 (January 24, 1974), 26-27.

[38] Gabriel Kolko, The Roots of American Foreign Policy (Boston: Beacon Press, 1969), 9.

[39] C. H. Anderson, Toward a New Sociology: A Critical View (Georgetown, Ontario: Irwin-Dorsey, 1971), 9; John W. Warnock, A Socialist Alternative for Canada, (Saskatchewan Waffle Movement, Regina 1973) 5; and Raymond Williams (ed.), May Day Manifesto 1968 (Harmondsworth, Middlesex, England: Penguin, 1968), 20.

[40] Göran Therborn, "The Swedish Road to Capitalism," Canadian Dimension, 9, 7 and 8 (1973), 61-66.

[41] J. H. Westergaard, "Sociology: The Myth of Classlessness," in Robin Blackburn (ed.), Ideology in Social Science (London: Fontana/Collins, 1972), 119-163.

[42] Gajo Petrovic, Marx in the Mid-twentieth Century (New York: Garden City, N.Y. Anchor Books 1967), Svetozar Stojanovic, Between Ideals and Reality (New York: Oxford University Press, 1973); and Mehailo Markovic, From Affluence to Praxis (Ann Arbor: University of Michigan Press, 1974).

[43] Ernest Mandel, An Introduction to Marxist Economic Theory (New York: Merit Publishers, 1969), 23-24.

[44] See the careful critical discussion of some extant 'socialist' societies (East Germany, Czechoslovakia, North Korea, and Cuba) in Kursbuch 30 (December, 1972) and the discussion there of 'revolutionary tourism'. The theoretical implications of this are well articulated by Hans Magnus Enzensberger, The Consciousness Industry (New York: The Seabury Press, 1974), 129-157.

[45] For two complementary models for societies such as our own, one stressing political organization and the other economic organization, see Gar Alperovitz, "Socialism as a Pluralist Commonwealth," in Richard C. Edwards, Michael Reich, and Thomas E. Weisskopf (eds.), The Capitalist System, First Edition (Englewood Cliffs, New Jersey: Prentice-Hall, 1972), 524-539; and David Schweickart, "Worker-Controlled Socialism: A Blueprint and a Defense," Radical Philosophers' Newjournal, 8 (April, 1977).

[46] Hans Magnus Enzenberger, Consciousness Industry.

[47]Noam Chomsky, "Introduction" to the English translation of Daniel Guerin's _L'anarchisme: De la doctrine a l'action_ (New York: Monthly Review Press, 1970), 7-20.

[48]Charles Taylor, "Interpretation and the Sciences of Man," The Review of Metaphysics, 25, 1 (September, 1971).

[49]Horkheimer, _Critique_; and his interviews in _Der Spiegel_ (January 5, 1970) and (July 16, 1973).

[50]Ludwig Wittgenstein, _On Certainty_, English translation Denis Paul and G. E. M. Anscombe (Oxford: Basil Blackwell, 1969). For a brief and clear introductory elucidation of some of the threads of thought in _On Certainty_ most relevant to what I say above, see G. H. von Wright, "Wittgenstein on Certainty" in G. H. Wright (ed.), _Problems in the Theory of Knowledge_ (The Hague: Martinus Nijhoff, 1972).

[51]Flew, _Presumption of Atheism_, 7; I try to show something of this in Flew's work in my article cited in footnote 16. See also my "Religion and Groundless Believing" in Mostafa Faghfoury (ed.), _Analytical Philosophy of Religion in Canada_ (Ottawa: The University of Ottawa Press, 1981).

DISCUSSION

B. G. Smillie, Response . . .

It is a pleasure to respond to an atheist and a socialist from the position of a Christian and a socialist.

I will start by examining Kai Nielsen's critique of religion. Professor Nielsen, in Part 2 of his paper, attacks North American cultural religion. I am sure that from the Husky Oil Tower in Calgary "the all pervasiveness of neanderthal evangelicals" is very apparent.

Nielsen compliments academic theologians as being "staggeringly at a distance from where plain religious folk are at," particularly in contrast to political leaders like Carter, Nixon, Ford, and Reagan. Let me return the compliment and say that his position is refreshingly different from where many academics are.

He bears little resemblance to the academic mandarins whom Noam Chomsky talks about in American Power and the New Mandarins[1] who used the allegedly value free models of stimulus-response in behavioural psychology to carry out a cruel pacification program in South Vietnam. Nor does he settle for a hedonistic pragmatism touched with cynicism which is such an easy academic posture.

What I want to emphasize is that when we engage in political criticism of the church, most of it justified, and we compare it with an institution we take for granted, namely the university, we find the university is just as culture-bound, just as chameleon in representing the uncritical value system of an oppressive capitalist society. In fact in comparison, I believe the Canadian church represented in the Canadian Council of Churches and the Canadian Catholic Conference has in recent history a better track record of political concern than the university. In 1973 the main line churches were first into the arena in condemning the Allende coup in Chile and Canadian complicity in that event. They have been in the forefront of investigation of Canadian bank investments in South Africa. They have shared in condemning the exploitation of native peoples in the Canadian North under the guise of benevolence. They have provided a strong critique of Canadian neo-colonialism hiding as development aid to the third world countries. This does not give them any excess of virtue for these acts because under the mandate of their call to the service of God they are unprofitable servants who have only done what it is their duty to do.

In the third section where Kai Nielsen elaborates his form of atheism we find it is very dependent on theism. He says, "to be an atheist one need not assert the non-existence or even the probable non-existence of God. One, to be such an atheist, only need not be a theist." One can't help reflecting on what would happen to this dependency state of atheism if all theists disappeared. These atheists would have to set up a propositional rational God so that they could refute its existence.

When one examines the credo of this atheism we find it starts with 'I believe in a moral universe.' "Torturing human beings is vile, exploiting and degrading human beings is through and through evil, cruelty to human beings and animals is morally speaking unacceptable, and treating one's promise lightly or being careless about the truth is wrong." There is no attempt made to explain how we know these things are wrong. There is a contextual awareness of morality recognized when Professor Nielsen says that in certain extraordinary circumstances there might be an occasion to lie or to break a promise or to harm someone, but what would be the guiding principle in these exceptional circumstances is left unexamined. In fact, Christian ethicists would say that an ethical system that did not know how to deal with exceptions would lead to the most brittle moralism; "the sabbath was made for man not man for the sabbath."

To go on with the Nielsen Credo, I believe that human kindness is a good thing and is timelessly true. I believe that there is purpose in life but it is ambiguous. Rather than seeking a purpose for which we are made or a goal of history like a New Jerusalem or a classless society, he says, "There are things in our environment that are worthwhile doing, having or experiencing, things that bring joy, understanding, exhilaration or contentment to ourselves or to others."

In section four on his presumptions of socialism, Professor Nielsen presents a model of socialism in contrast to a dehumanizing capitalism and every right-thinking socialist would have to say "Amen."

My criticism of his exposition of the presumptions of socialism is that in his attempt to find an Archimedean point to assess social institutions and indeed whole societies, he constructs a model of an ideal socialism that resembles Gaunilo's perfect island in the ontological proof for the existence of God. It seems to me to be a construct that cannot be falsified on philosophical grounds, nor could it face the test of Political Theology where the constant insistence is that God's activity must be seen in this world and not in some distant celestial city.

In making my response I will not engage in any lengthy debate which I believe is a barren discussion on whether the presumptions of atheism make untenable the presumptions of theism of the Judeo-Christian-Islam faith stance. That is for me a "Ho-Hum" battle. However, let me say this much about it. The Nielsen philosophical position centres on a metaphysical question on what one considers to be criteria of evidence. William Hordern has struck at the centre of the weakness of this method of doing philosophy in his criticism of the main prop of logical positivism in its attempt to banish metaphysics.

> The metaphysical nature of logical positivism is revealed when we ask what kind of statement is its own verification principle...its statements must be a priori or empirical. Some of the early logical positivists tried to argue that it is an empirical hypothesis, but it is clear it is not. There is no empirical evidence that could tend to verify of falsify it.[2]

Hordern concludes that if, as A. J. Ayer says, the verification principle is a priori and definitional, then all one has to say is, "that is not the way we intend to define what is meaningfully true."[3] Professor Nielsen can quite justifiably claim that he is not a hard core logical positivist. He repudiates the Humean rationalistic empiricism of Flew, but at the same time he carries the same vocabulary and the same implications for verification in propositional form when he says, "the burden of proof" is on the Christian to prove that he worships a cosmological god, or a teleological god, or a moral god. It is not that Nielsen denies causal relationships, or purpose, or morality, he just states that for the presumptions of Christianity to stand up it would be beholden on the Christian to prove that his God is the <u>sine qua non</u> for these things to exist in the world.

Let us go into the presumptions of socialism using Nielsen's method of "appealing to not very controversial <u>facts</u>" and see if he "escapes defeat" for his position. To set the scene for this method of finding evidence, let us review the verifiability principle established by John Wisdom and Anthony Flew. The Wisdom-Flew parable is a story developed from a tale told by John Wisdom in his haunting and revelatory article "Gods."

Once upon a time two explorers came upon a clearing in the jungle. In the clearing were growing many flowers and many weeds. One explorer says, "Some gardener must tend this plot." The other disagrees, "There is no gardener." So they pitch their tents and set a watch. No gardener is ever seen. "But perhaps he is an invisible gardener." So they set up a barbed-wire fence. They electrify it. They patrol it with bloodhounds. (For they remember how H. G. Wells' The Invisible Man could be both smelt and touched though he could not be seen). But no shrieks ever suggest that some intruder has received a shock. No movements of the wire ever betray an invisible climber. The bloodhounds never give cry. Yet still the Believer is not convinced. "But there is a gardener, invisible, intangible, insensible to electric shocks, a gardener who has no scent and makes no sound, a gardener who comes secretly to look after the garden which he loves." At last the Sceptic despairs, "But what remains of your original assertion? Just how does what you call an invisible, intangible, eternally elusive gardener differ from an imaginary gardener or ever from no gardener at all?" Flew concludes, "A fine brash hypothesis may thus be killed by inches, the death by a thousand qualifications."[4]

Professor Nielsen describes the oppressive dehumanizing power of capitalism and in contrast the major tenets of socialism where production is for human use and where wealth is distributed. When he goes in search of some country that might approximate an ideal socialist state we find his examples very vague. He insists that "ought" implies "can," but where is it to be found? He mentions Chile under Allende--Allende certainly retained a Marxist ideology, but at one most fundamental point was a deviationist in that in a classical Marxist sense Allende did not arm the workers. This Allende interpretation of socialism supports Professor Nielsen's principle of democracy, but hardly lasted long enough to be a convincing empirical reality. The United Kingdom and Sweden with their economic inequalities and their support of a wealthy elite are classed in the capitalist grouping. But later Russia, China, and Cuba are all condemned on the grounds that they do not have a democracy.

In facing the difficulties of establishing socialism in Europe and North America where there is no self consciousness of a working class and where capitalism is adaptable and resilient, he pushes his hope into an unsubstantiated future when he says "we are really in no position to be so sure that socialism in a decade or so is not a reasonable possibility first in Western Europe, starting in the South and then in North America." But where in the South of Western Europe may we see the first fruits of this compelling socialism--Monaco? Turkey? Greece? Southern Italy? Spain? Portugal a few years ago might have shown some promise but it hardly makes a good example today. So one has to ask what is the difference between this ideal socialist state and no socialism; a fine brash hypothesis seems to have been killed by inches, undergone the death of a thousand qualifications. This lack of evidence to show an actual existing socialist state does not, in my view, reject the case for socialism. It only questions Nielsen's method which he uses to attack Christianity and theism. In his attack on Christianity he is charitable enough not to identify political theology with the "moral majority," yet he uses the evangelicals and fundamentalists of the moral majority to discredit all Christianity. If his method of arguing is valid, then his own position on socialism is discredited by the fact that the majority of academics (particularly philosophers) are ardent supporters of a status quo not significantly different from the status quo supported by the evangelicals. A philosopher ought to know that it is an _ad hominem_ fallacy of the worst kind to discredit political theology by referring to what they do not believe and lump them with what Alberta's religious evangelicals do believe. In summary Nielsen's "well grounded" socialism as an "Archimedian principle" cannot be verified by his own criteria.

If I were looking for a socialist theoretical construct that risks being observed in our contemporary scene (but which also has problems meeting empirical verifiability tests), we have an interesting analysis by C. B. Macpherson in his outline of a type of national populist socialism emerging in third world countries, particularly in Africa.[5] Macpherson sees these third world countries drawing from western democracies the important liberal principle of democratic freedom but rejecting the possessive individualism. He sees the same countries laying hold of the Marxist critique of capitalism, but rejecting the Marxist emphasis on the dictatorship of the urban proletariat which does not fit the scene where class is replaced by a tribal populism and a charismatic leader emerges from the midst of the tribal family. This might be represented in Tanzania where there seems to be an important measure of local autonomy and accountability. Certainly this populism which is based on a Rousseau-like "general will" retains the importance of freedom and has units of accountability that are close at hand. Yet it keeps the people united in a common socialist political ideology. This populism we have seen in western Canada in the agrarian revolt. It died in the progressive movement because it was issue orientated and lacked a strong socialist critique of the capitalist society we live in. Could such a socialist populism be rejuvenated in Canada? My own personal viewpoint is that it could be. To be truly populist it would have to leave a large measure of autonomy on how this socialism would emerge in the different areas of Canada, but it would be a refreshing contrast to the broker liberal pragmatism that presently dominates our Canadian political arena.

The question that always haunts us, particularly when we look at the political scene from a theological perspective, is how can we keep our socialist analysis from becoming idolatrous. A very useful critical theory of society that Professor Nielsen uses has been developed by Jürgen Habermas and the Frankfurt school. Habermas has recognized that every critical theory runs the risk of becoming disassociated from praxis and thus of losing its critical power. In his condemnation of Russian Communism whose credo was "The Party is to represent the highest form of proletariat action," Habermas says, "Stalinist praxis has furnished the fatal proof that a Party organization which proceeds instrumentally and a Marxism which has degenerated into a science of apologetics complement each other only too well."[6] In fact, Habermas suggests that both capitalism and the ineffectual Communist parties are judged by their failure to bring emancipatory results. There can be no meaningful theory which, per se and regardless of the circumstances, obliges one to militancy. In any event, we can distinguish theories according to whether or not in their structure they point toward possible emancipation.[7]

The Catholic scholar Edward Schillebeckx, in supporting and yet criticizing Habermas' critical theory of emancipatory praxis, asks the penetrating question: what makes "emancipation" and "freedom" beyond reproach when ideological positions are under scrutiny? They could be the ideals of a thoroughly repressive and despotic society. There is no empirical justification for basing this critical emancipatory theory on objective facts. Schillebeckx supports these criteria of freedom as laudatory, but insists that this position presupposes an interpretation of humanity. It is not some objective meta theory. So finding a hermeneutic principle that best explains and helps interpret our human condition still remains the quest.[8]

The hermeneutical circle I wish to support as a Christian in developing a political theology is based on the belief that God is the controller of the world and is revealed in the events of history, not in ambiguous speculative arguments that prove or disprove God's existence. In this historical arena God has become visible in Jesus Christ, who in the Holy Spirit continues to guide us in the development of a more humane society. I believe that in the Scriptures of the Old and New Testaments God has given us a hermeneutical principle for understanding how to know ourselves and how we can live as good stewards of the world God loves. The tools for understanding the political arena have been greatly enhanced by a new understanding of the structure of the Bible. Sölle points out that the great Bible scholar Rudolf Bultmann, as a child of the Enlightenment, has contributed to this hermeneutic by subjecting the canon of scripture to the questions of what can the modern person believe. This was a very useful device in illuminating the scenes of scripture and freeing the events from an anachronistic cosmology. But the problem with Bultmann's critical approach to the Bible was that although the text was illuminating to our understanding of the world, it remained politically quiescent in the face of the takeover by National Socialism. Ironically Bultmann and other Biblical scholars, in trying to assume no political bias, have in fact assumed the oppressive ideology of the status quo. In other words, the hermeneutical circle is incomplete.

Helping us complete the circle, there is also a very useful heuristic source of political understanding in the biblical understanding of freedom. It is a very biased freedom for the captive, the poor, and the oppressed. "God has put down the mighty from their seats and exalted the humble and meek. God has filled the hungry with good things, the rich have been sent empty away."

In conclusion may I express my appreciation of Kai Nielsen's paper. He has exposed the way in which Christian evangelical pietism has become the cultural religion of the powerful who become the agents of plundering the poor. His espousing of a socialist framework for creating a more humane society makes him an ally in our struggle to develop a more just society.

NOTES

[1]Noam Chomsky, American Power and the New Mandarins. (New York: Vintage Books, 1967).

[2]William Hordern, Speaking About God (New York: MacMillan,1964), 32.

[3]Ibid.

[4]Alastair MacIntyre and Anthony Flew, New Essays in Philosophical Theology (London: SCM, 1955), 96-97

[5]C. B. Macpherson, Democratic Theory: Essays in Retrieval (Oxford: Clarendon Press, 1973), 157-169.

[6]Jürgen Habermas, Theory and Practice, trans. John Viertel (Boston: Beacon Press, 1973), 36.

[7]Ibid., 32.

[8]Edward Schillebeckx, The Understanding of Faith (London: Sheed and Ward), 125.

DISCUSSION (cont'd.)

Question, Kai Nielsen

This is something I want to put generally to all of you. Let me say something autobiographic at the beginning. I am a socialist through and through, neither a Christian nor a Jew. One of the things that puzzles me is that you Christian intelligentsia sound to me like good comrades. I could identify with you in the struggle for a changing society. But one of the things that perplexes me, and I would like to see how you face this, is that in North America at least--Quebec less, but in English Canada, and in the United States--the dominant Christianity has almost nothing in common with what you say. It's the Billy Graham, Ronald Reagan, Gerald Ford, the peanut baron Carter, who are Christians and who dominate the religious scene: reactionary, privatistic, anti-communist, anti-socialist, anti-progressive, powerful, dominant, and completely reactionary. Now you Christian intelligentsia are not even in the ball game as far as I can see. (laughter)

Response, Yves Vaillancourt

I would like to give a few hints of an answer to this provocative question. I would make the question a little larger: Why, in North America, are the majority of university professors so much in favour of the status quo? Why are the majority of the mass media people so much in favour of the dominant capitalist system? Why are the majority of the staff of labour unions in North America so much in favour of the capitalist system? If you start to answer these questions you begin to have an hypothesis about the church as an institution within an historical society at an historical moment. To me, the church--in my own analysis, the institutional church--is under pressures of the dominant mode of production as much as any other institution within our society, but why remain as a Christian with such a contradiction? I would say that some institutions, some organizations, are on the side of the dominant class. They are at home there; for example, the Chamber of Commerce. These institutions are not lost when they are on the side of the bosses in a society like ours, but in my own Christian reflection and experience, the church as an institution is lost when it is on the side of the powerful forces; it is in contradiction with its own original message.

Therefore, political theology for me is a daily life thing. It is a preoccupation first of all to gather this family of Christians, many of whom were isolated in the beginning. This is a grouping of Christians evolving in the direction of Marxism and in the direction of a socialist position who were a little separated one from the other and who needed a nourishment that was not coming from the institutional church. The first task was to gather this family, and after that the challenge we discovered and we still have is to develop in a collective way a Christian reflection about faith and hope, but a reflection about the very basic points of the Gospel and of Jesus Christ's practice that can be a support for the practice we have with other comrades who are not Christian but who share a common concern in our own context.

Response, D. Sölle

I'd like to add something in the same direction. I think the church is mainly middle-class people, whatever that means exactly, and so it shares with other middle-class institutions what Marx called disfavouring between two positions. It's not totally defined by its economic interests. Take the example of teachers--they are dependent on the administration but have also relation to the kids and parents, so they are in between. And I think this favouring of middle classes, sometimes going to the right wing and sometimes going to the left wing, is very characteristic of the situation, and this is the place where churches are moving and organizing. I am as sceptical as you are about the mainstream churches and the mainstream middle-class, because the experiences of history tell me that when it comes to the battle, then the middle-class may decide to go to the right. This happened in Germany when the middle classes in 1933 decided out of anti-Communism to go to the Fascists; it happened as well in Chile in 1972 when the middle classes, not only by American dollar bribes but also by their own fears, went to the side of the Fascists. Now the problem for me is simply that I am working inside of a part of the middle classes which is called the church, and I think there is always, somehow, hope for all my people in an option for socialism. This openness of the middle-class existence is based in the economical and social basis of these people; they have some liberties. That's dangerous, of course, but it also can turn out as a sign of hope, and I think that it turns out to be more and more as a sign of hope in these Christian circles. And I want to give you this as an ironic example which I got from Nelson Rockefeller, who said in 1976 that he thought there was a certain contradiction between our Christian heritage (as he said) and the structure in which we live (or the life we enjoy, as he liked to say). Even Nelson Rockefeller sees the split, so we have some hope, too, that we are not totally absorbed, or in other words, that the compatibility of capitalism and Christianity is not so unquestioned as it was, say, some 20 years ago. There is a shift, and it is an increasing number of Christians in the whole world who make the socialist option, and that's simply a fact. You'll find them in the concentration camps and tortured in Latin America, these people, and that's new after 2,000 years of Constantianism.

Question, Alan Richards

Dr. Nielsen, I too am from Alberta and I like to think of myself as a socialist in that place, and so I can sympathize with the kind of frustration you speak about in developing a socialist strategy in Alberta. I am a little disappointed, though, that in taking the question, "Is there a need for political theology?" you didn't discuss this in the historical context of Alberta. It seems to me the question is not: Is there a need for a political theology? but, Is there a need for political theology, given the kind of Alberta that presently exists? And so if we are going to look at some sort of socialist program, we need to address the questions of a society that is rich in oil. We need to look at the whole question of oil vis-a-vis our native people and the demands that we are placing on the Mackenzie Valley. The development of a petro-chemical industry is the base for the Alberta economy to the neglect of development of sound agricultural practice and land management. This it seems to me is the context in which we ask whether or not there should be a political theology. This is not to overlook what you have described as the function of religion in Alberta, which as you point out has had a very conservative influence in political movements. But given the Alberta scene, we can't start with a Marxist basis because the people aren't Marxist, but we might be able to start from a Christian perspective, because they claim to be Christians: "They are Christian and should be held accountable to that tradition." Addressing them within the Christian faith, you can say you believe in love; then you have some accountability to the question of social justice. I was disappointed that that context was missing from the discussion.

Response, K. Nielsen

I can understand your being disappointed and it's probably a function of labour, an academic deformation; that is to say, I'm a philosopher, I know about abstract theoretical things in some way--I can speak to those. The kind of specific knowledge to say other than obvious things that I sometimes say over television I don't have. You need someone else; you need an Alberta equivalent of C. B. Macpherson, or somebody like that. (Lawrence Pratt would do very well indeed). I couldn't do it, though I think it is very important to do. My last remark was precisely designed to meet that. I can well imagine somebody saying, "Look, you completely leave out the tactical question: What do you do in a Bible belt to try to build toward social change?" I don't know how, and I'm perfectly prepared to say that somebody might use the language of Christianity, even in a fairly figurative and Luddite fashion, to try to effect a social transformation. As I said in my final remarks, after I departed from my text, I would be perfectly prepared to go along with that. I doubt that it will be effective, but one cannot be sure of that, and in itself I have no criticism of it. I think it's a very good thing, I welcome it.

However, I was speaking in a different cultural context. I was speaking to a group of academic intellectuals, all of whom are theologians, and what I wanted to do was drive home the theoretical point that they may have been bringing coals to Newcastle. I was challenging the belief that we must hang on to the Jewish-Christian tradition in order to give an adequate theoretical basis to transform society or to make sense of our lives. I was challenging the old belief that somehow Marxism, or critical theory, if it were only supplemented by this Christian-Jewish tradition, would give a stronger foundation for the social transformation that a number of us look for. I assumed that was the kind of audience I was speaking to. The thing you were asking, which is probably a much more useful question, certainly a question which is more useful generally to Canadian society, I could hardly speak to in any reasonable way, beyond voicing a few platitudes.

Question, Paul Newman

Professor Nielsen asked the question, "why theology?" There seems to be more interest and common agreement in, yes, politics, and even, yes, Marxism, as a tool of analysis, as a tool of strategy, but he's asking the question, "why theology?" and I hope somebody gets around to answering that question. To be more precise, is anybody going to talk about the way in which Jesus is normative for political theology, and that was the question you asked; you said that the burden of proof is on Christians to show why God or why Jesus is normative. Why are Jesus and God related to this whole enterprise of concern for injustice?

Response, Gregory Baum

I would like to speak against that. It seems to me that an old-fashioned Christian theology divided people into believers and atheists, and I think that today we--I mean those of us who live after the holocaust--realize that this distinction is really quite inadequate. This distinction should be between people who are with the little ones, who identify with the people to whom we do the dreadful things, and those who shrug their shoulders, and therefore to introduce God or theology as a kind of dividing principle between people who identify with the little ones is, I think, a terrible strategy that leads to the perpetuation of the cruelty for which this world is at fault.

4

THEOLOGY AND LIBERATION

Dorothee Sölle

Biographical Statement

I want to begin with some personal remarks about my own theological political autobiography. The question I wish to pose is the way that one becomes radicalized. This is an important question, not only for oneself, but it also gives hints as to how other people become radicalized. Radicalization in Christian language could be called conversion. Radicalization or conversion happened to me in two of the most important political events of my lifetime. The first was that I am a German raised in the 1930s; this makes me a citizen of the country which produced the holocaust. I spent a lot of my time as a young student during my university years with the questions of my generation: How could it happen? and, What did you do? we asked our fathers, our teachers, our mothers, the men in the local shops. We persisted with our questions: Where were you when the trains carried the Jewish people to the East? What did you do about it?

Theoretically this was later discussed under the whole notion of collective guilt. This affected me by making me recognize in the development of my political theology that sin is not being unkind to my mother, or having some sexual problems sometimes, but it has to do with my existence as a member of a community. In my case, this was the German Reich. This deepened my understanding of the Christian faith, more particularly my awareness of sin and forgiveness as a member of the church. During the Hitler period, a very small group of Christians went with the Nazis. There was also a very small group who were against it and joined the resistance in the confessing church. The mainstream church still preached what they always did, they sang the same songs, they had the same liturgy, they thanked God when He made spring and all the other seasons. In other words, everything went on just as it had always been. In this tranquil church, totally and completely politically quiescent, I began to see that the most common sin in Christians is making invisible what you don't want to see. It is business as usual. This is my background in German church history.

The second event that radicalized me was to notice that no event in history stands alone. Auschwitz was re-born in the Vietnam war. This brought me into socialism and taught me to understand that if we really want to avoid further Auschwitzes and Vietnams, our only hope is the hope for a socialist world. This was a long process for me. My awareness of oppression and domination began not domestically, but in the Third World, as it did for many people of the New Left.

My first point of entrance into this whole political question was to ask why helpless women and peasants were bombed or burned with napalm. I had a similar experience in my home town of Cologne with the burning and bombing war. I was a child there, so I related my own fears to these people who had had the same experiences. I learned very slowly, coming from a liberal bourgeois background, to relate this Third World oppression. I saw that it was two sides of the same coin; on the one side imperialism, on the other capitalism.

I am still in this process of radicalization, and it struck me as I listened to Bill Hordern's presentation that I would no longer like to label myself under the word "political theology." The word "political theology" has a form of academic cautiousness. It doesn't seem too open; it is ambiguous in a way because there is right wing political theology (as was advanced in Karl Schmidt's "Father of the Nazi Activists"), as well as a left wing political theology. So I would like to have a more open language, both less ambiguous and less neutral.

When I wrote my book on political theology in 1968-1969 and I used this terminology, I was caught in an academic setting, still oppressed by the white male theological education I went through; I was still using their language which is neutral, male, scientific and formalistic. If we shift from political theology to liberation theology, we go from this formal description--and you don't know exactly what the substance is--to liberation, which is a more substantial description. So I would like to do that, and to go this way in a more conscious way as I did in these first steps, and to develop this further. I am a member of Christians for Socialism in Germany; I was involved in building this up in my country. So to take some steps toward the de-privatization of religion, the convertization of it, means mainly to think more in terms of organizational structures. That is how I hope to overcome my own idealism (in which everybody in our class is brought up, of course). That's a process we have to work on. To overcome idealism would mean for me to organize myself with others to work together, to spend all of my time not only on academics and writing academic tracts, but in meeting groups, talking with people, trying to organize people around concrete issues. In this way I come to the last point I want to make; I come closer and closer to a sharp critique of Protestantism and my own heritage in liberal Protestantism.

Let me just give you one anecdote: I was at a meeting with the Christians for Socialism in Italy two years ago, and I got into an argument with two comrades, both priests, Catholic priests. I felt them so anti-Protestant and so anti-enlightened, and I didn't like it. Then I said, "What the hell have you against Protestantism?" They thought about it and said, "I think you have the same analysis as we do. There is a gap between the modern world and Christian religion. We have the same problem. Everybody has to bridge the gap, but what you Protestants do is to change religion, so that it fits." Now after thinking a little bit about what that meant, I really understood, and I reflected, I reviewed my theological past, the years I had spent at university and conferences and faculties. And what essentially was done there was to make it fit; to make religion understandable, and enlightened, and de-mythologized, so that it might fit into this modern world--instead of reflecting how we could change this modern world so that it might fit again with the promises of the Gospel.

My theological father was Rudolph Bultmann. I do not think I would have gone into theology without him. I was brought up in a liberal family where the church didn't play any role, and my father used to say, "Go to Sunday School, kids, its a little bit better than Hitler Youth." That's my background. (Laughter) They were anti-Nazi and I am thankful for that, but they didn't give me any more than a tolerant view of an out-dated institution. So Rudolph Bultmann was the personification of the theology of enlightenment. He taught me that I didn't have to give up my reasoning or my thinking before becoming a Christian. It was a great help for me and helped me to understand what Christianity is. This is the first step I took and I tried to draw some consequences out of Bultmann's approach. This led me close to what was in that context the death of God theology. I was pretty close to that. In fact, I still have difficulty with a heavenly master who rules history from up there. Consequently, I have no need for an after-life. I have a need for a life here with all people. In my concern for this common need, I am less dependent on private and worldly needs. In fact I have to overcome them. Radicalization and deprivatization go hand in hand. The other point I wish to make is that it is most important to do theology collectively; to give back the act of Jesus and the exegetical business of searching the scriptures to the people. In this way we will remove it from the domain of the learned ones. One of my church fathers, Thomas Muentzer, talked about the ruling priest class as "evil Bible thieves." They stole the Bible from the people because they didn't teach them; they didn't give it to them; and I think that's a part of the shift we are going through, to give this back to the people. I just got a note from the Christians for Socialism in Italy, where this movement is strongest in Europe. They asked these groups what their priority was in terms of study, and astonishingly they said, "We want to have Bible study from a socialist perspective." This is also part of the shift I'm going through.

Theology and Liberation

This paper[1] will be introduced with a quote from Christopher Blumhardt, a German pastor and social-democrat in the 19th century. The word social-democrat at that time had a totally different meaning from today's. A social-democrat then was what we would now call a Communist. He says:

> I am thinking of a completely new society. . . I have thought that very soon now a religion would have no value if it did not transform society. . . that is why I feel related to those people who are reproached for pursuing a Utopia, and I feel linked to them. . . . May the time come when we will succeed in giving society a new order, in which money will no longer be the principal object, but life and happiness of men. . . . Where has Christ been present? Among the lowly. That is why they called him riff-raff, sinner. That was really what he was since he was a socialist. He took twelve proletarians and made them his disciples. Who then can accuse me of denying my Christian faith because I have chosen solidarity with proletarians and because I myself desire to be a proletarian?. . . Before God, there are no differences among men. . . . It is life lived in the spirit of Christ that has brought me to socialism.[2]

A new spectre is racing through the parishes and offices of the church, its synods and theology schools, its study circles and communication media--the spectre of a Christian's option for socialism.

For a long time, the message of Jesus could only be encountered in a canalized form--domesticated by scientific exegesis and historical-cultural considerations opposed to any action, limited to small church-related groups which became more and more marginal in relation to society as a whole, and at the service of a quasi-automatic and unconscious identification of Christian behaviour with social conformism. But against all expectation, even on the part of those who believe in progress, this message drives those who identify with it beyond themselves, it exiles them, making them guilty of criminality. It destroys tacit agreement with the permanent injustice of society. It makes impossible what is asked of us each day--the submission of all human desires and needs to the imperatives of a system of production and consumption. But is such a domesticated love, such a limited value of truth, the meaning of the Gospel? Is the Gospel simply a consolation useful for the stabilization of society and a rejection of change? Is the Gospel limited to an occasional thirst for justice?

"Don't upset our children with your Jesus." These words were recently hurled at a young pastor by a parent who added, "We want our confirmation." "_Our_ confirmation" and "_your_ Jesus" cannot be reconciled. Christ has become "subversive," a word adopted some time ago by the Latin-American police to describe those elements which would be named in Germany today as "radical," "against the constitution," someone who has become "perverted" (as one newspaper said) by an exaggerated love of neighbour. It is this subversive message which has led a growing number of Christians around the world to take a stand for socialism.

What I want to present in this paper is this new identity. It is born of the experience of class struggle and of a faith that has been lived; for an increasing number of men and women, these two experiences can no longer be separated from each other since they are reciprocally conditioned, nourish each other, and are expressing and organizing themselves in a new language. We are Christians and at the same time socialists; it has become impossible to define ourselves by a simple designation, I am Christian, because that expression allows for too many misunderstandings and tends rather to obscure the fact of being Christian "for the kingdom of God." It is precisely because there are a majority of Christians "for capitalism" (even if this is not expressed and not always completely conscious) that we must work out a more clear-cut definition in attempting our own self-description and, in that very act, expose ourselves increasingly to attacks. Of course, the statement "I am a socialist" also includes many possible misunderstandings and may evoke doubts about the fundamentally democratic character of the socialism we are talking of. Let me recall the saying of Rosa Luxemburg, the German Communist leader. She said, "There is no democracy without socialism." She adds, "There is no socialism without democracy, without self-control of workers, and self-determination of people." I think most Christians for Socialism will agree with this statement.

The movement of the Christians for Socialism was born in Chile in 1971. At that time, left-leaning Christians had lost their "home" because the right (at first under the moderate influence of the Christian Democrats) had entered an alliance with the far right, and by every means at its disposal (parliamentary opposition, boycotts, hysterical propaganda, currency manipulation, and financially supported strikes) tried to overthrow the Popular Unity government of Allende. Christians of the left in the face of this challenge were obliged to redefine themselves. They recognized the legitimacy of the Allende government and tried to avoid being marginalized by the churches which considered them as simply leftist cells, hence they defined themselves as Christians for Socialism.

It is not only on behalf of Chileans, but also of European Christians and of Christians in the Americas who are committed to socialism, that we point out two essential tasks that should be taken into account in each national political situation. First, we intend to unmask the unconscious confusion between Christianity and bourgeois ideology, and second, to make a more radical effort to refute the presumed incompatibility between Christianity and socialism and to develop the possibilities for alliance and the necessity of such an alliance. In the two stages of this "conscientization," Christians for Socialism have demonstrated this new identity by their struggle and reflection.

A new identity doesn't grow out of theory, and especially not theological theory. Theology can only be a "second act," a reflection on practical experiences which are analyzed and can then provide a basis for a new theology. Hence, we would completely misunderstand the Latin American theology of liberation if we reduced it to a new theological recipe alongside the theology of hope. On the contrary, we must take it seriously as a response to a liberation that has been experienced and lived. Theology is something derivative, a discussion "about" something which can not substitute but only return to and be a reflection of genuine language: it could be called genuine language, a song, a call to struggle, marching orders, a prayer. Then it is theological language, a secondary order of language, of reflective language. Christians do not possess a "theological theory," for example, about revolution that they could apply in political terms, but in the very living out of their faith they have a certain number of experiences which they have to interpret in a theological and critical manner.

What does faith signify in such a context? What does one believe? It is the capacity of saying "yes" to oneself, of saying "yes" to the world, and of accepting it as loved, willed, and possible for man. None of all this is automatic, and for more and more people, the earth becomes "just as uninhabitable as the moon" (Zwerenz). Faith stands in opposition to such an attitude; it makes spots on the earth habitable and returns us to experiences that have made this possible. Faith makes use of the relationship between vision and experience while moving toward productive change instead of cynical analysis (the direction of those who always seem to know the properties and circumstances of each social situation). Hence, one believes in the possibility of realizing love and justice, the possibility of experiencing meaning and happiness.

By this very fact, faith enters into a different relationship to the present than that practiced by numerous leftist groups who always satisfy themselves with a sort of total elitist negation of all that exists. Theodore Adorno, a philosopher of the Frankfurt School, had a famous phrase. He said, "There is no true life in that which is false" (a German translation). This is a dialectical phrase which is true if taken in a messianic horizon, but if it is taken as an absolute phrase robbed of this messianic significance (as it was by the students of Adorno of the Frankfurt School), then it becomes this elitist negative position of people who always know how bad and hopeless everything is. Our hope is based on the contradictions in society; it's not our business to unmask everything that's senseless, meaningless and hopeless. Instead of continually analyzing present experiences when all current events appear to be too complicated because specialized knowledge is required, we should have enough faith to believe that alternatives are possible.

Faith is believing in something that does not exist--like peace. To realize this, to begin to walk ahead in this direction, is faith--vision, process, and praxis all together. It is the vision of a new earth. If faith were only the beata visio of a new heaven, we would more easily be able to renounce the assurance and the aid which tradition offers us. The real Utopias (visions without the power to burst the structures of what now exists) have need of nourishment; they cannot feed on mere needs and promises; they require living experiences which can be transmitted. From my understanding, the greatest help we get comes out of tradition, and in this sense I would say that I am a traditionalist who knows that she lives out of given experiences of my fathers and mothers and grandfathers and grandmothers.

It is possible to escape from the captivity of Egypt; that is one of the basic Judea-Christian experiences I am talking about, a hope that is confirmed in my tradition. Five loaves and two fish have already been enough for thousands of men and women. And there have been some dead people whom no one has been able to kill. A critique of religion which pretends to offer a total explanation overlooks the necessity of anticipating a life moving toward fulfilment.

There are experiences that can be shared, images of hope which have become language. One of the questions which always comes up for discussion in groups like this is when people ask, "Are your goals as a Christian in any way different from socialists and humanists? What is there specifically Christian in what you say?" My answer is our tradition. I can tell the stories of victories, and I can tell these stories even in the time of defeat. To abandon these stories or this tradition could only signify an impoverishment, a restriction, a canalization, made in terms of a utilitarian rationalization. In Christian history the abandonment of these visions of hope, the withdrawal from these apocalyptic expectations, have always led towards the growing destruction of meaning and of an excessively "spiritual" approach to reality. Sometimes I ask myself, could there not be a parallel danger in socialist history? Doesn't the loss of vision and the retreat from utopian socialism in favour of scientific socialism present the same danger of a growing loss of meaning and a constantly more abstract understanding of what the achievement of socialism might imply? I see this very much realized when I listen to some East German philosophers who tell me that alienation is no longer a problem in East Germany because the means of production are state-owned by the workers. They say that the meaningless form of production has been removed. This pedantic answer shows the barren self-assurance of scientific socialism in contrast to the more mysterious vision of utopian socialism.

One must at least say that the role of vision has not been entirely clarified. The suspicion remains that it might be seen as pre-scientific and hence superfluous, as religion. In this context the interpretation of Marx given by Louis Althussier represents the deadly invasion of an exaggerated scientism. Under the slogan "progress without subject," Althussier has purified Marxism of all its teleological and anthropological elements and has disqualified the humanist and utopian features of the young Marx as so much ideology that must be removed from a Marxian that should be understood as science. In this way the surplus of hope and vision coming from utopian socialism has been definitely reduced and instrumentalized.

But vision and the objectively knowable process of history should not exclude each other. Faith, which has its full impact within the interior of utopian socialism, signifies both. It is participation in the process of realizing a higher justice; an interest in justice flows into analysis but would not know how to rest content with limited intellectual and abstract objectives. This mediation between vision and precise analysis, in other words between the Bible and Marx, is realized by faith through subjective practice, something that transforms also the individual ego.

This development is confirmed by experience. If someone asks me, How does one become a Christian for socialism? I would reply: love your neighbour in this society. Above all, be down to earth. Love implies an unconditional concern for others. The more you become involved with you neighbour, the more you must care about each person's world, their lives, their living and working conditions, their social environment. Then you want to understand the causes of your neighbour's misery and to bring about changes. I am talking out of experiences with a group who tried to work--political Christian housewives who didn't feel fulfilled in what the church offered and whose neighbour love was a little bit deeper than the usual one--they tried to love their neighbour and they were basically compassionate, and so they got to the roots of the problem and became more and more radicalized. After meeting with frustration, at first they saw the causes of social problems in people who are unconcerned, egoistic, and brutal. Ironically, in accepting such an explanation, the person is in danger of losing her compassion and becoming cynical. Next she comes to agree with those who have always known that nothing could be done. She has now reached the point of losing faith, and loss of faith is a cancer that spreads and kills. But if her compassion is even more basic, perhaps she will take a step beyond this false search for causes and become involved with the humanity that is around her. She will then discover objective social causes--for example, the legal structure which makes it possible for a landlord to raise rents in an old building. If she is patient, she begins to see the problems a person has in a particular position in the overall system. She may then turn her attention to another point. But the person who is genuinely compassionate will eventually hit granite--the structures of property and society, in other words, the injustice inherent in the class system.

When such a new phase has been reached, it is high time to read Karl Marx. I personally consider it foolish to believe that charity and Marxist analysis are opposed, as many academic left-wingers believe. It is precisely the small reformist steps and the ensuing frustration which kindles revolutionary fire. One soon makes the discovery that it is only property that is inviolate, not persons.

From this alliance of Christians and socialists, however, a new Christian-socialist identity begins to develop, in which one no longer asks questions of socialists--such as those about guarantees for civil liberties--but rather actively seeks the creation of a new socialism that is concerned with the significance of work and the participation of workers in decision-making processes. People then stop presenting these suggestions "as Christian" to an alien ideology, as was the case in the Christian-Marxist dialogue of the 1960s which was the period before an alliance. We can call recent developments the movement "from dialogue to alliance." Dialogue in the academic form of the 1960s is dead; it was killed when Russian panzers invaded Prague, but the alliance goes on. The problem of the development of a socialist future then has become our problem. It's not something which we bring to the socialists asking them for grants for the civil liberties; it's our own problem. We have to find our socialism. The question must be addressed in groups with the various partners in alliance.

Christians for Socialism understand themselves living in a world of theological pluralism: there are many paths to a new understanding of Christian existence. In German Protestantism, to talk about the part of the world which I know best, there are three different ways to come to socialism from a Christian perspective. One is the religious socialism represented in the early Paul Tillich before he came to America. He says in one of his early socialist writings, "The measure by which the seriousness of religious socialism may be judged is the place it gives to class struggle." I think that is a clear statement. Another important tradition is the Barthian left, as carried on today by Gollwitzer and Marquardt, and through the discovery of the young Karl Barth and his position in various real conflicts. A third theological strain is that to which I myself belong, stemming from the radical historical criticism of Rudolph Bultmann.

Let me try to elaborate on this question of what the Christian and socialist identity means. The common experience that we all have is that there is often a dualism between faith and social analysis. We learn that it is a matter here of two very different things which certainly are related to each other but which nevertheless exist independently and are a part of our theological education. Now from this dualist point of departure, very different possibilities of conceiving of the relationship between faith and Marxist analysis may be derived. If faith is understood as the acceptance of a certain number of elements on a conscious basis, then the option for a precise social analysis can appear as the consequence of faith, saying "I am a Christian, and therefore socialist." The relationship is then one of cause and effect. But in such a case one of the two parts of this affirmation will not have been taken completely seriously. Traditionally, it is that the consequences of the Christian point of departure appear to be a secondary thing; they can be the object of different decisions, and are submitted to reason understood within a framework of rational plurality. It is relatively common and clear that, in this model of faith, whatever the consequences that one might draw from it for the politics of development, its concrete application is left to experts. Experts decide about the application, as they call it, of faith. The social "application," the relation between faith and political reality, appears to many as something that one ought to make, but that one also can leave aside. In this model, religion is first seen as apolitical; it can and ought--above all, in extreme situations--to lead to political consequences; but in principle, the dimension that is called "vertical," or divine, can perfectly well be separated from that which is considered as only human, or "horizontal."

Such a conception of Christianity is bourgeois. I mean this in the double sense of this word; in one sense it means simply that it is an expression of an historical epoch of the bourgeoisie or of liberalism, as you might call it. But I mean it also in the critical sense of a new point of view where bourgeois means an out-dated class system or class-based system. I think this theology which teaches us to separate faith and its so-called application in politics is bourgeois. It reflects dualist divisions of life which are so characteristic of bourgeois consciousness in general, as the separation of public and private life. Bourgeois theology separates love into two dimensions, love for God and love for man. The "horizontal versus vertical" schemata is almost exclusively employed in a reactionary sense, in order to devaluate the horizontal demension, to deny any relationship between it and the vertical demension, and finally, to make it only a part, a moment out of Christian life. In this process some like to refer to the Bible, which, in fact, does indeed speak of relationships to both God and men. But the Bible does not consider these relationships in terms of a dualism between religion and politics, between the love for God and love for one's neighbour, between religious conduct and human conduct. On the contrary, the tendency of Jesus is firmly to hold on to the unity of these two lines of conduct. For him, life does not consist in two parallel paths, but essentially in their meeting and in their intersection. And at every moment it is God who is involved.

You will remember a number of stories in the Gospels. In one, a lawyer asks Jesus about eternal life. Jesus does not respond with a profession of faith, but with the story of the man who fell into the hands of robbers on the road between Jerusalem and Jericho. And the rich young man, whose question is strictly bourgeois, asks much the same question, "What must I do to inherit eternal life?" He receives the answer: "Go, and sell what you have and distribute to the poor." When Jesus, in the language of the fourth Gospel, says, "My father and I are one," it's not a matter for him of a unity understood in a religious sense, and which would have no meaning except for him, it is a matter of the unity of life and love, in which we all are one with God, reconciled and comforted. This consciousness of unity, the experience of being one with men and women who are struggling and suffering, might well be called solidarity--all this is what is treated piecemeal in bourgeois theology and hence totally enfeebled. The separation between the horizontal and the vertical result in the enfeeblement of the human ego, in the incertitude and separation of people from God as they are faced with an unknowable truth. The anthropological pessimism which is so clearly expressed in classical Protestantism leads to this uncertainty; we don't know what to do, we are helpless, powerless. We know God but we don't know what to do. Now this is today combined with the whole overspecialization of all the particular domains of life; we end up bound hand and foot, incapable of acting.

It is against such a piecing out of love that I would like to recall at this point the story of Jesus curing the paralytic. The Pharisees had prepared a trap for Jesus and made the distinction between curing the sick man and pardoning his sins. They didn't believe in either of the two--they had confidence in neither the vertical nor the horizontal dimension of Jesus. It was a trap, the same trap that many bishops and other authorities are making for theologians today.

That is why Jesus ironically formulates their dualist thought in terms of a question: "Which is easier, to say to the paralytic, 'Your sins are forgiven,' or, 'Arise, take up your bed and walk ?'" Which is easier, we ought to ask today, the vertical or the horizontal? Which is more decisive, happiness or salvation? What can we do as Christians? Announce to everyone the pardon of their sins and salvation, or liberation. I think it is clear from the Christian perspective that the question is absurd. It is the dissembling tactic of the Pharisees to cut the horizontal off from the vertical; it is not the approach of Jesus. For him to cure and to pardon are only one thing; spirit and body are not two parts of a person that can be separated from each other.

The conditions of misery in our world cannot be separated into various domains; there is no area reserved to the exclusive competency of any group. The selection process that goes on in schools destroys children both psychically and physically. The piecing out of work into absurd small details destroys the capacity of the worker to think, and make plans, and project a future. It ends up making people sick. It also makes people deaf to the Gospel, for fundamentally it destroys one's capacity to accept oneself. As I talked in the beginning, to say "yes" to life, is destroyed by the way we organize work in our society. Time does not permit me to analyze the mechanism of repression which is at the root of this language of separation between the vertical and the horizontal, as if they were two dimensions of reality, but if we accept such an analysis, we are abandoning reality as if it were merely a secular domain, submitted to its own norms. This would constitute the most subtle form of atheism--in my understanding it is the rejection of God. In appearance there would be a pious insistence on the vertical dimension, love of God, on the theological foundation of questions of realist politics, and an insistence on the long-sought specificity of Christian faith. But this pious accent ends up quite simply in separating the relationship with God from reality; it signifies nothing but the theologically camouflaged incapacity of discovering God in reality, in the least of the brothers of Jesus on the road between Jerusalem and Jericho. That is why this whole separation of the vertical from the horizontal is emphasized.

The ideology of this incapacity to believe formulates some very sharp criticisms when Jesus, as it claims, is transformed into a "social-revolutionary." Its essential argument is formulated in terms of the various domains of life, such as politics, economics, and religion. Now, first of all, one has to say that historically the process of this differentiation was just beginning in the civilizations of the peoples of Asia Minor in the time of Jesus, this separation of domains one from another. For example, separating religion from other spheres of life, like health, which for us is normal, was not at all normal for Jesus; separating religion from the norms of law; separating religion from the norms of social relations: I think Jesus fought against all that. These germs of dualism had no soil in which to produce anything in the world of Jesus, the world of the country-side and of ordinary people. In contrast such dualism corresponded very closely with the developed consciousness of cultivated citizens of the metropolitan centres of antiquity--in other words, types like Pilate are at home in the separation of the different domains. He says, what is truth? That's the enlightened, skeptical, educated citizen, dweller in one of the metropolises, who is bored by being in Jerusalem and with the dull people there. But the friends of Jesus were not in this class. They had another understanding of life. For someone like Pilate the separation of the domains of life and their autonomy is normal; for Jesus it is in contradiction with the kingdom of God.

I think one of the characteristics of today's efforts of cultural revolution is to reject this separation of the different domains of existence, whereby each would have particular norms that characterize it. But again, this separation itself is to be attacked and the Christian faith helps us with that. Now I would go a little bit into the opposite danger in regards to the Christians and socialist identity, one that also comes from a dualist conception of things. If faith and social analysis are understood in their relationships as cause and effect, faith could then be understood as a sort of "additional energy," useful for political struggle. What then remains to faith? The domain that is then reserved to it is called by the rather technical expression, "motivation." "My motivation is Christian, my action socialist." This manner of expressing oneself, in the last analysis, springs from the same bourgeois and dualist framework; faith is conceived as a point of departure, a basis for setting out, but it is a "beginning" which can be replaced and is ultimately employed simply as a support force. Faith is no longer looked at and understood in its relationship with praxis, but reduced to a particular conception of things. I think that most of the people here in this room know people like this who became involved in social criticism and social action. As they became activist they lost their faith. First, their faith was only their motivation, but you can't live on a motivation; that's really a rather technical split of the human person. Then if you don't need faith, it will die. This happened to some of my friends too, and I am concerned about that. I think Christians for Socialism have to work on the whole identity of Christian faith and being a socialist.

Faith for them is no longer looked at in its relationship with praxis, but reduced to a particular conception of things. We thereby abandon science to Marxism and radically separate it from a motivation that is considered completely private. If traditionalists consider the application of faith as an unimportant and variable consequence, depending on each social context, to progressives who very often equally lay claim to dualism, motivation often appears as of no importance and equally variable, depending on the necessities of socialization. Looked at through the spectacles of the Marxist criticism of religion, faith seems then like a pair of baby shoes in which one learned to walk, and which at best retains private and nostalgic importance. But you don't need your baby shoes when you become adult. Such a conception reifies faith in my understanding and makes a fetish of science, destroying the human subject of both one and the other. That precisely among theologians who consider political questions there are many who fall into this conception of things only shows that they have not yet broken out of the bourgeois schemas of academic theology, and they succeed in saving their own subjective non-existence only by surrendering themselves to a theological and/or political dogmatism.

But it is possible, and since I am living in this country I am more and more convinced, that this danger is passé and more and more Christians consider themselves obliged to conceive of faith as more, as a private conception. In the struggle that they have led against church directives, against clearly reactionary mass media, they have openly insisted on the misunderstandings that have been linked to the love of neighbour. They have indicated that the latter ought normally to imply political consequences, and it is in these combats that Christian socialists are learning to discover their political identity. They have experienced for themselves that opposing positions are not simply political, but are also and fundamentally enrooted in faith and theological understanding, and this kind of oppositional polarization which takes place in the churches, as everybody knows, can no longer be dealt with if one does not have anything more than the theory of the "two domains absolutely separate from each other." They no longer think of the world in terms of placing it at the door of the church and of Christianity, and abandoning the Gospel to the forces of the right. Their option in the class struggles has not separated them at all from faith, but made them capable of understanding more clearly what it means to believe. They therefore are trying to affirm that they have the right to be at home in the faith and to discover again its subversive traditions.

The manifestation of Christians for Socialism is not only a political necessity but a Christian necessity. Faith itself requires that one take a position in the class struggle on the side of those who are exploited. The realization of faith requires participation in the revolutionary process. The congress of Christians for Socialism at Avila in January 1973 declared: "We consciously live our aspirations by the Gospel and our militant commitment as a unity, and it is this unity which permits us to carry in us the hope of a new world. . . . According to what we believe, the Resurrection of Jesus Christ can be understood and accepted in its full sense only if each form of the exploitation of people has been eliminated. It is here that Marxism has taught us, with a greater and more scientific depth, our historic task in the process of liberation. Thus we have learned to rediscover and to realize, in all the intention of our life, the subversive and radically new character of the Gospel." This is what the Christians for Socialism declared in one of their meetings.

The purpose, therefore, is not to make faith an instrument in the service of politics, as the reactionaries tell us, but to destroy the calculated utilization which is made of faith at present. Even now this utilization of Christian elements in the psychological consolidation of the dominant ideology is scarcely recognized by us. Another quotation from this document: "In bourgeois society religion has become a private affair, with the result that the Church would be able to define Christian identity by reducing it to an individual dimension (the relationship between God and me), totally abstract (separated from social conditioning). This privatization and abstraction have been the price that the Church has had to pay bourgeois society in order to be able to claim a universal action and influence." Someone who stands up against the utilization of the Gospel for partisan ends ought especially to understand this defense as a contribution to a practical withdrawal of Christianity from the "embrace" of capitalism.

Let me end with another short quotation: It's a part of a judicial examination of Robert Davezies, a French priest and a Christian for Socialism, which took place during the Algerian war, after he had taken the side of the Algerians:

The Judge: Why have you done this?

Davezies: I have read the Psalms.

The Judge: I have too, but I have not drawn the same consequences from them.

Davezies: I have read in the Psalms that God is the God of the poor.

The Judge: I too.

Davezies: Today those who are most poor are Algerians.[3]

I think it is precisely this question--who are the most poor today?--which is decisive. To answer it, scientific Marxism can help us. We do not understand it as a complete world-view but use Marxism as an instrument--the best available tool--that is, as a scientific method permitting us to make correct analyses and which itself should be corrected by new experiences.

It does not mean that all the contradictions between faith and socialist commitment are transcended when we have said this. We have not yet discussed the central questions of the love of enemies, and of non-violence and others. But it is only in the struggle for liberation that they are able to be transcended; this is the message of the Christians for Socialism. Unity is no longer conceived in dualist but in dialectical terms. In other words, the synthesis that we find will not place in relationship an achieved faith and an achieved socialism. Both will transcend the level they have reached in the history of mankind until now; our praxis, by transcending what is given, will manifest, as Marx said, "the truth--that is, reality and power, the historical rootedness of our thought."[4]

NOTES

[1]The public lecture was based on an article by Dorothee Sölle, "Christians for Socialism," Cross Currents, Trans. Sally and Joseph Cullen, 25, 4 (Winter 1976), 419-434.

[2]Ibid., 419. Christopher Blumhardt (1842-1919), Pastor and Social Democrat.

[3]Ibid., 433.

[4]Ibid., (Marx, Second Thesis on Feuerbach).

DISCUSSION

Response, Gregory Baum, "A Canadian Catholic Perspective."

Professor Hordern has told us in his essay that modern Christian theology has become more involved in political reflection and in fact moved to a critical position in regard to contemporary capitalism. This shift to the Left, according to the lecture of Professor Sölle, has taken a good number of Christians to a socialist position. She has given us an interesting and perceptive account of 'Christians for Socialism' in Western Europe. Allow me, in response to her lecture, to present a summary of the shift to the Left that has taken place in the official teaching of the Catholic Church.

In 1965, Vatican Council II produced a document, Gaudium et Spes, that looked upon the modern world in a positive way and encouraged Catholics to take an active part in it. The Catholic Church declared itself in solidarity with the whole of mankind and defined as its mission to serve the human community and tighten the bonds that bind man to man and peoples to peoples in the creation of a just and peaceful world. Gaudium et Spes was written by bishops and theologians associated with the developed Western nations; it reflected the optimistic view characteristic of the sixties. The answer to the world's problems was development and expansion.

Three years later, in 1968, at the Medellin Conference, the Latin American bishops looked at the same modern world and tried to define the role of the Christian community in it, this time from a very different perspective, that of the underdeveloped countries. The Medellin Conference recognized that development and expansion promoted by the North Altantic nations was in fact creating a state of dependency and increased exploitation in Latin America. Latin America had become part of a world-wide economic system which oppressed the hinterland for the benefit of the metropolis. While the Western nations were becoming more prosperous, the third world nations were thrust more deeply into misery. The Medellin Conference recognized that, in this situation, the Christian community must be in solidarity with the poor and exploited and struggle with them for their liberation. This new Latin American perspective had a strong influence on the Catholic Church's official teaching, especially at the Third Synod of bishops held at Rome in 1971.

This Third Synod of bishops became a turning point for Catholic social teaching. In a document entitled Justice in the World, the bishops adopted positions that went far beyond Vatican II. They introduced the notion of 'social sin' and declared that the gospel of Jesus Christ redeems us from sin, including this 'social sin.' We are told that the Christian understanding of redemption includes "the liberation from all oppressive conditions of human life." Salvation, in other words, has a social dimension. Divine grace has a political direction. While Catholic theology has never wholly forgotten the social side of divine salvation, popular piety and congregational preaching have only too often presented salvation as God's merciful rescue action delivering individuals from the catastrophe decreed upon the world. Such a privatized view of salvation is wholly irresponsible in today's world. The Synod adds "action on behalf of justice and participation in the transformation of society" is "a constitutive element" of the gospel life. In other words, holiness has a social dimension. The Christian life includes a socio-political commitment toward the reconstruction of society in terms of greater justice.

With this teaching the Third Synod of bishops rejected a distinction recently introduced into theology between the vertical and horizontal dimension of the Christian life. The vertical dimension, it is argued, deals with man's relationship to God, and the horizontal dimension with his relationship to others and society as a whole. Following the logic of this distinction, it is man's primary vocation to worship God and relate himself to God interiorly; to assume responsibility for the human community is important but secondary. On the basis of this distinction, some Catholics have criticized the new ecclesiastical emphasis on social justice and social criticism. What counts first of all, they argue, is personal surrender to the invisible God. But in the light of God's self-revelation in Christ and God's self-communication in the Spirit, the two dimensions, vertical and horizontal, are inseparably intertwined and fused. The God whom we seek is present in us and in others as a source of new life and the remaking of society. And conversely, action on behalf of justice is not a self-willed effort but surrender and obedience to the divine Word. Social commitment is, therefore, "constitutive" of the gospel life. The promised salvation includes "liberation from all the oppressive conditions of human life." The gospel has a political *élan*.

After the Third Synod of bishops, the Canadian Catholic bishops entered into ecumenical relations with the other major churches in Canada, Anglican, United Church, Presbyterian and Lutheran, and created permanent inter-church committees whose task it was--and still is--to examine from a critical Christian point of view the social, political, and economic problems of Canadian life. Basing themselves on the careful reports written by these committees, the Canadian bishops addressed the Catholic community in a number of important statements and, conjointly with the other Christian churches, submitted briefs to the Canadian government.

In a brief entitled "Justice Demands Action," submitted to the Prime Minister and the Federal Cabinet in 1976, the Canadian church leaders, including the Catholic bishops, asserted that they "stand in the tradition of the prophets" and recognize that "to know God is to seek justice for the poor and oppressed." The brief then explains that "the present economic order is characterized by the maldistribution of wealth and the control of resources by a small minority" and pleads for "an alternative to the present unjust order, a new international economic order." This reasoning is repeated by the Canadian bishops in their 1976 Labour Day Statement, "From Words to Action." Here the bishops give the same two reasons why the present economic system is unjust: it expands the gap between the rich and the poor, and it leaves the control of resources in the hands of the few. Again they ask for the creation of a more just social order.

Is there something new in these texts? In the past, Catholic teaching has often judged international monopoly capitalism severely, but on these occasions the ill effects of capitalism were attributed to the greed of the rich and powerful. If they and the rest of society became more generous, more just, more Christian, then these ill effects could be made to disappear. The brief passages quoted above seem to operate out of a different logic. They accuse the economic system itself of leading to the maldistribution of wealth, of producing a growing gap between rich and poor nations, and of assigning power to a corporate minority. These are presented as systemic effects of capitalism. They occur whether the men who run these institutions be saints or sinners: the ill effects are built into the system.

In the 1975 Labour Day Statement, "Northern Development: At What Cost?" the Canadian bishops demand that the government not allow the industrial development of the Canadian North without consultation with the native peoples. For if the large corporations and the departments of government carve up the land with purely economic goals in view, they will destroy the matrix of survival for the native peoples. Why, the Statement asks, do corporations and government agencies act in this way? "The maximization of consumption, profit and power has become the operating principle of this society." This is not a reference to the attitudes of the men in charge of these institutions, it refers rather to the operational logic associated with them. Again, in a letter on world hunger, called "Sharing Daily Bread," the Canadian bishops suggest that for the distribution of food the free market is no longer adequate. Why? Because the free market following the law of supply and demand distributes food only to those who have the ability to pay. Food is not available to people without money. What we need, in the area of food distribution first of all, is the democratization of the economic system. The ideals of equality and participation must be extended from the political to the economic order.

This shift to the Left in the official Catholic teaching does not mean that the Catholic Church has endorsed or approved of socialism in any of its forms. I recall at this point that in 1931, in the encyclical *Quadragesimo anno*, Pope Pius XI condemned not only revolutionary, atheistic communism but also what he called 'mitigated socialism,' i.e. democratic forms of socialism, even when they are not opposed to religion and do not intend to abolish all forms of private property: "No one can be at one time a sincere Catholic and a true socialist." One of the main arguments against socialism was the concentration of power which the public ownership of the means of production placed in the hands of the government. Socialism, according to papal teaching, made the state an all-powerful instrument of domination. But already in the same encyclical of 1931, Pius XI described a new development taking place in capitalism which he called "the new imperialism of money," i.e. the growing power of transnational corporations which hold monopolies, determine prices, and regulate the flow of money on a world scale. In more recent papal documents, there is the clear recognition that these vast corporations transcend the boundaries of the nations in which they were founded and hence escape the control of the government. In many instances, especially in the case of the smaller nations, these corporations exercise a power greater than that of national governments. Governments are no longer able to protect and promote the common good. The monster of power which frightens people everywhere is no longer necessarily the centralizing national government but the transnational corporations. In *Populcrum progressio*, Pope Paul VI recommends, therefore, that government assume more powers, try to regulate the economic life of the nation, and fulfill their assigned task of promoting a more just distribution of wealth among the people. Here, too, we observe a significant shift to the Left.

This does not mean, of course, that the Catholic Church recommends socialism. What it does mean, it seems to me, is that the question of socialism, resolved by ecclesiastical decree at one time, must be posed anew from a contemporary Catholic point of view. In Catholic countries we observe that a considerable number of active Catholics turn to socialism as, in fact a social outlook in keeping with Catholic principles, even though in many instances these choices have been frowned upon by bishops and popes.

In the Canadian context, especially the English-speaking, any talk of Christians opting for socialism recalls the radical Social Gospel of the twenties and thirties and its association with the Canadian socialism of the CCF. It is certainly worth while to clarify the features of this Canadian form of socialism. It is my impression that the Marxist language and Marxist style which are adopted in the socialist parties in Europe and Latin America create obstacles in the English-speaking world, in particular in English-speaking Canada. At the same time, a Marxist-style class analysis has become part of sociological methodology so that social thinkers make use of it without adverting its Marxian origin and without thinking of themselves as Marxists. Canadian socialism certainly utilized sociological class analysis and understood the main problem in Canada and the world as the conflict between two basic classes, the owners and controllers of industry and resources on the one hand, and the dependent and disadvantaged classes on the other.

There were, however, special features of Canadian socialism that deserve to be spelled out. I can only mention them briefly here. Canadian socialism in the thirties and forties followed the British labour movement in its attachment to democracy and the parliamentary system. Canadian socialism also entertained a strong libertarian position: it defended the freedom of expression, the freedom of association, and other constitutional liberties. While Marxists look upon these two trends as the creation of the bourgeoisie and hence suspect them of serving the interests of the present economic system, in the Anglo-Saxon world and in certain parts of Europe these trends in fact preceded the emergence of the bourgeoisie: they were grounded in Protestant religion. Against pope and prelate, Protestants sought to organize their churches democratically, and finding themselves under pressure from royal governments, advocated religious liberty as a basic human right. Canadian socialism stood in this Protestant tradition. It trusted populism, especially in the prairies: and since the Cooperative Commonwealth Federation was founded on a union between farmers and workers, Canadian socialists avoided the word 'proletariat': they sought a language that would promote unity between the several disadvantaged sectors of Canadian society. Moreover, while Marxists usually appeal to 'scientific' arguments analyzing the contradictions of the present system, Canadian socialists provided 'moral' arguments against capitalism and demanded the reconstruction of society in the name of the biblical idea of justice. It is also instructive to compare the party organization of the CCF and that of more Marxist-oriented parties in the thirties and forties. The CCF tried to remain a grass roots party: it rejected the elitism, the secrecy, and the authoritarian style of the Marxist parties contemporary to it. The organization of the CCF embodied democratic and populist ideals, remained in touch with local groups, and presented itself as a federation of provincial groups with distinct character and styles.

Now Catholics on the whole didn't have very much to do with Canadian socialism. Catholicism is a pre-industrial religion, and because it is pre-industrial it has resources: it has a sense of community, and it has resources to critique industrialization and modernity that deserve to be taken very seriously, and also on this continent, Roman Catholics have resources for radicalism because they have been surrounded by bigotry and exclusion. Coming from orange Toronto I suppose it is not surprising that I say this. Catholics in this country were a minority; the country was owned by Protestants, and therefore they have a real experience of being marginalized and being kept away from participation in the important institutions of the country. I think there are resources for radical critique within the Catholic tradition that are to be explored.

I think it is important, listening to Dorothee Sölle, that we as Christians heed the call to link into that which has taken place, not to create something totally new and impose it from without on Canadian experience, but to be in touch with Canadian history as we seek to outline an indigenous Canadian socialism. Where are the Movements in Canadian society? Where are the memories? Where are the events of past and present into which we can tie? Where can we find friends? Where can we find solidarity so that together we work for the reconstruction of society?

It is my personal view that Canadian socialism today, while making use of scientific analysis, should at least in English-speaking Canada--use a language and adopt a style that reflects this democratic populist, libertarian, and biblical heritage. This, to my mind, is in keeping with the Christian gospel.

Response to G. Baum, Y. Vaillancourt

I am surprised to see to what extent the comments you made about the interpretation of the last official documents coming from Rome was a positive interpretation. I think it's possible to use scissors and to find nice sentences in some places and others, but I wanted you to go on and point out also how much there is a strong anti-socialist action coming from Rome in these years. There is a strong and well-organized participation in an anti-communist campaign and an anti-theology of liberation campaign, and there are some very Fascist methods being used to give names of people from South America to North America and to Europe. There is a very conservative and efficient network trying to kill what Dorothee has been trying to develop, i.e. Christians for Socialism. The Pope has spoken against socialism at least once a week; this cannot be forgotten and has to be said.

Secondly, I think sometimes it's important to identify the word 'socialism.' As you pointed out we see the danger of an imported model which is not adapted to our situation. But there is another danger which is to so emasculate the word 'socialism' that finally we wonder if it is still socialism at all. What is the Canadian socialist tradition we are talking about? I wonder to what extent our socialist tradition is not a British import from the Labour Party in Britain. History has shown us that the British Labour Party experience cannot be named socialist; it's a form of social democratic capitalism because the ownership of the means of production is still in private hands. Social democrats like Callahan and Wilson are capitalists, and they go along with Carter and all the people of his type.

I have another point I want to make; the question you raise about what happened to Marx in Great Britain. He had hopes in the 1850s and the 1860s--similar to Lenin's hopes for Germany during the First World War. These hopes were not fulfilled in Britain or in Germany. Marx at the end of his life, and Lenin after, developed a specific contribution to the theory about imperialism. Their hypothesis was better than yours. The imperialist countries like Germany and Britain at that time, and now North America, create objective conditions which permit the local bourgeoisie to exploit the satellite countries they live in. They can save enough out of profits to produce a well paid working class in the rich countries. With this phenomenon they establish division within the working class. Marx and Lenin developed a concept of l'aristocratie ouvrière theory, explaining why in Great Britain and in Germany the temptation of the socialists was to turn themselves into collaborators with the bourgeoisie in a social democratic style. Therefore, in conclusion, I interpret what Dorothee Sölle has said as being in the line of the Christians for Socialism, but I wonder if what you said, Gregory, even if you are a good friend of mine, is not in the line of Christians for social democracy. This can be respected, and there are Christians struggling for social justice in both trends, but it would be good to have a discussion on this because these are two ways chosen by people doing political theology, and this debate is important.

Response, G. Baum

First of all, about the repression of Christians for Socialism in the Catholic Church: I certainly agree that there were meetings organized in Rome recently; Rome continues to be against the theology of liberation; and pressure is being applied to reduce the influence of this theology.

At the same time, popes and bishops have written the documents that I have quoted and I think they have to be used by Catholics. I think that if you belong to a church that expresses itself in documents which sometimes transcend the narrow interests of the writers and signers, the documents have to be used. When people of any church get together to write about their vision of the world, there is, after all, something going on that is simply the ideology which defends their class, but there is also a wrestling to deal with the symbols of Christianity. Again and again at significant instances one can point to documents which I think transcend significantly the class interests of the people who wrote them in the Christian church, and I think that they have to be used.

Secondly, when it comes to the question of socialism, obviously we have a much larger argument. Let me say first of all, that in this country, in English-speaking Canada, the great danger of the left is sectarianism. At English-speaking universities we are surrounded by splinter groups of true-line Marxists, six or seven different kinds, who have severed themselves from public life, who have very little relationship with the working class, and, furthermore, who have severed themselves from the public discussion.

It seems to me that in English Canada we have a tradition which certainly expresses itself in the Regina Manifesto, the founding document of the CCF in the 1930s. This movement, which carried momentum into the early 1940s but declined at the end of the Second World War, deserves to be studied.

There is a body of literature that teaches us the way solutions to certain problems were attempted here in Canada. This can serve as an inspiration and a rallying point, and as a way of presenting socialism as something that is really Canadian--I am talking about English Canada now--where we link ourselves to a uniquely Canadian experience. It is beholden on us to introduce a socialist position and discussion by referring to Canadian documents, by referring to Canadian class struggles and strikes, and significant arguments that took place in Parliament, positions adopted by the CCF and NDP party in Parliament. In spite of the impoverishment of the Left experiences in Canada, there is a resource that we should under no circumstances abandon, and while I agree with you that looking at the social democratic parties in Europe, Germany in particular, and England as you mentioned, there is perhaps no encouragement, yet, looking at the socialist countries that are not democratic, is no encouragement either, and therefore I don't want to use this kind of argument. I think we want to trust that the new is possible; we want to trust that history is open; we want to believe that if we involve ourselves in creating as wide a base as possible for the socialist struggle, life can be different, and for that reason I do not despair, neither turning to the socialist countries of Eastern Europe nor to the social democracy in the west. In this way I would justify my concern for tying into the Canadian socialist tradition.

Question, D. Sölle

I want to make one or two remarks on the whole question of social democracy, specifically in Germany. As we know, in the middle and end of the 1960s, some people in West Germany had more hope for a more socialist social democracy. We had these Young Socialists inside of the social democratic party who developed a theory which was called "system transcendent reforms." They tried to distinguish between reforms which are only binding the wounds and veiling the real problems, and other reforms which could transcend the system of capitalism. For example, if you increased the public transportation and in this way decreased the use of private transportation, that would be such a system of transcendent reform, which failed of course. Now this whole concept has more or less failed and the line of the social democratic party in West Germany is much more rigid and rightist now than it was some years before. I appreciate very much the point you made in respect of Lenin that has to do with imperialism, and even if the social democracy in West Germany has made working-place conditions in some respects really better--and social conditions in terms of job security, pension funds, health, are quite good--there are two things where a non-socialist trend of social democracy comes out. The one is the clear stand for imperialism in the business with South Africa and the atomic plants for Brazil. Here are clear imperialist alliances with other Fascist countries. The second point, is our repression within West Germany, which comes out in different laws, domestically repressive laws, concerns the cultural sector. I mention only two: one is a law which requires every young teacher to pass a political examination before he or she is employed by the state, and this examination includes questions so naive as, "Did you read Habermas?" I was told this story by a friend who went through such an examination. He was accused of being in this and that Viet Nam demonstration. Then when the student said, "How do you know?" they said, "Your car was parked in a side street." Things like that make clear how many people are constantly overshadowed by the secret police. There is another law against the propagating of violence which concerns books, and publishers, and teachers as well, so that our friend Gustav Guttierez is in danger of being forbidden to come to Germany because he is seen as propagating violence. Now that's the inner situation in this part of the world, and I think really we have a lot of reason to fear this type of social democratic policy.

Question, Anonymous contributor,

Even before I came to the conference, as I read the brochure, two statements came into my mind. One of them was that Jesus did not say, "Take from the rich and give to the poor," with a sense of personal responsibility. I also feel that he did not say, "Demand justice" so much as he said, "Be just, you and you and you and me, be just to people." I suppose I see sin as personal sin with personal responsibilities for that sin which I feel may not be inherent in movements, political, and especially, in this context, socialist movements.

I feel, however laudatory the cause of socialism, and it's something I personally have a great deal of feeling for, that it's possible to hurry to a socialist conference with the idea of aiding mankind and pass by the beggar in the street and not hold out our hand and give him something, however small. That is the way we are tested personally in the eyes of Christ. He said that we should take seriously and personally what we do to the least among us. I suppose I could pull in Mother Theresa's statements to Malcolm Muggeridge on the BBC broadcast, that she did not want her movement to grow large because it depended on personal contact, person to person, delivering love, in effect, delivering Christ to each person that was lost in large movements. I might ask you to comment on Mother Theresa's work too. I suppose I bring in possibly erroneously the example Jesus set by avoiding political reformers, especially the zealots of his time, although I suspect that you may have a ready answer for that. Your response would be very instructive. You talked about the rights of man and it made me think of Simone Weil's statement that man has no rights, only obligations, and that we do not demand our rights but we fulfil our obligations.

My general feelings, just to sum up quickly, were that movements of the kind you describe so often lead to bad spirit, contention, and division. He indicated very clearly that there would be; he brought the sword and not always unity. You referred today to radicalism. If I'm not mistaken, and I'll have to go back to my sources, the root of the word "radical" means root, and to go back to being radicalized means to go back to roots. It seems to me that Christian roots, maybe the Christian's tap root, is patience, and I wonder about the feeling of impatience that I sometimes pick up in the radical socialism that you speak of. So I suppose I speak as a skeptic here. I wonder if things are really changed in movements, specifically political movements; whether the love that St. Paul talked about as being all-important isn't very often lost. Thank you for your patience.

Response, D. Sölle,

Patience is not a gift I got from our Heavenly Father. A book I have written is entitled Revolutionary Patience. I feel it's not the same as what you are talking about. I think patience without this adjective revolutionary makes me rather impatient. The problem I have with your talk is really that I feel offended by a certain insensitivity to human suffering; I feel as if you don't want to live in this society but maybe in a better one where I am not. To say that Jesus said, "Be just, be just, be just, you and you and you" is simply not true, and if it is true that God is just and I believe in that, then God isn't here. This society in which we live is not unjust in doing certain unjust action; it is basically unjust; it is built on injustice, built on exploitation of other people. That is the case with the whole first world, the industrial west. It is a basically unjust society. Exactly in this context, the personal imperative to say "be just, you and you and you," is not enough because you allow others to continue in injustice, and that isn't really theology. If you understand salvation as your individual rescue, being taken off from this bad world to another one, then you don't understand the justice we are looking for. The justice we speak about is not fulfilled in being a just individual.

Were you aware that the statement you quoted by Simone Weil was from her last book which was put together by friends from her diaries after her death? To understand the content of this woman's life you have to realize that she was a militant champion of workers in labour unions. She organized strikes and in fact her whole life, which was concerned with the obligations of people to their social history, stands in complete contradiction to the individualism you are supporting.

But let me make one other remark. I think what capitalism does to people is not only to exploit them but also to destroy the silent exploiters which we are. It destroys our compassion, our capacity of seeing and hearing the cry of others. It destroys really our roots, and so many people are in search of their roots, because in a society like this our roots will be destroyed more and more under the dictatorship of capitalism. I have, of course, a deep respect for people like Mother Theresa and others who are trying to live the lives of saints, but I cannot accept her as a model for the church. I am interested in the church in which we could again pray and sing and live as Christians; I think we need that for all of us, and therefore this individual model is for me simply not acceptable. I also want to have a community in which justice and doing justice is not the exception for radical people but just what people are trying to learn; in which solidarity is not a superhuman characteristic but just what normal people become used to in schools where they are not educated for competition but for solidarity. I want my children to go to schools in which they learn real solidarity. I can't accomplish this with the personal peity you are proposing. It is not because I have something more than the Christian has, it is simply because I have tried to take seriously the sayings of Jesus and his proposals for our lives.

Question, K. Nielsen to D. Sölle

I want to say initially how extremely grateful I am to discover that there are people who are Christians and have the set of commitments that you have. You are not the sort of Christian I am accustomed to meeting, and I am most grateful I can say this. Now after having said that, I am not taking anything back. I want to make only one remark about something you said that puzzles me. Suppose someone asks the questions that I was trying to ask, "What does 'Christian' add to 'socialism'?" This is what I have been trying to smoke out. You said, there is a tradition available to someone like myself, or Engels, or Marx, or Lukacs, and I don't think that's right.

I mean, we atheists know very well, if we understand our history, that we grew out of the Christian and the Jewish culture. Engels wrote movingly and powerfully about Thomas Muentzer; it is often said by Christians and sometimes by anti-Marxists that there are eschatological elements in Marx which come out of the Christian tradition and the Jewish tradition. But what I want to say is that they are available to people like myself and important people like

Marx and Engels and Lukacs, and yet we are not fettered by them. The young gentelman who got up and spoke to you seemed to me to be fettered by his Christian tradition, and many Christians are. We may be fettered by other things; perhaps I am fettered by too rationalistic presuppositions. I am sure that I am in certain ways, but I don't see, in short, why the tradition that you spoke about is not equally available--unless you are going to say some rather funny things like, "you know you really have to be in a tradition and accept a tradition for it to be available"--to people who are no longer Christians but who know what it's like to live in the Christian tradition. That is one of the reasons why I find the Christian images that you use profoundly moving. Thank you.

Response, D. Sölle to Kai Nielsen

There is something I wanted to say this afternoon in listening to you. I think part of our problem is language and which language do we have and do we use. I was angry at you this afternoon because I felt so much of the language you used was oppressive. It was an oppressive language in terms of a language which does not allow any expression of feelings. The so-called scientific language which I feel is inhuman or male--I have real trouble with it, and I become more and more impatient with it. I think we have to learn how to create a language which allows a more holistic expression of ourselves, in which our emotions are not hidden or suppressed but are shared. I think that what the Christian language gives me is really an attempt at a cultural means of production, an expression, which transcends the atheist's language or the scientific language. I can't imagine humanity without dreams which transcend ourselves. Even the horizons we get through the socialist tradition must be transcended. That is the richness of the religious traditions, all of them, I think. I understand Marxism as Marxism understands itself, as an heir of humanity's traditions, but sometimes you get the feeling that they don't take on the heritage, they don't use it, and I wish we could use it together in a better way and find more and new liberating language. That I would see as a common task of Christians as well as socialists in a liberated society.

5

THE APOCALYPTIC TRADITION: LUTHER AND MARX

Abraham Rotstein

Nothing might seem more dubious than the attempt to bring together the rabid foe of the peasants with the evangelist of the proletariat.[1] Their doctrines lay more than three centuries apart, while their goals were literally worlds apart. The substantive differences between them would fill volumes.

Yet a modicum of detachment from the great struggles in which Luther and Marx were engaged may offer glimmers of a different perspective. Both were outstanding figures in the Western apocalyptic tradition, a tradition that conceives of the world as bearing an overwhelming burden of domination and oppression and proceeds to offer to the oppressed a vision of perfect community. Luther's kingdom of God whose presence on earth he felt could already be discerned, promised a regime with surprising similarities to Marx's socialism.

But nothing lies further from the aim of this essay than the attempt to turn Luther into a latent communist, nor Marx into a latter-day Christian *malgré lui*. What they do share in common is a rhetorical structure, namely, the characteristic process of the apocalyptic tradition that moves step by step in a systematic fashion, from the original condition of domination and oppression to the culmination of perfect community.

Such an intermediate process may not be readily apparent, particularly when abrupt rhetorical leaps are taken by both authors from overwhelming "oppression" to a total "salvation." Nevertheless, certain discrete elements of Lutheran theology that fall into place en route to his kingdom, serve as an unexpected road-map for Marx's dialectical path to socialism.

Standing as a bridge between Luther and Marx is the towering and enigmatic figure of Hegel. His thought derives from many sources, particularly from the ancient Greeks and from his contemporaries, but the Lutheran strand of his philosophy has largely been overlooked. As a troubled and skeptical graduate of the Lutheran seminary at Tübingen, Hegel was nevertheless able to affirm in later life: "I am a Lutheran and am just as rooted in Lutheranism through philosophy . . . it contains within it a higher Spirit than merely that of human tradition."[2] He regarded the Protestant Reformation as

Die Haupt-Revolution, the great revolution[3], and its central doctrine of Christian freedom was the cornerstone of his own philosophy. Christianity, in its Protestant expression, was the truth of the universe and of individual self-consciousness, but was presented, in Hegel's view, in outmoded forms--in myths, miracles, and legends. For the generation of the Enlightenment it was necessary to render "the language of religious myth into that of thought."[4]

My chief debt in this exploration is to Hegel, although I can do little more than acknowledge this debt with occasional references to his work.[5] The essential premises of this essay are derived in modified form from Hegel's famous parable on lordship and bondage in the Phenomenology of Mind,[6] but the ramifications of the parable extend far beyond our present subject. (Nor is there a semblance of unanimity among the various commentators as to how this parable may be interpreted.)

The modern political interest in lordship (Herrschaft) and bondage (Knechtschaft) tends to view the meaning of these terms as "domination" and "oppression," respectively, the starting point of the present analysis. The neglected dimension, however, is the underlying religious foundation of Hegel's thought that recognizes in these terms the "Lord" (Herr) and "servant" or "slave" (Knecht) of the Bible. Ever since Luther, the terms Herrschaft and Knechtschaft have been central to German Protestant theology.

The German language permits both a political and theological interpretation of these terms, and Hegel's attempt to exploit and to reconcile this ambiguity is the key to the breadth of his perspective. He had in mind a two-fold constituency, the Protestant believers and those who were fleeing orthodoxy into the Enlightenment, and he tried to hold them together on his own ground. Even though his intentions were not realized (in part because they were so difficult to grasp), he attempted a general framework to encompass all manifestations of lordship and bondage; theology and politics were to be united within the common transcending experience of human consciousness.[7]

The present attempt, from a largely Hegelian vantage point, to compare the antecedent Luther with the posthumous Marx can be viewed as an application of Hegel's theme of lordship and bondage to the apocalyptic tradition in both religion and politics. The rhetorical properties of our common terms Herrschaft and Knechtschaft are traced throughout their widely different contexts.

This necessarily involves us in a framework that is much older than the three centuries that separate Luther and Marx. Luther adhered scrupulously to his biblical sources, particularly to Paul, and in that sense we may speak of a time span not merely of three centuries but of three millennia of the apocalpytic tradition.

The chief rhetorical mode on which I rely is that of inversion, closely related to what is more commonly known as the dialectic. Heidegger drew attention to this Hegelian discovery as a specific and discrete phenomenon of consciousness,[8] but the present investigation indicates that there is a more extended _system_ of inversion at work. Its starting point is invariably the antithesis of lordship and bondage, and its conclusion is the characteristic reconciliation of this antithesis in a vision of ideal community. It is this systematic formal pattern which I have termed the "rhetoric of transfiguration."

The limitations of this endeavour should also be apparent. An analysis of the rhetorical structure in Luther and Marx will have little to add to the substantive doctrines of either theology or socialism and must bypass the economic, social, or theological settings in which these originated. I hope, in turn, that nothing is detracted from these doctrines, and I have attempted to avoid any suggestion of reductionism. The exalted expressions of the human mind stand on their own merit, and, as Hegel warned (in a slightly different context), are uncompromised by an analysis of the "medium" of articulation.[9]

At best, the rhetorical structure acquires a _sui generis_ even if limited interest in its own right and may perhaps raise some novel questions that I shall touch on in the conclusion.

In its pristine form, the rhetoric of transfiguration comes to us in the Old and New Testament. Some brief illustrations will be cited from both to accompany our schematic outline.

Lordship and bondage are reciprocal or complementary terms, not unlike teacher/student, or doctor/patient. The existence of one term implies the existence of the second term of the pair. For much of human history, such as in the greater part of the feudal period, lordship and bondage exist in some more or less benign relationship of mutual dependence. It is necessary to posit these two terms in some form of opposition--what Luther, Hegel, and Marx called an antithesis--for the systematic process of inversion to begin.

Diagram 1 below may facilitate our analysis of this process if the limitations of the diagram are kept in mind. I hasten to warn the reader that the four analytic stages presented below do not necessarily occur in successive discrete steps and that there are important qualifications and differences in emphasis to which I cannot do full justice here. The process of systematic inversion, moreover, never occurs in this abstract form but is deeply embedded in the theological, social, and political circumstances of the particular periods we are considering. These serve to "mediate" the process. Furthermore, the elements I shall subsequently identify are scattered throughout the writings of Luther and Marx and form a systematic structure only when viewed from an analytic perspective of which these authors were only partly conscious.

Diagram 1 unfolds through four stages (columns 1 to 4 respectively), from the initial antithesis to the final community. Above and below the horizontal line, the movement takes place along two circuits, each moving horizontally through these columns. These are the circuit of lordship and the circuit of bondage respectively.[10] The dotted symbols are used to indicate inverted forms of the initial designations of lordship and bondage. Apart from the close link between Paul and Luther, the definitions of lordship and bondage change in the different basis we are considering here, but the systematic process of inversion stays the same.

DIAGRAM I

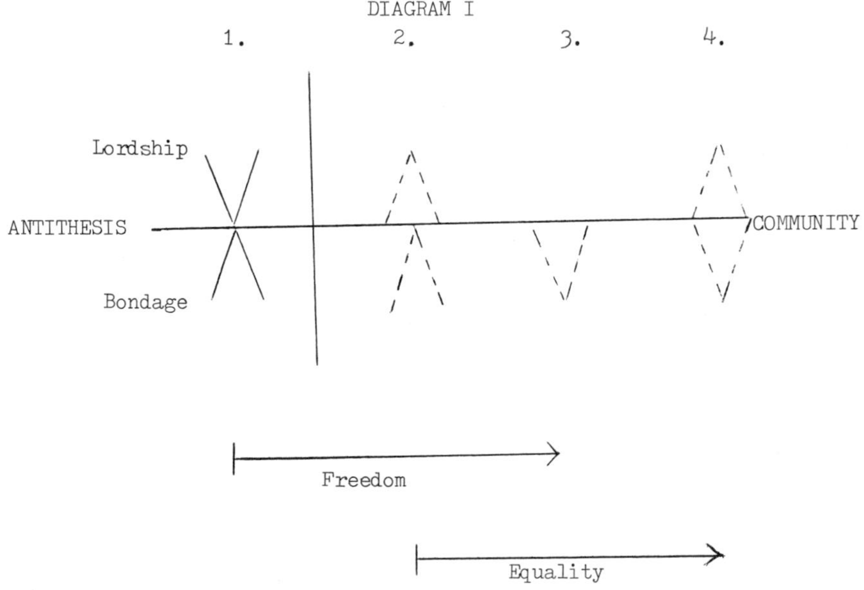

In column 1, the bondage is of a totally oppressive kind and reflects the subjection to a tyrannical lordship. The two terms are pictured here in an antithetical relationship reflecting the full burden of domination and oppression.

In the Old Testament, the Covenant at Sinai stands as the central moment and has its rhetorical origin in the oppressive bondage to Pharaoh in Egypt. In the New Testament, the equivalent role is played by man's bondage to his mortality: to the body, sin, and death.

Along the lower circuit, the dotted symbol of column 2 shows an inversion of bondage from a totally oppressive to a highly exalted state. In the Old Testament, the Hebrew _eved_ means both "slave" and "worshipper." Thus "we were slaves unto Pharaoh in Egypt" (Deuteronomy 6:21) is rendered in inverted form in God's statement: "For unto me the children of Israel are slaves; they are my slaves. . ." (_avadei_, Leviticus 25:55). In the New Testament, we may note the similar inversion of "slaves (_douloi_). . . of sin unto death" (Romans 6:16) to "slaves of Christ" (_douloi Christou_, Ephesians 6:6). The same word "slave" is retained, but a transfiguration has occurred to a bondage that is man's highest vocation. I call this an _inversion of substance_ where the identical term has, so to speak, been turned "inside-out."

In column 3, the exalted "slaves" now become "lords" in their own right, equal in status to each other. This is an _inversion of form_, or a turning, so to speak, "right-side-up." In the Old Testament, the Jews as slaves of Yahweh become the "chosen" (i.e. blessed) people, "called by the name of the Lord": "And the Lord shall make thee the head, and not the tail; and thou shalt be above only, and thou shalt not be beneath." (Deuteronomy 28:10, 13) In the New Testament, Christians as slaves of Christ become correspondingly "joint-heirs with Christ" (Romans 8:17), "sharers of Christ" (Hebrews 3:14), and "a chosen generation, a royal priesthood" (I Peter 2:9).

From the original oppressive bondage of the first column, we can now specify a process of differentiation along the lower circuit through two different forms of inversion. The first of these, the inversion of substance, is generally given the name, or linked with "freedom." It forms the basis, for example, for the remission of slavery in the Old Testament and for Christian liberty in the New

Testament. The second inversion, the inversion of form, is occasionally called "equality."[11] Freedom and equality wear different faces in the respective periods discussed here and remain formal designations in our schema.

Along the upper circuit, the movement to column 2 indicates that tyrannical lordship has been vanquished or destroyed by a new exalted lord. Yahweh, for example, defeats Pharaoh (Deuteronomy 29:2), and Christ abolishes death, which is "swallowed up in victory" (II Timothy 1:10; I Corinthians 15:54); Christians receive eternal life. (This corresponds to what I believe Hegel had in mind when he referred to "absolute negation" of lordship.[12]) The upper figure in column 2 indicates a single total inversion, but it may encompass within it further internal differentiations in particular instances (such as in Marx, as we shall see below).

Column 2 now presents a complementary or reciprocal relationship between the new "lord" and the new "slave" instead of the previous antithesis.

In column 4, the "lords" (of column 3) join with the exalted lord of column 2, to create a new vision of "community" such as the "kingdom of priests and an holy nation" (Exodus 19:6) of the Old Testament, or the kingdom of God in the New Testament whose inhabitants are "fellow-citizens with the saints and of the household of God" Ephesians 2:19). This is represented by the closed figure of column 4.

There are two important political characteristics of this community: there is a total identity of interest between the new lords and the supreme lord; secondly, the lords are explicitly declared to be powerless and all power is said to reside in the supreme lord (cf. I Corinthians 15:24; Colossians 2:8). The attributes of freedom and equality are retained within this perfect community and the original antithesis is completely resolved.

Speaking therefore only of the structure of the rhetoric, the perfect community results from a characteristic process of inversion: both terms of the original antithesis are turned 'inside-out' and 'right-side-up.' Allowing for some important qualifications and differences, such a schema forms a vital component of the rhetorical structure of the old Testament, the New Testament, Luther, Hegel, and Marx.

This essay is organized under three themes that run parallel in

Luther and Marx respectively. Lordship and bondage, the first of these themes, elucidates the common structural basis, i.e. the rhetoric of transfiguration as outlined here. But we are concerned with other levels of rhetorical similarity as well.

"The Theology of Negative Transcendence" offers a brief overview of Lutheran theology as a parallel to "The Politics of Negative Transcendence," an overview of Marxian politics.

Common semantics were transmitted in the course of time from Luther to Marx in part due to the remarkable achievements of Luther's German. In his translation of the Bible, Luther "created" the past while laying the linguistic foundations of future German culture and philosophy. Much of this was bound to be reflected in Marx's vocabulary and figures of speech. Vital conceptual links between the two arose indirectly through the intermediation of Hegel. Our third theme deals with the semantics of both authors.

But the underlying rhetorical structure which Marx and Luther shared did not ultimately depend on a common linguistic basis nor even on the influential role of the Lutheran Hegel on Marx, however important and illuminating these influences were. The structure of the apocalyptic tradition can equally well be discerned, as we have noted in abbreviated form, in the Old and New Testament in their original languages. This tradition was carried forward in Western society with a powerful inner momentum of its own.

1. Luther

1.1 Lordship and Bondage

Lutheran theology is an epic structure of paradox. The key to its paradoxical character is generally antithesis and inversion. The major essay, "On the Freedom of a Christian" (1520), threw into high relief the inner life of the Christian living simultaneously in "the freedom and the bondage of the spirit." As Luther indicated to Pope Leo in the accompanying letter of transmittal, the essay "contains the whole of Christian life in a brief form, provided you grasp its meaning."[13]

Luther's central paradox as presented in this essay turns on the meaning of lordship and bondage in the context of Christian freedom: "A Christian is a perfectly free lord of all [*freyer herr über alle ding*] subject to none. A Christian is a perfectly dutiful servant of all [*dienstpar knecht aller ding*] subject to all."[14] The resolution of this paradox--how a Christian may be simultaneously a lord and a servant, and yet at all times free--goes to the heart of the theme of lordship and bondage.

Luther followed Paul very closely in his elaborations. The spiritual and the carnal natures of man are in an antithetical or contradictory relationship: according to his spiritual nature he is an "inner or new man"; according to his bodily nature he is an "outward or old man." We find that "these two men in the same man contradict each other." This contradiction is based on Galatians 5:17--"for the desires of the flesh are against the Spirit, and the desires of the Spirit are against the flesh."[15] Through the process of inversion we have outlined, the antithesis is resolved and a characteristic vision of perfect community follows the outcome of such a resolution.

Luther explored the structure of Pauline theology and commented on it in various ways. "_Antithesin facit Apostolus_" ("the Apostle creates an antithesis"), Luther stated of one of the passages in Paul's Epistle to the Romans.[16] He was fully aware of the role that antithesis played in the New Testament and followed this consistently in his own work: "_Observanda autem hic est Antithesis_. . . " ("it should be noted moreover, that here is an antithesis").[17] In his debate with Erasmus on the bondage of the will, Luther reiterates that "Scripture speaks through antithesis" and that everything that is opposed to Christ reigns in him.[18] This notion was to emerge once more in the antithesis (_Gegensatz_) of Hegelian philosophy and later again in Marx.

The "oppression" under which we live is that of the body (rendered by Luther as _leyplichen unterdruckung_).[19] Death, suffering, the lusts of the flesh, sin, and the transience of this earthly existence, all are interconnected features of bodily existence and the elements of the Christian's oppression or slavery.

There is also a vital institutional component to this oppression. Luther reiterates Paul's injunctions against the law. Paul had in mind the structure of Jewish religion, the Mosaic code, and offered salvation through the church. But it was the Catholic church of his day that Luther saw as oppressive bondage, the "popes, bishops and lords" who exhibit:

> so great a display of power and so terrible a tyranny that no heathen empire or other earthly power can be compared with it, just as if the laymen were not also Christians. Through this perversion the knowledge of Christian grace, faith, liberty, and of Christ himself has altogether perished, and its place has been taken by an

unbearable bondage of human works and laws until we have become, as the Lamentations of Jeremiah say, servants [knecht] of the vilest men on earth who abuse our misfortune to serve only their base and shameless will.[20]

The notion that righteousness may be sought through good works is a "perverse notion," a "leviathan." Luther says that "in truth they (works) are not good. They deceive men and lead them to deceive one another like ravening wolves in sheep's clothing."[21]

The response to this compendium of oppressive bondage--the body, the Church, and works--is twofold: The Christian as servant and the Christian as lord. As a servant, he serves his neighbour, voluntarily and with love. He follows Christ as his model:

Although the Christian is thus free from all works, he ought in this liberty to empty himself, take upon himself the form of a servant, be made in the likeness of men, be found in human form, and to serve, help and in every way deal with his neighbour as he sees that God through Christ has dealt and still deals with him. This he should do freely, having regard for nothing but divine approval.[22]

The operative phrase is that the Christian "ought in this liberty to empty himself," but the translation is elliptic. The original Latin text of the essay (rursus se exinanire) conveys the sense of reverting to, or coming back again to empty himself by undertaking 'works' intended to serve his neighbour. Thus the Christian turns, so to speak, his oppressive bondage inside-out, i.e. he inverts it by becoming a servant, as Christ did, in selflessness and love.[23]

The Christian "servant" now becomes a "lord." The Christian, Luther states, is "lord over sin, death and hell," and he is "free from all things and over all things so that he needs no works to make him righteous."[24] The lord, moreover, has no need, spiritually, for kings, or priests, or the oppressive church hierarchy, but through his "priestly glory" and his "royal power," the Christian lord rules over life, death, and sin.[25]

This is a remarkable inversion of status once again as the Christian servant acquires the powers of a lord. How does this take place? Luther's answer is through faith: "every Christian is by faith so exalted [erhaben] above all things that, by virtue of a spiritual power, he is lord [eyn herr wirt geystlich] of all things without exception, so that nothing can do him any harm."[26]

Inner freedom is the name which Luther gives to the new status of the Christian both as a servant and as a lord. This must first be distinguished from external freedom: "It is more excellent than all other liberty, which is external, as heaven is more excellent than earth." Luther also warns against using this freedom as "an occasion for the flesh."[27]

The Christian lives simultaneously, as we noted, in "the freedom and the bondage of the spirit," for to become the "servant of all. . . is the highest freedom [*summa libertas*] for it lacks nothing and receives nothing, but rather gives and bestows."[28] Luther follows closely the Pauline doctrine of Christian liberty and points to Christ as a model of freedom for the Christian as a servant: *simul liber et servus, simul in forma dei et in forma servi* (at the same time a free man and a servant, in the form of God and of a servant).[29]

Likewise, the Christian as a lord is free by virtue of rising above and disengaging from mortality and from finite reality when he is free from all works, fulfilling in this way his Christian mission: "Thus we are now free and the victors over death, sin, the law and the devil, freed moreover from all that is given to man."[30]

Binding together these two vocations within this inner freedom, the Christian as lord and the Christian as servant are united. In brief, Christians are "servants of our neighbours, and yet lords of all" and are "Christ's one to another and do to our neighbours as Christ does to us."[31] As Luther summed up the matter at a different point: "In Christ, the lord and servant are one" (*Das Ynn Christo, herr und Knecht eyn ding sey*).[32] This offers the resolution of Luther's paradox of Christian freedom.

Such freedom is never fully realized in man's life and is, for Luther, always a process of "becoming."[33] This is achieved through faith, the cornerstone of Lutheran theology: "Christian liberty (is) our faith" and "faith alone, without works, justifies, frees, and saves."[34]

How are we to understand the practice of faith? Luther offers a traditional metaphor from the New Testament and from medieval theology and an elaboration of his own. Faith "unites the soul with Christ as a bride is united with her bridegroom. . . . Christ and the soul become one flesh."[35] This unity is then the basis of Luther's oft-repeated notion of a "joyous exchange" (*fröelich wechszel*):[36]

> Now let faith come between them and sins; death and damnation will be Christ's, while grace, life and salvation will be the soul's; for if Christ is a bridegroom, he must take upon himself the things which are his bride's and bestow upon her the things that are his.[37]

Christ is the mediating agent, but Luther delineates this mediation more sharply. The "joyous exchange" is an evocative way of suggesting how the human could divest itself of its burdens and is thus turned "inside-out." Luther is most explicit when he states that the person is emptied or "evacuated from himself" if he determines to pay no attention to his works so that Christ may live and work in him.[38] The Latin phrase evacuator a seipso approaches closely our theme of self-inversion, and is the key, we believe, to Luther's notion of faith.

Turning now to our first diagram, we may note that schematically Luther's paradox of Christian freedom unfolds along the lower circuit. In column 1, the Christian in oppressive bondage to the body, to the Church, and to works, inverts his bondage to willingly become a servant of his neighbour following in Christ's example (column 2). Oppressive bondage turns into exalted bondage. This exalted bondage (an inversion of substance) is followed by a second inversion (column 3) where the Christian, through faith, disengages from finite reality and becomes a lord (an inversion of form). Both these vocations are encompassed within the Christian view of freedom (as indicated in the diagram).

The movement on the upper circuit is not treated here explicitly by Luther, and the portrait of Christ remains that which we have touched upon previously from the New Testament. Christ as Lord abolishes death and sin and offers eternal life. Thus the dynamic movement within Luther's essay "On the Freedom of a Christian," turns, as seen from this perspective, on the power of inversion which approximates closely to what Luther calls "faith."

As Luther puts the matter more poignantly, faith consists of turning ourselves away from "the vain no" and "of holding fast to the deep and hidden 'yes' under and above the 'no'. . . ."[39]

Out of man's two natures emerges Luther's portrait of a bifurcated world, one segment of which is inner and spiritual (ynnerlich, geystlich), and the other, outer or bodily (eusserlich, leyplich). The most important political expression of this dualism is Luther's doctrine of the two kingdoms:

> God has ordained two governments; the spiritual [das geystliche], by which the Holy Spirit produces Christians and righteous people under Christ; and the temporal [das welltliche], which restrains the un-Christian and wicked so that--no thanks to them--they are obliged to keep still and to maintain an outward peace.[40]

Christ's kingdom is hidden to the eyes and senses but "already exists in this world"[41] and rules side by side with the temporal world until all those who belong in the spiritual kingdom have entered. Thereupon Christ "will destroy everything [alles auff heben] at one time and lay about him."[42] This will occur on the last day, when Christ's kingdom of faith is handed over to God "so that we will behold Him most clearly without veil and obscure words." It will be a transformation from "hidden essence" (verborgen wesen), to "manifest being" (offentlichen wesens).[43] At that point "God himself will be Lord alone [allein Herr sein] and rule alone in us, His children."[44] Further, all institutional structures of power will be abolished "making us all equal and erasing every distinction among emperor, kings, nobility, burghers and peasants. God alone will be everything."[45]

Equality is an explicit feature of the spiritual kingdom: "ubi Christus est suo spiritu, ibi nulla differentia" (where Christ is in His Spirit, there no distinction exists).[46] Luther repeats this in different contexts: "wir sollen alle gleich sein" (we should all be equal, even though the gifts of God give more to some than to others).[47]

Dut in the temporal kingdom the opposite prevails: "A worldly kingdom cannot exist without an inequality of persons, some being free, some imprisoned, some lords, some subjects, etc; and St. Paul says in Galatians 5 that in Christ the Lord and the servants are equal."[48]

In the spiritual kingdom, there is a perfect correspondence between individual and community. When God alone rules in each citizen of the kingdom and invests him with the Holy Spirit, the citizen can only want and do what the Holy Spirit requires that he want and do. Luther calls this condition "spontaneous" (das da heisse Spontaneus), that is, where "willing, desire and love is to obey and be subject to this Lord without hypocrisy. . . to be upright and obedient gladly and voluntarily."[49] "They thus conform themselves purely to the will of God," Luther states, and man thus "wills what God wills."[50]

A further paradox now becomes apparent and is resolved. The Christian lord, with "royal power," who "rules over all things, death, life and sin," is on the one hand "omnipotent with God because he does the things which God asks and desires. . . ."[51] On the other hand, Luther often declares that Christians must be made aware of their "impotence" (impotentia).[52] The latter reflects Paul's "My power is made perfect in weakness" (II Corinthians 12:9). But it is this condition of being "spontaneous" with God in the spiritual kingdom which reconciles the two. If man is totally conformed to what God asks, and performs only those deeds, both his impotence and omnipotence emerge from affirming his faith and allowing God's power to work in him. (The nature of God's power is discussed in the following section.) But it should be apparent that the Christian lord's citizenship in the spiritual kingdom carries with it no contradictions or conflicts.

Column 4 of our diagram conveys this sense of complete community in the spiritual kingdom. The Christian as lord (column 3) is a perfect inverse image of God. His wishes and God's are identical; all conflict (or antithesis) is ruled out. God's omnipotence is now his and at the same time he remains powerless in his own right.

Luther's spiritual kingdom exhibits the characteristic qualities to which we have pointed in the resolution of the basic antithesis of lordship and bondage: freedom, equality, the total identity of individual and community and the absence of power and conflict. These are the essential elements that reiterate in Luther the entire system of the rhetoric of transfiguaration.

The spiritual kingdom is not a regime that will be confined to heaven for "we shall be wherever we wish, in heaven, on earth, above or below as we please." It will be an answer to Adam's fall and "the restoration and renewal of the creation and for the liberty of the children of God."[53]

1.2 The Theology of Negative Transcendence

Lutheran theology emerged sporadically out of an intense series of struggles: with the Catholic Church, with the peasants, and with Erasmus on the question of the bondage of the will. The details of all of these events must be bypassed here while we present a necessarily brief overview of the theological formulations that emerged.

Throughout, an apocalyptic vision dominated Luther's view of the world and animated his theology in a characteristic way. The real world, as he saw it in its outward form, "does not seem to be a kingdom but a place of exile, or to be living but to be constantly dying, or to be in glory but to be in disgrace. . . ."[54] He added that "the more we preach, the viler and more ungrateful the world becomes. It seems to me that the world will not last much longer."[55] This sense of an imminent transformation when the world has reached its low point closely shaped his theology which we call here the theology of negative transcendence.

Touching only on the highlights of its logical development, we may begin with the two natures of Christ and, in a closely related fashion, the two natures of man. Ultimately there emerges Luther's formulation of the nature of God the Father.

Man's two natures, the spiritual and carnal exist, as we have seen, in perpetual contradiction and struggle--in antithesis. But Christ's two natures are presented in much the same way. A joint portrait of Christ and man is offered in symmetrical form: "So Christ empties himself [eussert sich] of his divine form, and thus he is and assumes the form of a servant which he is not. We however, empty ourselves [eussern uns] of the form of a servant, which we are, and take on or are subject to the divine form which we are not."[56] There is the effect here of a "mirror image," where Christ and man, each with two natures, reflect each other in inverse form. It was precisely this problem which haunted Luther's theological imagination and was the matrix of several other doctrines. Christ's two natures of "Lord" and "Servant" are designated by Luther as Creator (der Schopffer) and creature (die Creatur).[57] These two natures of Christ are "inseparable" (unzutrennlich beinander) as if they were "intertwined and unified" (geflochten und vereiniget). "Where one of these natures exists, there the other must also be, and neither can evermore be split from the other nor parted from it."[58] This forms the basis of the doctrine of communicatio idiomatum, the communication of properties, namely that "anything which is attributed to one nature is also attributed to the other, because one person results [from it]."[59] Discussing the Gospel of John, Luther adds:

> Now if the true God dwells in Christ, who was born of Mary, that is, the God who made and created all, we must say that the deity and the humanity joined not only their natures but also their properties, except for sin. . . . Since His incarnation the two natures are united; and the divine nature confers its properties on the human, and vice versa, the human on the divine.[60]

This sense of two spheres, Creator and creature, lordship and bondage, existing in an inverse relation but united, and attributing mutual properties one to the other is a position that was basic to

Hegel's parable of lordship and bondage. In a more attenuated form, it was reiterated in Marx's view of lordship and bondage as capital and labour.

Luther moves in an easy and self-evident way from Christ's suffering to man's suffering. Christ is the model for man and man's cross rightly "destroys man's self-confidence" while he allows God to do everything in him.[61] Christ's "fearful symmetry" is thus recapitulated in man who is: spiritualis et carnalis, iustus et peccator, bonus et malus" (spiritual and carnal, righteous and sinful, good and evil).[62] This leads to man's afflicted conscience, the afflicta conscientia, or the trawrigkeit des gewissens which was to re-emerge in Hegel later as the unglückliches Bewusstsein, the unhappy consciousness.[63]

This pervasive dualism was pressed onward in several directions and received its most dramatic statement in the theology of the cross. This theology evolved in a sharp attack on the practice of indulgences in the Catholic church--the purchase from the church of the remission of one's sins.

As early as 1518, Luther refers in the Heidelberg Disputation to true theology as the theology of the cross (theologia crucis) standing in sharp opposition to the theology of glory (theologia gloriae) ascribed to the Catholic church. In the theology of glory, God is known from his works, his glory, and his power. But according to the theology of the cross, God wishes to be known by a standard that is the precise opposite, namely by his suffering and his weakness.[64] "Crux sola est nostra theologia" ("the cross alone is our theology"). states Luther.[65]

The theology of the cross had its basis in Christ's two-fold work, a work that is "characteristic" and a work that is "alien" (proprium et alienum).[66] The "characteristic" work includes grace, righteousness, truth, patience, and gentleness. The "alien" work includes "the cross, labour, all kinds of punishment, finally death and hell in the flesh. . . ."[67] Luther states that it is to Christ's alien image that we must be conformed: "Just so must we be conformed to the image of the Son of God."[68] This forms the basis of Luther's attack on the indulgences: "Whoever does not take up his own cross and follow him, is not worthy of him, even if he were filled with all kinds of indulgences."[69]

Luther's complaint against the Catholic indulgences was summed up in a significant formulation echoed much later in an almost identical vein but in a thoroughly different context by the young Marx. Luther states: "the theology of the cross has been abrogated, and everything has been completely turned up-side down" (evacuata est theologia crucis suntque omnia plane perversa).[70] For the young Marx, as we shall see, it was the power of money in a capitalist society that created "the world upside-down" (die verkehrte Welt).[71] The complaint in both cases was against the dominant institutional structure, against the constricting role of money, and was articulated as a complaint against an inverted world.

Pursued to its furthest extreme, the theology of the cross offers a view of God the Father as the negativa essentia, the negative essence. Luther means "the negation of all things which can be felt, held and comprehended. . . ," or alternatively that God "cannot be possessed or touched except by the negation of all of our affirmatives."[72]

Luther's negativa essentia is not an isolated reference, for he refers to God's power at another point as Nichtigkeit[73] nothingness, and further in Latin as "nothingness and worthlessness." Luther bases this theology on Paul: "For everything in us is weak and worthless: but in the nothingness and worthlessness, so to speak, God shows His strength, according to the saying (II Corinthians 12:9) 'My power is made perfect in weakness'."[74]

This negation, the negativa essentia, corresponds to what I have termed here the power of inversion. A leading Lutheran scholar, Paul Althaus, sums up Luther's Divinity as the power of inversion (Umkehrung) as follows:

Sie ist die Macht, aus dem Nichts, aus dem Gegenteil zu schaffen. Sie erweist sich gerade in der Umkehrung aller irdischen Mässtabe und Verhältnisse.[75]

(God) is the power that creates out of nothing or out of its opposite. It is manifested by the inversion of all earthly standards and relationships.

Luther's notion of negation and inversion reappear in virtually identical form in Hegel, particularly in Hegel's definition of the lord, in the parable on lordship and bondage as "die reine negative Macht, der das Ding nichts ist"("the negative power without qualification, a power to which the thing is naught").[76] In other designations Hegel refers to the lord as "absolute universal Being as . . . mere nothingness" (allgemeine Wesen als der Nichtigkeit),[77] "the negative essence" (negatives Wesen), or simply "nothingness" (Nichtigkeit).[78]

Within the context of the theology of the cross and the power of inversion, there emerges a portrait of man's alienation and salvation. In Jesus' "alien" work man may see himself as "emptied and alien" (ledig und frembd).[79] In the Heidelberg Disputation Luther is more explicit:

He, however, who has emptied himself [cf. Phil. 2:7] through suffering no longer does works but knows that God works and does all things in him. . . . He knows that it is sufficient if he suffers and is brought low by the cross in order to be annihilated all the more. It is this that Christ says in John 3:7: "You must be born anew."[80]

In "On the Bondage of the Will," the path for the elect (electos) is "that being humbled and brought back to nothingness by this means they may be saved."[81]

Stated succinctly, Luther's prescription for man was as follows: ". . . nos ipsos deserere et exinanire, nihil de nostro sensu retinendo, sed totum abnegando. . . "("to forsake and empty ourselves, keeping nothing of our senses, but negating everything. . .").[82]

It is precisely from this point of departure in Lutheran theology, man's own "emptying" of himself and negating everything, that Hegel takes up the matter and develops his thesis on man's work and activity in the world. Hegel brings to bear the same mode of reasoning and the same resolution. But Hegel turned the problem the other way, from man as creature to man as creator of his own artifacts. It was in this mirror image, so to speak, that the theme of alienation reappeared as a central concern in Hegel and in a further variation in the early Marx. (A full treatment of the alienation theme is beyond the scope of this paper.)

Hegel was influenced by one further theological dispute in which Luther was engaged--that of the Sacrament. Luther's rivals in this dispute, Zwingli, Münzer, Karlstadt, and Oecolampadius argued that the Holy Spirit was fundamentally separate from material things and worked through an "inner word." Luther argued instead in defence of the Sacrament that the spiritual and material were interlocked:

They think nothing spiritual can be present where there is anything material and physical, and assert that flesh is of no avail. Actually the opposite is true. The Spirit cannot be with us except in material and physical things such as the Word, Water, and Christ's body and in his saints on earth.[83]

Instead of this drastic separation between the inner and outer in the Eucharist, Luther argues in a telling phrase that "God inverts this order" (Gott aber keret das umb), that is He "sets before us no word or commandment without including with it something material and outward, and proffering it to us. . . . You find no word of God in the entire Scriptures in which something material and outward is not contained and presented." "Christ," Luther continues, "is present in his Word and in the outward things of which his Word speaks."[84]

It is this formulation that became the basis of Hegel's notion of "finite Spirit," in the everyday world where consciousness and material existence are interwoven, and formed the lower circuit of bondage in his schema (see Diagram 1). Hegel called this circuit "Life."[85]

For Luther, this was a thoroughly consistent elaboration of the central problem of the two natures of Christ: "Here there is God and man, the highest and the lowest, infinite and finite in one Person, emptying and filling all things--by this wonderful union God has joined the human nature to Himself."[86]

Man in both his alienation and salvation is the product of God's handiwork, and is conformed to Christ's alien image. Luther's injunction to man is: "stand fast, however, in such contradictory experience and nevertheless believe most constantly, for you wait for what cannot be seen."[87] Put differently: "For what is good for us is hidden, and that so deeply that it is hidden under its opposite" (*sub contrario absconditum sit*).[88]

Luther's theology culminates in a telling and poetic image of man's fate. As one sinks outside oneself and out of all creation into nothingness, one falls into the hand of God which embraces creation from all sides.[89]

1.3 Luther's Semantics

The elucidation of Christ's (and man's) dual nature was a semantic struggle for Luther as well as a theological one. It absorbed his genius for language and bequeathed eventually a vocabulary that included some of the key words of the Hegelian and Marxian systems.

One of the most important is the word *entäussern*, which is used in the modern translation of Philippians 2:7: "[Christ] emptied himself" ("*entäusserte sich selbst*"). When Luther first approached this Philippians passage in 1518, he found no immediate German equivalent to the Greek *heauton ekenosen*, nor to the Latin translation *semetipsum exinanivit*. His first solution was simply to add a German suffix to the Latin, and he coined a new word: *hat sich exinanirt*.[90] Only in 1522 did Luther begin to use *eussern* as a translation (literally "to outer"), a word which he retained in different forms to the end of his life.[91]

At one point, Luther used the same word (geeussert) for the subsequent process of Christ's exaltation to heaven.[92] A further important usage (reminiscent of the "joyous exchange") is the way in which Christ is contrasted with man in symmetrical but inverse form around this term eussern which we cited above.[93] Entäussern became a central term in both the Hegelian and Marxian theories of alienation which were thus rooted semantically in Christ's Incarnation.[94]

Luther's antithetical dualism was embodied occasionally within his semantic usage, that is, the same word might come to have opposite meanings. The most important modern word is aufheben, meaning on the one hand "abolish," and, on the other, "raise up" or "preserve." a word that is crucial to both the Hegelian and Marxian vocabulary. (It is often translated as "supersede" as when one economic class supersedes a second in the Marxian schema.)

Luther used the word unselfconsciously in its two discrete meanings, but these two opposite usages of aufheben were fused in the later German. We believe that Hegel recognized explicitly that one of the roots of this term, "raise up," was related to Jesus' exaltation. Hegel's use of aufheben was one example of his attempt to translate religious language into that of philosophy.[95]

Many other characteristic words from Lutheran theology are strewn throughout Hegel's texts in close variants. To mention only a few: Äusserlichkeit (externality or outwardness), Innerlichkeit (inwardness), Versöhnung (reconciliation), Entzweiung (disunion or division), Geist (spirit), Zeugniss (witness), Offenbarung (revelation), entfremdet (alienated), and the words that are central to this discussion, Herrschaft (lordship) and Knechtschaft (bondage).

God's power, the negativa essentia, the power of inversion and negation, received its popular expression in many contexts in one of Luther's favorite words, umbkeren (to overturn). Luther speaks on behalf of Christ, whom enemies have crucified, and states (typically mixing Latin and German): "But I will completely overturn (invert) this" (Sed ich wils blat umbkeren).[96] The editors of Luther's works add in a footnote that Luther uses this expression frequently: Sehr oft bei Luther.[97]

Hegel's notion of Umkehrung (inversion) is adapted from Luther.

In The Philosophy of Religion, Christ's death is explicitly stated to be an inversion (Umkehrung) and should be understood as a paradigm for every individual where he yields up his natural will.[98] A variety of uses of this term in Hegel is reflected further in Marx's extensive use of the related Verkehrung which we shall see below.

Schmitz (following de Negri) remarks on the common structure of Luther's and Hegel's vocabulary that "these two vocabularies are perfectly interchangeable" and are invested with a common spirit, that of "contradiction."[99] De Negri for example, traces the origin in Luther of the famous and difficult Hegelian phrases an sich and für sich.[100]

We may also note the Lutheran resonance of the very title of Hegel's chapter on lordship and bondage: "Die Wahrheit der Gewissheit seiner selbst" ("The Truth Which Conscious Certainty of Self Realizes"). It has the ring of an oft-quoted Lutheran expression: "deyner warheit gewiszheyt macht mich, das ichs festlich glewb" ("the certainty of your truthfulness. . . leads me to believe this firmly").[101]

But it was out of Luther's ceaseless preoccupation with the two natures of Christ that the most pregnant suggestion for Hegel emerged. How these two natures could still be one person, Luther thought, was ultimately "inscrutable," and "foolish reason" would not help. In the midst of a Latin text he breaks into German: und ye mehr man im nachdenckt, ye weniger man Davon verstehet ("the more one reflects on this, the less one understands it"). But he then adds immediately that it was necessary to believe and to know that we were dealing here with regulae dialecticae, the rules of dialectics.[102]

2. Marx

Marx carried on an endless diatribe against theology and religion with occasional grudging praise and perceptive insight. His views would warrant much fuller treatment than can be allowed here. But in his debate with Max Stirner, Marx put his finger on the nub of his argument, namely, that Christianity had focussed on the wrong definition of oppressive domination, that is on man's mortal existence:

> The only reason why Christianity wanted to free us from the domination of the flesh (Herrschaft des Fleisches). . . was because it regarded our flesh, our desires as something foreign to us; it wanted to free

us from determination by nature only because it regarded our own nature as not belonging to us. For if I myself am not nature, if my natural desires, my whole natural character, does not belong to me myself--and this is the doctrine of Christianity--then all determination by nature--whether due to my own natural character or to so-called external nature--seems to me a determination by something foreign, a fetter, compulsion used against me, heteronomy as opposed to autonomy of the spirit [Heteronomie im Gegansatz zur Autonomie des Geistes].[103]

While declaring his opposition to the "Christian dialectic" which regarded man's natural existence as an external alien force, i.e. a "heteronomy", Marx understood that it had issued from "an inverted world" (eine verkehrte Welt) and was thus "an inverted world-consciousness" (ein verkehrtes Weltbewusstsein).[104]

The root of the problem, Marx felt, was the social and economic order under which man lived; that was the true source of his bondage and it had reached its most oppressive form under capitalism. What Marx meant to express in his famous phrase "the fetishism of commodities" was that "the process of production has the mastery over man, instead of being controlled by his," that man's products "rule the producers instead of being ruled by them."[105] This fetishism, he stated subsequently, was an inversion (die Verkehrung) of the proper relationship that should prevail.[106]

The contradictions of capitalism were typically designated by Marx as phenomena of inversion. "Everything," he stated, "appears upside down in competition."[107] These phenomena were now found to be present in history and society rather than in "pure consciousness," as Hegel would have it with his "dialectic of negativity", or in the power of God as Luther maintained.

But there was also present in Marx a strong sense of continuity in the structure of his argument with what had preceded him, despite his firm and oft-repeated dissociation of himself from religion and from Hegel's "spirit." Both Marx and Engels saw their task within the mainstream of the "German revolution." For Engels, Luther had composed "that triumphal hymn which became the Marseillaise of the sixteenth century."[108] Even though this revolution had taken a theoretical form and had still to transcend its religious basis, yet the line with Luther and Hegel was continuous in their own minds: "Germany's revolutionary past is precisely theoretical: it is the Reformation. As at that time it was a monk, so now it is the philosopher in whose brain the revolution begins."[109]

But in a more general sense, this "revolutionary past" extended even further back into history. Each epoch, Marx explained, levelled a similar critique at its immediate predecessor. The bourgeois critique against the feudal era "resembled the critique which Christianity levelled against paganism, or also that of Protestantism against Catholicism."[110] Thus the "German revolution," in a more attenuated sense, had its antecedents as far back as the origins of Christianity. It formed part of Marx's sense of the dialectical movement of history.

Marx was particularly impressed by Luther's shift in focus from what was external and alien to man to what was internal and indigenous to man's nature: "It was no longer a question of the laymen's struggle with the priest outside of him, but of his struggle with his own inner priest, his priestly nature." Marx saw the continuity with the next step which he was advocating: "so the philosophical transformation of the priestly Germans into men will emancipate the people," and finally that "if Protestantism was not the real solution it at least posed the problem correctly."[111]

Marx saw the coming of Protestantism as a characteristic ideological expression of the new bourgeois society. He viewed the problem of the relation of capitalism to Protestantism within the context of his general position on the relation of production to its political and cultural superstructure. He notes that: "definite relations of industry and commerce are necessarily connected with a definite form of society, hence, with a definite form of State and hence, with a definite form of religious consciousness."[112]

Even though Luther had preceded Adam Smith, the apostle of the market economy, by some two and a half centuries, Marx was inclined to draw a parallel between Luther's aims and those of Smith. What had happened in the Protestant Reformation was reiterated in similar fashion in the subsequent structure of bourgeois society. Marx (following Engels) calls Adam Smith "the Luther of Political Economy." Just as Luther shifted the locus of religious feeling from the external structures of Catholicism into "the inner substance of man," so had Adam Smith shifted our understanding of the economy and of wealth from the perception of an external and independent system to one where we now understood private property as "incorporated in man himself being recognized as its essence." Marx refers here to the central role played by Adam Smith's labour theory of value in the new political economy. The result was similar for both capitalism and Protestantism: "man is brought within the orbit of private property, just as with Luther he is brought within the orbit of religion."[113]

The economic system of private property is thus internalized in man and so is rooted within his very essence. This makes the effective domination of the system immensely more powerful. But that simultaneously provides the greatest moral basis for the complaint of estrangement; the economic system subverts the individual at his core, and thus subverts as well the entire human species. A new transcendence was imminent, and "the problem" common to both capitalism and Protestantism in Marx's view could now be solved. But how different was Marx's solution in the end from that of Luther?

Marx's definition of "bondage" had changed drastically from that of his predecessors; nevertheless the rhetorical structure of their argument left its mark on his own view of history. Inversion and reinversion became the key to man's oppression and to his liberation.

We turn our attention to Marx's treatment of lordship and bondage as a schema of economic and social development. Herrschaft is now domination by changing forms of private property, and Knechtschaft is the bondage of different forms of alienated labour, entäusserte[n] Arbeit.[114] In a few elliptic notes at the end of the second manuscript of the Economic and Philosophic Manuscripts of 1844 (E.P.M.), Marx outlines the process relating capital and labour as Herr and Knecht. They develop first reciprocally even though separated and estranged and "promote each other as positive conditions." They then develop in opposition (Gegensatz).[115] The motive force of change is not the benign or complementary side of this reciprocal relationship but their antagonism, "the antithesis of labour and capital" (der Gegensatz der Arbeit und des Kapitals).[116]

In a strictly formal sense, "antithesis" plays the same role for Marx that it plays in Paul's designation of man's two opposing natures, in Luther's elaboration of Pauline theology as the two natures of Christ mirrored in the two natures of man, and in Hegel's general schema. It sets the stage and provides the impetus for the drama which now unfolds to an apocalyptic resolution.

Private property begins with the domination of land (Herrschaft des Grundeigentums)[117] in the feudal period, based on the labour of the serf. With the shift to commercial agriculture (called physiocracy after its theoretical exponents, the physiocrats) serfdom is abolished, giving way to the freed agricultural worker who then becomes "labour in general." Labour is now a mobile commodity on the capitalist labour market, as freely disposable in principle as any other commodity. The capitalist and the power of money of which he is the instrument win out over the landowner and other fixed forms of private property. But this is contingent on the transformation of the serf into the free worker.[118] Thus we have the second or bourgeois stage of economic history when private property had to complete "its dominion (Herrschaft) over man and become, in its most general form, a world-historical power." It was a "historical necessity."[119]

There is a further contingent development of "lord" and "servant" in the capitalist period: "As the bourgeoisie develops, there develops in its bosom a new proletariat, a modern proletariat; there develops a struggle between the proletarian class and the bourgeois class. . . ."[120]

In the Grundrisse, which laid the basis for Capital, Marx sums up by stating that the master-servant relation (Herrschafts- und Knechtschafts-verhältnis) is part of a formula that "forms a necessary ferment for the development and the decline and fall of all original relations of property and of production. . . ." This formula, he adds, also forms the basis for the dissolution of capital.[121]

In Capital, Marx returns to this theme in historical perspective: "from the moment that men in any way work for one another, their labour assumes a social form."[122] Initially, such as in the feudal period, these social forms are based upon "direct relations of domination and oppression" (unmittelbaren Herrschafts- und Knechtschaftsverhältnissen).[123] It is this antithesis which gives rise to further internal forms of differentiation and to the transformation from feudalism into the factors of production, labour, and capital in a developed capitalist society. This antithesis is a "dynamic relationship moving to its resolution."[124]

Some idea of the process entailed in this antithesis of capital and labour is provided by Marx's discussion of money (one manifestation of capital) in the E.P.M. Money is the motive force that dominates man and creates the oppressed and alienated society. It derives its special power because it holds captive "men's estranged, alienating and self-disposing species nature. Money is the alienated ability of mankind."[125] Money is designated by Marx as "this overturning power" (diese verkehrende Macht), and he elaborates on this theme of inversion. Money is "the general overturning (allemeine

Verkehrung) of individualities which turns them into their contrary (in ihr Gegenteil umkehrt) and adds contradictory attributes to the attributes."[126]

Perhaps Marx was not consciously aware of how closely he followed along in the footsteps of Lutheran rhetoric. There was both an intended and an unintended irony when he described money as "the visible divinity--the transformation of all human and natural properties into their contraries."[127]

But the question of inversion was not merely limited to money. In the Grundrisse, this theme is pursued further into the realm of economics. Marx finds that "inversion [Verkehrung] is the foundation of the capitalist mode of production, not only of its distribution." He states that "this twisting and inversion [Verdrehung und Verkehrung] is a real [phenomenon], not merely supposed one existing merely in the imagination of the workers and the capitalists."[128]

This general inversion of the individual, the human species, and the entire economic system, forms the basis for the most compelling response: from this complete undermining of his human essence, man moves to total liberation. This takes the form of a systematic reinversion of man and society to their true human form and proceeds through the mediating role of the proletariat. The proletariat moves from its own "complete loss of humanity and can only redeem itself through the total redemption of humanity"; the German text contrasts völlige Verlust (complete loss) and völlige Wiedergewinnung (complete redemption).

The proletariat, as we will recall, is Marx's Knecht, and we see here the characteristic inversion of bondage. With it, in turn, comes the promise of total freedom or emancipation. The proletariat proceeds from "universal suffering" to "emancipating itself from all others spheres of society, thereby emancipating them."[129] As stated in the E.P.M.: "the emancipation of society from private property etc. from servitude [Knechtschaft], is expressed in the political form of the emancipation of the workers . . . because the emancipation of the workers contains universal human emancipation. . . ."[130] Marx highlighted the prospect of freedom in the Communist Manifesto: "In place of the old boureois society, with its classes and class antagonisms, we shall have an association, in which the free development of each is the condition for the free development of all."[131]

A dehumanized and enslaved proletariat becomes a redeemed and free proletariat. This is the movement from oppressive to exalted bondage--the inversion of substance referred to earlier. But now the second inversion makes its appearance--the inversion of form--and the exalted bondage turns into lordship. In Germany, Marx foresaw a partial or political revolution where the working class would emancipate itself and achieve universal dominance (allgemeinen Herrschaft).[132] He adds: "Only in the name of the universal rights of society can a particular class lay claim to universal dominance."[133] Marx refers several times in the Communist Manifesto to this 'lordship' of the proletariat, i.e. their "supremacy" (Herrschaft). His graphic instruction reads: "the first step in the revolution by the working class, is to raise the proletariat to the position of ruling class. . . ."[134] It is reminiscent, rhetorically, of Moses' promise to the Jews: "And the Lord shall make thee the head, and not the tail; and thou shalt be above only, and thou shalt not be beneath." (Deuteronomy 28:13)

One of the aims is the achievement of equality: "Equality as the basis of communism is its political justification. . . ."[135] Marx also refers to the "equality of wages" under communism.[136]

Thus we have the parallel movement of Marx's Knecht to Luther's Knecht (servant) moving from oppressive to exalted bondage and then the further inversion to the status of ruler or "lord."

The resolution into "perfect community" now looms as the final step. Society is the indispensable framework for viewing life, "a mode of appropriating human life."[137] For Marx, "the subject, society must always be kept in mind as the presupposition."[138] But man's social experience in history thus far leaves a relentless negative imprint on him. As long as there is any form of division of labour in the community, which Marx calls the "natural society," there we find that "a cleavage exists between the particular and common interest." Consequently "man's own deed becomes an alien power opposed to him, which enslaves him instead of being controlled by him."[139]

In a society dominated by private property, moreover, social appropriation appears as estrangement (Entfremdung) and as alienation (Entäusserung), but these necessarily form the very basis that constitutes this society (als die wahre Einbürgerung).[140]

In The German Ideology Marx distinguishes between "the illusory community," based on the antagonism of classes and on the division of labour, and genuine community, where the division of labour is abolished. "In the real community [wirklichen Gemeinschaft] the individuals obtain their freedom in and through their association." He adds that "only in the community, therefore, is personal freedom possible."[141]

The movement towards socialism is a movement towards community in two institutional stages. The first is crude communism, "the first positive annulment [positive Aufhebung] of private property."[142] This forms the basis, in its positive expression, for the notion of communism: "communism is the positive expression of annulled private property--at first as universal private property." ("Der Kommunismus endlich ist der positive Ausdruck des aufgehobenen Privateigentums, zunächst das allgemeine Privateigentum."[143]

The first phase is, by itself deficient since it is merely the negation of private property. There is a more basic need yet to be fulfilled--"the need for society,"[144] that is, a further negation of universal private property. It is to the resolution of this overall historical problem of "society," to which the final stage, socialism, is directed. Its aim is to put an end to man's historical alienation, "the destruction of the alien relation between men and what they themselves produce."[145] It aims as well for a "unity of being of man with nature."[146] Man is the "awareness and real mind of social existence" and as such becomes the "totality of human manifestations of life."[147]

This formulation from the E.P.M. is reiterated in the Grundrisse. Marx invokes "the absolute working-out of [man's] creative potentialities. . . the development of all human powers as such." This is "the end in itself" that "produces his [man's] totality."[148]

It is this sense of "ideal totality" (die ideale Totalität)[149] which characterizes Marx's ultimate solution, totally integrating man and society. This vision of society appears as an ideal image of man writ large. The active agent is now "the proletariat organized as a ruling class" (als herrschende Klasse) i.e. as the State.[150] In this vision, the proletariat "associates, fuses [zusammenfliesst] and identifies itself with society [mit ihr verwechselt] in general, and is felt and recognized to be society's general representative. . . ."[151]

The rhetorical structure follows closely Hegel's resolution of the parable of lordship and bondage as a "complete and thoroughgoing fusion and identification," or as he put it alternately, the "reflexion into unity."[152]

When the proletariat is thoroughly fused and identified with society as a whole its "dominance" becomes short-lived, and the identity of its goals with those of society as a whole becomes complete. The final stage of our schema is recapitulated in Marx in the explicit abolition of power. Political power, Marx claims, is merely the result of class antagonisms, and with the abolition of the latter, a society will evolve where "there will be no further political power as such."[153] In a well known passage from the Communist Manifesto, he reiterates this notion:

When, in the course of development, class distinctions have disappeared, and all production has been concentrated in the hands of a vast association of the whole nation, the public power will lose its political character. Political power, properly so called, is merely the organized power of one class for oppressing another. If the proletariat during its contest with the bourgeoisie is compelled, by the force of circumstances to organize itself as a class, if, by means of a revolution, it makes itself the ruling class, and, as such, sweeps away by force the old conditions of production, then it will, along with these conditions, have swept away the conditions for the existence of class antagonisms, and of classes generally, and will thereby have abolished its own supremacy as a class.[154]

The German text of this last clause reads: "_hebt...damit seine eigene Herrschaft als Klasse auf._"[155] Compare this with Paul's prescription for the kingdom of God when Christ "shall have put down all rule and all authority and power" (I Corinthians 15:24). In Luther's translation (1546): "_Wenn er auffheben wird alle herrschaft, und alle oberkeit und Gewalt_,"[156]

This comparison reveals the common culmination of the apocalyptic vision. In its rhetorical structure, Marx's socialism is as comprehensive and all-embracing a vision of community as the _totus Christus_ of the New Testament, as Luther's kingdom of God, or Hegel's ideal Protestant state.

Marx's analysis of capitalist development and his prescription follow very closely the schema presented in Diagram 1. Some minor changes are incorporated in Diagram 2 below. One modification may be included by adding an identical column prior, but exactly similar, to column 1 in Diagram 1. These two columns reflect the fact that Marx's economic history is briefly laid out in two general stages, corresponding to the two historical periods of feudalism and capitalism, each with its particular antithesis of lordship and bondage as private property and labour.

DIAGRAM 2

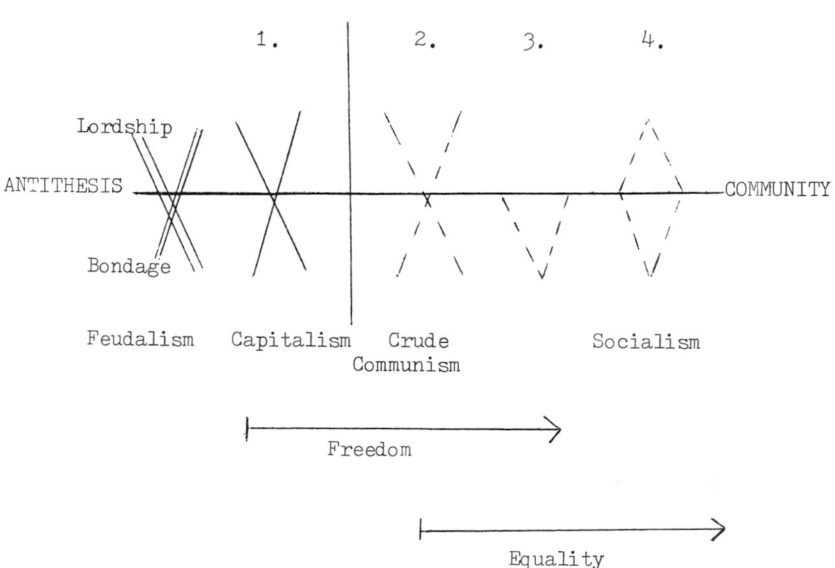

Beginning with the lower circuit in column 1, the proletariat moves, as we have seen, from its oppressed to its redeemed status (column 2) and thence to its "lordship" as ruling class (column 3). Freedom and equality accompany these two movements.

Along the upper circuit, there is a differentiation of lordship rather than the single total inversion portrayed in Diagram 1. The movement from column 1 to column 2 reflects the movement from capitalism to "crude communism" which is the negation of private property (<u>aufgehobenen Privateigentums</u>) as "universal private property" (an inversion of substance). A further negation (to column 4) produces true socialism in a community where the proletariat as the ruling class (column 3) is thoroughly fused and identified with society. Its goals and those of society are identical, and all power is abolished.

This recapitulates the entire system of the rhetoric of transfiguration in Marx. What we have tried to establish is that the final apocalyptic vision necessarily follows from the systematic process of inversion of the basic antithesis.

2.2 The Politics of Negative Transcendence

> It is above all the task of philosophy, which is in the service of history, to unmask human self-alienation in its secular forms, once its sacred form has been unmasked. Thus, the critique of heaven is transformed into the critique of the earth. . . the critique of theology into the critique of politics.[157]

"Consciousness," Marx notes in the Critique of Political Economy, "must be explained. . . from the contradictions of material life, from the existing conflict between the social productive forces and the relations of production."[158] This consciousness of which Marx speaks is a consciousness of oppression, of deprivation (from the objects man has produced), and of exploitation. When the worker recognizes the products he produces as his own, and his separation from them as improper--forcibly imposed--there is an enormous advance in consciousness (ist ein enormes Bewusstsein), which spells for the system "the knell to its doom."[159] The active agent is the working class, animated by "the communist consciousness," which Marx describes as "the consciousness of the necessity of a fundamental revolution."[160]

The communist consciousness which Marx invokes stands in sharp contrast to the conventional consciousness and ideology of bourgeois society which acts as a form of domination and which sees the world upside-down:

> the conditions of existence of the ruling class. . . are more or less consciously transformed by the ideologists of that class into something that in history exists independently. . . and which are set up as a standard of life in opposition to the individuals of the oppressed class, partly as an embellishment or realization of domination [Herrschaft], partly as a moral means for this domination. It is to be noted here, as in general with ideologists, that they inevitably put the thing upside-down [auf den Kopf stellen]. . . .[161]

But how does a communist consciousness come into being when a society's political institutions and ideological expressions reflect the existing forces of production and their accompanying social relations? With the development of the division of labour in society, "a division of material and mental labour appears." Marx foresees that "the forces of production, the state of society, [or what he calls "social relations"] and consciousness, can and must come into contradiction with one another. . . ." Consciousness, in this new, contradictory role, may now acquire a catalytic function of its own when it becomes conscious of "something other than existing practice."[162] Subsequently, "from forms of development of the productive forces these [social] relations turn into their fetters. Then begins an epoch of social revolution."[163]

In short, "the communist consciousness" carries within it, in dialectical fashion, both the contradictions of society and the basis for the resolution of man's social oppression: "the categorical imperative to overthrow all conditions in which man is a debased, enslaved, neglected, contemptible being."[164] It is this consciousness which Marx calls "that genius that animates material force into political power," and it is based on the recognition of a revolutionary class as "the negative representative of society."[165]

The notion of the proletariat as "the negative representative of society," as well as a communist consciousness that is transformed into political power, is suggestive of some of the elements of our earlier discussion of Luther's theology of negative transcendence. We shall try to show that what Marx had in mind as the dynamic elements of a communist consciousness bears a clear resemblance to what Luther had in mind by his central notion of "faith" and the nature of God's power. This may seem, initially, to be a rather "heroic" exercise, for their overwhelming substantive differences have been completely set aside. It is not a general but a limited comparison of rhetorical structure in which we are now engaged.

First there is the central role played by antitheses which provide the initial tension in both systems and prefigure within them the path to "salvation." For Luther, we turn once more to the two natures of Christ. Within Christ "two extreme opposites are contending" (duo extreme contraria concurrant).[166] Everything that is opposed to Christ reigns in him. Luther uses many expressions for this antithesis in God, and for the corresponding antithesis in man.[167]

In Marx, the basic antithesis, as we have seen, is between capital and labour.[168] But this is echoed in a cluster of related and similar antitheses. Marx refers to "so many antithetical forms of the unity which itself brings the antithesis to the fore."[169]

These antitheses in Luther and Marx evoke a compelling response from man in broadly similar ways. But initially Marx's rhetoric appears as a mirror image or "negative" of Luther's rhetoric in curiously symmetrical form. For Luther, man following Christ's example "empties himself," moving to a state of nothingness by conforming himself to Christ's alien image, shedding his works and bearing death, sin, and punishment. For Marx, man is forcibly coerced into "self-emptying" and is shorn of his "works" or his products by a cruel, relentless system. Marx refers to alienated labour as "labor of self-sacrifice, or mortification" and thus to the labourer as a "sacrificed and empty being."[170] There is "a complete emptying-out, this universal objectification as a total alienation. . . sacrifice of the human end-in-itself to an entirely external end [ganz äussern Zweck]."[171] In both cases (but for very different reasons) man is voided or emptied of his objects or artifacts.

In Luther's theology of the cross, man conforms his own image to that of Christ but relies on God as the negative essentia, or Nichtigkeit (nothingness) to work in him and to bring about his salvation. For Marx, there is a corresponding negativity in the relation of capitalist and worker. In an alienated society "the worker knows the capitalist as his own non-existence, and vice versa" (der Arbeiter weiss den Kapitalisten und umgekehrt als sein Nicht-dasein).[172] Marx reverts to this type of expression frequently in the Grundrisse. Capital operates in the worker to bring about his nothingness or non-being (ihr eignes Nichtsein).[173] For Luther, God shows his power "in that nothingness and worthlessness."[174] For Marx, the power of capital is shown in the "valuelessness and devaluation of the worker" (Wertlosigkeit und Entwertung des Arbeiters).[175]

These rhetorical expressions appear in Luther and Marx, so to speak, back to back, or in mirror image. God's power operates for Luther as His most exalted expression; for Marx the devaluation of the worker by capital is the source of his most oppressive condition. Nevertheless, this "negativity" is the rhetorical prelude to "salvation" in both cases. Marx envisions the final stage of capitalism as the growth of:

> the mass of misery, oppression, slavery, degradation, exploitation; but with this too grows the revolt of the working-class, a class always increasing in numbers, and disciplined, united, organised by the very mechanism of the process of capitalist production itself. . . . The knell of capitalist private property sounds. The expropriators are expropriated.[176]

Luther states that present suffering (following in Christ's path) will lead to ultimate salvation:

> For Christendom must take the same course as the Lord Himself (John 15:20). Christians must bear the brunt of the attack of the devil and the world, must be run over and trampled, so that they may feel it. . . [as Isaiah says]: 'But I will see to it that you trample those who trampled you, not merely for a time, as you now must suffer for a time; but you shall trample them forever.'[177]

In the Communist Manifesto, Marx and Engels state: "The

modern labourer. . . instead of rising with the progress of industry, sinks deeper and deeper below the conditions of existence of his own class. He becomes a pauper. . . ." But the fall of the bourgeoisie and the victory of the proletariat "are equally inevitable." The Manifesto concludes in the famous phrase: "The proletarians have nothing to lose but their chains. They have a world to win."[178]

Speaking in Christ's name Luther states: "When you think that you have been devoured and destroyed, I will force My way through and bring it to pass that you rise and reign."[179]

The basis of political mobilization in Marx is the deliberate striking of a strong polar antithesis. Marx provided what amounted virtually to stage directions for the conduct of the apocalyptic drama. He explains how the antithesis, that is an antithesis in consciousness, can and must be forced, how "the burden must be made still more oppressive by adding to it a consciousness of it. . . ."[180] For a particular class:

> To take over this liberating position, and therewith the political exploitation of all the spheres of society in the interest of its own sphere, revolutionary energy and spiritual self-confidence do not suffice. For a popular revolution and the emancipation of a particular class to coincide, for one class to stand for the whole of society, another class must, on the other hand, concentrate in itself all the defects of society, must be the class of universal offense and the embodiment of universal limits. A particular social sphere must stand for the notorious crime of the whole society, so that liberation from this sphere appears to be universal liberation. For one class to be the class *par excellence* of liberation, another class must, on the other hand, be openly the subjugating class.[181]

By comparison, Luther is more concise, and is concerned with a different antithesis in consciousness but he is equally evocative: faith "believes that life emerges from death and that perdition ends in salvation."[182] When God "exalts to heaven he does it by bringing down to hell."[183] "In short," Luther states, "God cannot be God unless he first becomes a devil. We cannot go to heaven unless we first go to hell."[184]

In a more succinct fashion, Marx refers to "that revolutionary boldness which flings at its adversary the defiant phrase: I am nothing and I should be everything" (*Ich bin nichts, und ich müsste alles sein*).[185] Paul's expression, standing, so to speak, back to back with Marx is: "for in nothing am I behind the very chiefest apostles, though I be nothing" (II Corinthians 12:11). In Luther's translation: "*da ich doch nicht weniger bin, als die hohen Apostel sind, wiewohl ich nichts bin*." This is preceded by Paul's phrase "for when I am weak, then am I strong," echoed in turn by Luther as "Thus Christ was strongest when He was death and weakest."[186]

It is in this characteristic rhetoric that Luther's "faith" bears its striking similarity to Marx's revolutionary consciousness. We may recall Luther's metaphor of Christ's marriage to the sinful human soul. Luther showed how this results in a "joyous exchange," or in effect how the human soul, burdened by death and damnation, inverts itself (through Christ's mediation) and acquires grace, life, and salvation. Paul Althaus sums up Luther's notion as follows: "faith is the art of comprehending God in his opposite. . . ."[187] For Marx, Man's consciousness of a cruel and exploitative history becomes fully developed and is transcended when it "affirms its opposite."[188] The call for revolution in the Communist Manifesto was a call to invert historical development as it had proceeded thus far (_umgekehrten Verhältnis zur geschichtlichen Entwicklung_).[189]

There are characteristic words in both instances that capture this apocalyptic resolution, that is the abrupt leap or inversion where the underlying contradiction is suspended and transformed into its opposite. For Marx, communism, as man's total salvation, will happen " 'all at once' and simultaneously. . ." (_auf einmal_).[190] One of Marx's favourite words is _Umschlag_, "the turn into its opposite."[191] He also refers to "_dieser dialektische Umschlag_" - "the dialectical reversal."[192] For Luther the characteristic word to which we have already referred is _umbkeren_--to overturn or invert: "Our Lord God can immediately overturn things despite the Emperor or the Pope." (_Unser Herr Gott kans bald umbkeren trotz Keiser, Bapst_).[193]

Summing up the two positions, we see that out of Luther's battle with the Catholic church where, as we recall, "everything has been completely turned up-side-down," there emerged the theology of the cross centered on God's power as the _negativa essentia_, the power of inversion. Marx in turn regarded capitalism as "an enchanted, perverted [read 'inverted'], topsy-turvy world" (_die verzauberte, verkehrte und auf den Kopf gestellte Welt_),[194] but communism "overturns the basis of all earlier relations of production and exchange."[195]

Thus Luther's theology of negative transcendence reappears more than three centuries later (via the intermediation of Hegel) in the guise of the politics of negative transcendence. For Marx, emancipation will come about as the result of "the formation of a class with radical chains. . . a class that is the dissolution of all classes, a sphere of society having a universal character because of its universal suffering. . . because. . . unqualified wrong is perpetrated on it. . . .[196] The proletariat already embodies "the negative result of society," and (in a characteristic reversal) "merely elevates into a principle of society what society had advanced as the principle of the proletariat," namely, "the negation of private property."[197]

As the notion emerges in the fully developed version of Capital, Marx maintains that "capitalist production begets, with the inexorability of a law of Nature, its own negation. It is the negation of negation."[198] Further, "it is evident that the laws of appropriation or of private property. . . become by their own inner and inexorable dialectic changed into their very opposite."[199]

Luther had noted that "the more we preach, the viler and more ungrateful the world becomes. It seems to me that the world will not last much longer."

Marx wrote to Kugelmann in 1857: "I am working like mad all through the night at putting my economic studies together so that I may at least have the outlines clear before the deluge comes."

2.3 Marx's Semantics

It is not surprising that Marx fell back now and then on the phrases and similies of Protestant rhetoric. These phrases had themselves filtered into conventional German speech, and often an awareness of their origins had been lost. Marx, moreover, borrowed, as he had stated, Hegelian "modes of expression,"[200] and Hegel was a professed Lutheran. Some of these words and expressions went to the heart of Marx's structure of thought. But at other times, Marx deliberately turned his sharp wit to good account with an ironic use of religious phraseology.

We cannot pretend here to a comprehensive discussion of Marx's semantics, but we can offer some suggestive notions of the influence of the Lutheran and Hegelian vocabulary. Hegel had attempted to adapt some of his philosophical concepts from their initial religious expression in Luther, such as the terms entäusserung and aufheben discussed previously. Marx borrowed many of these terms and adapted them in his own dialectical way. But his semantics were animated throughout by a reliance on antithesis and inversion.

That something is "external" (ausser) is one of Marx's consistent complaints. For example, Marx's complaint about private property is that it is "external to man"--"ausser dem Menschen."[201] This is to be resolved, as we have seen, by the "positive Aufhebung des Privateigentums."[202] We are reminded of Paul's dictum (II Corinthians 4:16): "but though our outward man (ausserlicher Mensch) perish. . . ." In Paul, Luther, Hegel, and Marx, the "outward" must be redeemed in their respective fashions.

What is outward or external is closely linked to a state of alienation. In reference to man's alienation from his own labour, for example, Marx used the phrase fremd[en] und ausser (alien and external). It is the same phrase (via Luther's translation) as Paul's fremd und ausser, his reference to alienation from the commonwealth of Israel.[203]

But there was an important difference as well in Marx's use of the term ausser. For Christian theology and for Hegel, man's entire finite or mortal existence was considered outward or foreign to his inner being.

Marx restricted his own use of the term, in its negative connotations, to what was external or foreign to the human condition in a social or institutional sense. Man's self-realization in the world, his genuine outward expression of himself could be (or should be) a positive event, and he also gave a positive connotation to ausser in words such as Lebensäusserung, the positive expression of life.

Ideally, Marx envisioned the full outward expression of man's talents and his natural endowment as his work and activity in the world. Such expression was indeed what made man, "man," namely "the total universal development of the productive forces of the individual."[204] Marx foresaw "the development of the richness of human nature as an end in itself."[205] Man exists as a member of a species and asserts that existence directly in his activity and in the objects he creates: "he can only express his life in real, sensuous objects." The object is "the direct embodiment of his individuality."[206]

But under capitalism, man was forcibly separated from the objects he produced when they became commodities on the market. This compromised fatefully man's human existence, and it was this connotation of entäusserung (alienation) to which Marx returned again and again. Man's work as the manifestation of his creative life

(Arbeit. . .[als] eigne Lebensäusserung) became subverted as entfremdete entäusserte Arbeit, estranged, alienated labour.[207] Other expressions of this antithesis were given in the contrast between Lebensäusserung,[208] the positive expression of manifestation of life and Lebensentäusserung,[209] the alienation or estrangement of life; between Wesensäusserung,[210] the expression of essential being, and Wesensentäusserung,[211] the alienation of man's essence.

Thus we see the dialectical gyrations of the term Entäusserung whose origins, semantically, in Christ's Incarnation (in Philippians 2:7--entäusserte sich selbst--discussed previously in "Luther's Semantics") shifted from Luther's positive, exalted use of this term (man's divesting himself of his material embodiment and his "works"), to Hegel's ambiguous use (man's coming-to-be within an alienated, objective existence), to Marx's entirely negative use (man's forcible separation or dispossession from his own artifacts).

But the blind spot on religion and religious rhetoric among Marxists was virtually total, and hence the origin of this term was lost. One of the greatest Marxian scholars, Georg Lukacs, in his work on The Young Hegel, devotes an entire chapter to the concept of entäusserung and offers a myopic conclusion:

In themselves there is nothing novel about the terms Entäusserung and Entfremdung. They are simply German translations of the English word "alienation". This was used in works on economic theory. . . . Philosophically, the term Entäusserung was first used, to the best of my knowledge, by Fichte. . . .[212]

Aufheben, cited above in regard to annulling the "outwardness" of private property, is a frequently used expression borrowed from Hegel.[213] It is often translated as "supersede" or "transcend" and became one of the central words of the Marxian vocabulary. Marx uses the term in regard to transcending private property,[214] transcending self-estrangement (Selbstentfremdung),[215] and transcending alienation (Entäusserung).[216] A basic polarity is built into the word itself, and the two connotations of "annul" or "abolish" on the one hand, and "elevate" or "preserve" on the other, run to the heart of Marx's conception of the revolutionary process. But the inner significance of Aufheben is summed up by Marx in a characteristic phrase cited previously, namely that it "affirms its opposite" (sein Gegenteil bestätigt).[217] This is entirely consistent with Hegel's general use of this term. We have commented previously on its Lutheran origins (see "Luther's Semantics") and on Hegel's explicit recognition that one of the roots of this term, as he used it, led back to Jesus' exaltation.

Because of the reliance on antithesis in the structure of his argument, Marx's style and vocabulary were often animated by the same polar tension found in Luther's and Paul's rhetoric, although this is sometimes lost in the English translation. Marx adopted this contrast of opposites as a stylistic device to point to the characteristic contradictions of capitalism or to their resolution. One such contrast can be seen in a chapter heading from the *Grundrisse*: "The realization process [*Verwirklichungsprozess*] of labour [is] at the same time its de-realization process" (*Entwirklichungsprozess*).[218] In the *E.P.M.* we have: "With the *increasing value* [*Verwertung*] of the world of things proceeds in direct proportion the devaluation [*Entwertung*] of the world of men."[219] Marx refers in *Capital* to the contradiction "between the personification of objects and the representation of persons by things" (*von Personifizierung der Sache und Versachlichung der Personen*).[220] In *The German Ideology* he refers to "replacing the domination of circumstances and of chance over individuals by the domination of individuals over chance and circumstances."[221] In the *Grundrisse*, "the violent destruction of capital. . . [is] a condition of its self-preservation."[222]

Religious metaphors abound in Marx. The analogy with Jesus' role as mediator (Hebrews 8:6) recurs from time to time. In his essay "On the Jewish Question" Marx argues:

> The state is the intermediary [*Mittler*] between man and man's freedom. Just as Christ is the intermediary [*Mittler*] to whom man transfers the burden of all his divinity, all his *religious constraint*, so the state is the intermediary to whom man transfers all his non-divinity and all his human unconstraint.[223]

But Marx had no inhibitions about using religious rhetoric and vocabulary in a satirical fashion, often with telling effect. Capital, land, and labour, the three basic factors of production he regarded as an "economic trinity."[224] Labour as embodied in instruments and materials of production makes these into "the body of its soul and thereby resurrects them from the dead."[225] Marx spoke of capital's "very mystic nature" since it seemingly absorbs all of labour's social powers of production.[226] Regarding Hegel's idealized view of the bureaucracy within his ideal state, Marx comments that the prerequisite examination for civil servants is "the bureaucratic baptism of knowledge. . . ."[227]

But these satirical devices are merely incidental to the general argument. I have attempted to show how some of the central terms of the Marxian vocabulary had been adapted, via Hegel, from Luther's original formulations.

The end result was a striking rhetorical similarity of structure and semantics in Luther and Marx amidst their profound substantive differences. Hence a partisan preoccupation with their differences alone hardly tells the full story. When Marx declared that "the worker becomes a slave of his object" (*wird der Arbeiter also ein Knecht seines Gegenstandes*),[228] a Lutheran theologian might have found his own reasons for full agreement with him. But the real basis of this agreement remained hidden.

3. Conclusion

Paul, in one of his letters to Timothy, warned against those who dealt only with the forms of godliness but stayed away from its substance. This essay on the apocalyptic tradition has been devoted to a neglect of that warning.

I cite in my own defence Meister Eckhart, who once stated that the Godhead "is free of all names and void of all forms. . . and no man can in any wise behold it." If Meister Eckhart is right, what are we to make of that *forma mentis*, that extraordinarily persistent cast of mind of the apocalyptic tradition? What significance can be ascribed to the unity of its theological and political expression such as in Luther and Marx? Whence the source of its millennial appeal?

Some may regard this very question itself as presumptuous and any answer that is offered even more so. Answers, moreover, may be addressed to many different levels of this issue. But restricting myself as I do to the rhetorical structure--the rhetoric of transfiguration--I am tempted to read this dramatic and long-standing record of the phenomenology of the Western mind as a portrait of the inner self.

Others, no doubt, will see many things of greater and more enduring significance. But I cannot overburden the question of rhetoric. It is neither more nor less than the most direct expression we have of that elusive and barely discernible realm of the inner self. Hegel preferred to call his subject the phenomenology of mind or spirit; others may prefer the expression "the structure of consciousness."

Whatever name we give to our subject, the conclusions we may draw at this stage must be considered tentative, referring rather to a silhouette than to a portrait of the self in the Western apocalyptic tradition.

First there is the pervasive sense of the dual nature of man which is portrayed within the recurrent theme of lordship and bondage. This dualism dates back to biblical religion. Paul, following Christ, wished to "create the two in himself into one new man" (Ephesians 2:15). Luther pursued this theme and concluded in regard to Christ's dual nature that: "*Duplex quidem est natura, sed persona non est divisa*"--"Though his nature may be two-fold, his person is not divided."[229] Man, for Luther, was an inverse image of Christ. Hegel's restatement of the Lutheran faith concluded that "God is thus in spirit alone. He is not a beyond but the truest reality of the individual."[230] Thus Hegel set as his aim "the transition from faith to knowledge. . . the transfiguration of faith in philosophy."[231] Out of such a transfiguration there emerged Hegel's insights into the phenomenology of mind and the dualism in consciousness: "consciousness contains a double element within itself," and he spoke of the "duplication of self-consciousness within its unity."[232]

This dualism was never benign but always existed in conflict, in antithesis. Hegel pointed to the universal dimensions of this antithesis in his parable of lordship and bondage. Marx relocated this antithesis in history and society, in capital and labour, rather than within the individual's consciousness. But he reverted to man's consciousness once more, man's revolutionary consciousness in its dialectical structure, as the road to salvation. The "Christian dialectic" was thus bypassed but the mandate ascribed to the communist consciousness bore its own similarity to Luther's credo.

This sense of an existential dualism of man's condition is both cosmic in nature and, at the same time, the deepest image of the self. But this very tension initiates, or is open to, a characteristic process of resolution. The bridge between these two selves has a name, and, indeed, the most powerful common intuition that pervades both the religious and political expression of the apocalyptic tradition is the certainty of inversion. This is the face which "hope" presents to us. It is the *sine qua non* of our present tomorrows and runs to the heart of every call for "liberation." The moral insights by which we live, such as freedom and equality, emerge in an intimate relation with the process of "becoming"; emerge, as we have seen, from our exodus from 'bondage' through inversion.

The rhetoric of transfiguration reveals as well the intimate link between domination and oppression on the one side and perfect community on the other. The process of inversion is the key to the way in which salvation is prefigured in oppression. "The promised land" is prefigured in the bondage to Pharaoh in Egypt; eternal life is prefigured in the bondage to the body and to death; socialism is prefigured in the bondage to private property. The oppression is in every case real and tangible, but when, as Marx stated, the oppression is made more burdensome still, it acquires hidden wings. The apocalyptic drama is launched to its foregone conclusion.

Seen from a theological perspective, man finds his perfection in community as an inverse image of God. Seen from a political perspective--in the apocalyptic tradition--man finds himself writ large in that community which is a projection of a totally reconciled self in perfect freedom and equality with his fellows.

Hence perfect community comes to us in both its universal and intimately personal dimensions. This vision of the kingdom--whether it be called socialism or the realm of God--unites the attributes of self and community in an indissoluble bond. That may be its greatest strength.

But for those who march to the promise of "Thy kingdom come. . . on earth as it is in heaven," this is also its greatest weakness. No sophisticated acquaintance with politics or society is needed to realize the immense vulnerability of such a vision. There is no human society where a total reconciliation exists between the goals of individual and community, where all conflict has been lifted, where power has vanished, and where absolute freedom and equality have been realized. Nor do I believe there can be such a human community, particularly in the nether-world of the modern technoligical society. Yet it sometimes seems that the passionate pursuit of this community grows inversely as the prospect of its realization recedes.

This sets the stage for the central dilemma in the present encounter between the apocalyptic tradition and modern society. In the renaissance today of political theology, and in the numerous new movements of "liberation"--blacks, women, the poor, the third world and so on--we have a testament to the ongoing power of that tradition. The surge to visibility of "domination and oppression" and the greater or lesser thrust to "perfect community" evoke primordial echoes. A new multitude of contemporary step-children of the apocalyptic tradition strive once more to transform oppressive slavery to an exalted status and hence to their own version of 'lordship' or power.

Within the last decade and a half we have had a further global encounter between the apocalyptic tradition in its radical variants and the complex, implacable "otherness" of man embodied in his globe-girdling technology and in the anonymous tyranny of his bureaucracies. The achievements of modernity have become its own oppression, and "liberation" now has a global echo.

Hence the problem of lordship and bondage first posed by Hegel in his own opaque and obscure fashion comes into its own today. There are more contenders than ever for the role of leading actor, but the script remains virtually the same.

But how are we to respond to these modern claims on our moral sensibilities and to these imperatives for institutional change? These claims are far from absolute, but have they become in their numerous expressions a trivialization of the apocalyptic tradition? Or have we reached instead a moral stalemate by our refusal to recognize these contemporary step-children of this tradition?

I do not address myself here to a direct reply to these questions. Instead I have introduced a prior question which seems to provide an avenue for setting these claims in the context of contemporary realities. The central issue, as I see it, is that of _consciousness and society_.

The exploration of this theme should begin with an examination of the "medium" of transmission of the "new apocalyptics." The faithful revival of the rhetoric of transfiguration is not _ipso facto_ a claim to social recognition, however resonant its validation in the chambers of consciousness. Too many inspired forays and radical visions have come to nought recently against the ultimate realities of modern society. We must distinguish, if we can, between the compelling but divergent claims of consciousness and content.

At the present juncture of modernity and the apocalyptic tradition, at least two routes lie open to us. For the first group, rooted in orthodoxy, the secularization of biblical religion appears as the Achilles heel of modernity. The modern descendants of that religion, proclaiming liberty, equality, and community in the patois of the left, are thus to be disinherited. The temporal priority of Revelation is asserted, while the moral claim of history itself is denied. A new pursuit is undertaken for a forgotten grammar to forestall the awkwardness of modern vulgarizations. It is as if an ancient citadel could yet be rendered impregnable with a wider and deeper moat.

For the second group the dilemma is more complex. An explicit recognition of the role which a dual consciousness has played in the transmission of the apocalyptic drama need not deny the universal significance of the moral codes that have emerged. But the ineluctable constrainsts of modern society put at risk the pristine integrity of the apocalyptic vision. The realities of power, of conflict; the divergence of goals between individuals, groups and communities; the weighing in some moral balance of the ubiquitous and increasingly strident claims of domination and oppression; all carry with them a moral challenge whose outcome cannot entirely be foreseen.

The imperative of a totally reconciled inner consciousness, projected as the vision of a perfect kingdom on earth, is unattainable. But in that self-distancing that is still open to us from a conscious exploration and awareness of the inner self, Hegel could promise the message of that which is _aufgehoben_, annulled and yet preserved and transcended. In Jesus' exaltation, Hegel foresaw the continuity of man's finitude transcended by the triumph of his spirit.

This turn to the structure of consciousness, and the assessment of the self and the world as the realm of inversion, does not, however, come easily. As Paul stated, "we see through a glass darkly. . . ." Faith is "the evidence of things not seen."

Marx, as one of the chief apostles of modernity, echoed Paul's notion in a more cumbersome way. Ideology, he claimed, comes to us as if it were filtered through a _camera obscura_, a darkroom, and thus appears upside-down, standing on its head. This is an inherent in the "historical life-process as the inversion of objects on the retina. . . (in) their physical life-process."[233]

But Luther may have put it best in the name of faith, hope, and a profound awareness of the human condition: Those things that are to be believed are hidden from us. "It cannot be hidden any more deeply than when it appears to be the exact opposite of what we see, sense and experience."[234]

NOTES

[1]This paper is an interim and partial summary of a research project that has been made possible through the generosity of The Walter and Duncan Gordon Foundation.

Many friends have offered helpful comments but I must defer acknowledgements till my forthcoming book on this subject. Suffice it here to mention my debt to the research assistants who have participated at various stages of this project: Ben Agger, Thomas Ledebur, Ray Morrow, James Reimer, Gernot Wieland, and Almos Tassonyi.

[2]Letter to Tholuck, 1826: "Ich bin ein Lutheraner und durch Philosophie ebenso ganz im Luthertum befestigt. . . es ist ein höherer Geist darin als nur solcher menschlichen Tradition." Cited in Heinrich Bornkamm, Luther im Spiegel der deutschen Geistesgeschichte (2nd. ed.; Göttingen: Vandenhoeck & Ruprecht, 1955), 235.

Note as well Hegel's statements: "I am a Lutheran and will stay the same," and that in Protestantism, "the subjective religious principle has been separated from Philosophy, and it is only in Philosophy that it has arisen in its true form again." Hegel's Lectures on The History of Philosophy, trans. E. S. Haldane and F. H. Simpson (London: Routledge and Kegan Paul, 1896; reprinted 1955); Vol. 1, p. 73, and Vol. 3, p. 152 respectively. This work will be referred to subsequently as Hist. Phil.

We will also cite the following works by Hegel: The Philosophy of History, trans. by J. Sibree (New York: Dover Publications, 1956). This will be referred to subsequently as Phil. Hist. The Phenomenology of Mind, trans. J. B. Baillie (New York: Harper Torchbooks, 1967). This work will be referred to subsequently as Phen. The German edition we will cite is Phänomenologie des Geistes (Frankfurt: Suhrkamp Verlag, 3, 1970). Further references to this edition will be noted as Phän. Lectures on the Philosophy of Religion, trans. E. B. Speirs and J. B. Sanderson (London: Kegan Paul, Trench, Trübner, 1895). This work will be referred to subsequently as Phil. Rel. Werke is the abbreviation used here for the second German edition of Hegel's work published by Duncker und Humblot (Berlin, 1840-47).

[3]Hist. Phil. 3, 146-147. Compare as well: "This is the essence of the Reformation: Man is in his very nature destined to be free." Phil. Hist., 417.

[4]"Wir die religiöse Vorstellung in Gedanken fassen." Werke 9, 25; cf. Phil. Hist., 20.

[5]There will be a fuller treatment of the Lutheran Hegel in my forthcoming book tentatively entitled Perpetual Apocalypse: Hegel, Luther, Marx.

[6]Phen., 229-240, or 218-267 for the more extended version.

[7]The original title of Hegel's major work which was later dropped was Erfahrung des Bewusstseins, The Experience of Consciousness, cf. Phän., 596. Both the religious genesis and the pattern of adaptation of Hegel's thought can be illustrated in the subsequent title Phänomenologie des Geistes, The Phenomenology of Mind or

Spirit. It is suggestive of an almost identical phrase in I Corinthians 12:7, phanerosis tou pneumatos, "the manifestation of the Spirit."

The "Spirit" of the New Testament became Hegel's own "Spirit" (Geist). Hegel states that "The nature of God as pure Spirit, (reiner Geist) is manifested to man in the Christian Religion." (Phil. Hist., p. 323). But Spirit was now to become aware of itself as "self-consciousness" (Hist. Phil. 3, 22). Such a Spirit already rests in man and man "cannot know anything which does not rest in him" (Hist. Phil. 3, 14). Compare with Romans 1:19: "Because that which may be known of God is manifest (phaneron) in them (i.e. men); for God manifested (ephanerosen) it to them."

Hegel adds: "the real attestation of the Divinity of Christ is the witness of one's own Spirit--not Miracles; for only Spirit recognizes Spirit" (Phil. Hist., 326). Compare Romans 8:16, "The Spirit itself beareth witness with our spirit, that we are the children of God."

The similarity of the above two quotations is borne out in the German. Hegel's phrase "the witness of one's own Spirit" is in the original das Zeugniss des eigenen Geistes (Werke 9, 396). The Luther bible translates Romans 8:16 as Der Geist selbst gibt Zeugniss unserm Geist. . . (Die Bibel, Württembergische Bibelanstalt, Stuttgart, 1968).

Hegel maintains that this is the meaning of Luther's work: "This is the Lutheran faith. . . God is thus in spirit alone, He is not a beyond but the truest reality of the individual." Hist. Phil. 3, 159.

The above comment is not to be regarded as an exhaustive treatment of Hegel's use of the term "spirit." We should also point to Hegel's debt to Kant for the term "phenomenology" as well as his differences with Kant on whether finite knowledge is "the fixed and ultimate standpoint" (cf. Hist. Phil. 3, 427).

[8]Martin Heidegger, Hegel's Concept of Experience (New York: Harper and Row, 1970), cf. 126-129ff.

[9]Phen., 131ff.

[10]For the reference to circuits, cf. Hegel Phen., 224, Phän., 142 for Kreislauf; also Phen., 221, Phän., 140 for Kreis.

[11]In the Old Testament, the special status of slavery to Yahweh is the basis for the remission of debt bondage. After seven years, a "Hebrew servant" (eved ivri) shall go free (lachof'shi, Exod. 21:2), and every fiftieth year, the jubilee year, "ye shall. . . proclaim liberty (d'ror) throughout all the land unto all the inhabitants thereof" (Lev. 25:10). Equality in the Old Testament is a more complex subject and must be bypassed here.

In the New Testament, in their exalted bondage to Christ, Christians are "free. . . as the servants of God" (os eleutheroi. . . os theou douloi) (I Pet. 2:16). Paul adds: "likewise also he that is called, being free, is Christ's servant" (I Cor. 7:22). The basis of equality lies in the spiritual unity with Christ rendered in the well-known passage: "There is neither Jew nor Greek, there is neither bond nor free. . . "(Gal. 3:28). Equality emerges explicitly, as we shall see, in Luther and in Marx.

[12]Cf. _Phen._, 233-234. Further references will be made to the corresponding Lutheran and Hegelian notions of negation and inversion below.

[13]J. J. Pelikan and H. T. Lehmann, Luther's Works: _American Edition_ (St. Louis: Concordia Publishing House and Philadelphia, Fortress Press, 1955) 31, 344. This edition will be cited subsequently as _L W_ with the first number that of the volume and the second, the page.

The German edition of Luther's works used here is _D. Martin Luthers Werke, Kritische Gesammtausgabe_, Weimar, 1883--This edition will be cited as _W A_ . Luther's spelling is retained in the original, which often differs significantly from modern German.

[14]_L W_ 31, 344; _W A_ 7, 21.

[15]Ibid. Luther cites as well Paul's well-known dictum: "Though our outward man perish, yet the inward man is renewed day by day" (II Cor. 4:16).

[16]_W A_ 56, 366. The comment is on Rom. 8:15.

[17]_W A_ 40, II, 423; cf. further references to antithesis: ibid. 409, 414; 374 for "_contradictoribus_."

[18]"Si Scripturas per contentionem loqui concedis. . ." _W A_ 18. 779. Cited in H. R. Schmitz, "Progrès social et changement révolutionnaire, Dialectique et révolution." Revue Thomiste (1974). I am substantially indebted to this article devoted to the continuity of the dialectic in Luther, Hegel, and Marx. Schmitz discussed at length the work of Enrico de Negri, _La Teologia di Lutero, Revelazione e Dialettica_ (La Nuova Italia, Firenze, 1967). I have drawn freely on this excellent study which links the Lutheran and Hegelian dialectic.

A leading Lutheran scholar, Gerhard Ebeling puts the matter as follows: "Luther's thought always contains an antithesis, tension between strongly opposed but related polarities. . . ." Gerhard Ebeling, _Luther: An Introduction to his Thought_, trans. R. A. Wilson (Fortress Press, Philadelphia: 1970). 25.

[19]_W A_ 7, 27.

[20]_L W_ 31, 356; _W A_ 7, 29.

[21]_L W_ 31, 363.

[22]_L W_ 31, 366.

[23]The Latin text reads: _debet tamen rursus se exinanire hac in libertate_ (_W A_ 7, 65). What is missing from the English translation is the adverb _rursus_, derived from _revorsus_ or _reversus_, i.e. to turn back or return. This is reiterated by the word _widderumb_ in the German version of the essay where the test reads: _Und ob er nu gantz_

frey ist, sich widderumb williglich eynen diener machen seynem nehsten zu helffenn (W A 7, 35)--"And while he is now entirely free, he willingly makes himself once more into a servant in order to help his neighbour."

This usage of rursus is reiterated in a somewhat similar context in "On the Bondage of the Will." Luther states: "Si autem fortior superveniat et illo victo nos rapiat in spolium suum, rursus per spiritum eius servi et capitivi sumus (quae temen regia libertas est)." (W A 18, 635). "But if a Stronger One [Christ] comes who overcomes him [Satan] and takes us as His spoil, then through his Spirit we are again slaves and captives--though this is royal freedom." E. Gordon Rupp, et al., editors and translators, Luther and Erasmus: Free Will and Salvation (Philadelphia: The Westminster Press, 1969), 140, my italics. This edition will be referred to subsequently as "Rupp."

Luther inverts the term for servant and slave, Knecht, in precisely the same way as the equivalent eved in the Old Testament and doulos in the New Testament mentioned earlier. Knecht is in fact Luther's translation for both the Hebrew and Greek terms.

[24] L W 31, 367, 356.

[25] L W 31, 355.

[26] W A 7, 27; L W 31, 354.

[27] L W 31, 371, 372.

[28] L W 25, 474; W A 56, 481.

[29] W A 7, 50; L W 31, 344.

[30] W A, Tischreden 3, 36.

[31] L W 31, 367, 368.

[32] W A 18, 327.

[33] W A 7, 337: "nit eyn weszen sunderen ein werden, . . . wyr seyns noch nit, wyr werdens aber."

[34] L W 31, 349, 348.

[35] L W 31, 351. Luther's reference is to Eph. 5: 31-32.

[36] W A 7, 25. Cf. also der wunderbarlich wechsel, the wondrous exchange, W A 10, III, 356 (cf. p.53, v. 101) the gnediger wechsell, the gracious exchange, W A 2, 749; the admirabili commertio, the admirable exchange, W A 5, 608.

[37] L W 31, 351.

[38] *W A* 2, 564.

[39] W A 17, II, 203. Cited in Paul Althaus, *The Theology of Martin Luther*, trans. R. C. Schultz (Philadelphia: Fortress Press, 1966), 32. The operative phrase in Luther's German is *Drumb mus sichs von solchem fülen keren*. . . .

[40] *L W* 45, 91; *W A* 11, 251.

[41] Cf. *L W* 13, 247-248--the spiritual kingdom "is hidden to eyes and senses." Cf. also *L W* 28, 125; *L W* 13, 254. "Already exists in this world," see *L W* 12, 103; also "extended throughout the world," *L W* 37, 282.

[42] *L W* 28, 129; *W A* 36, 575.

[43] *L W* 28, 125; *W A* 36, 570-71.

[44] *L W* 28, 124; *W A* 36, 568.

[45] *L W* 28, 128.

[46] *W A* 20, 308.

[47] *W A* 1, 269. Cf. also "*wir alle gleich werden sein*," *W A* 36, 574; *W A* 11, 270; *L W* 45, 117.

[48] *L W* 46, 39.

[49] *L W* 13, 287.

[50] *L W* 25, 381; *Quia vult, quod vult Deus*, *W A* 56, 391. Cf. also "so that we readily will and do what he wills," Rupp, 140; *ut velimus et faciamus lubentes quae ipse velit*, *W A* 18, 635.

[51] *L W* 31, 355.

[52] *L W* 33, 144; *W A* 18, 688; for "*Infirmitate (i.e. impotentia)*," *W A* 56, 366.

[53] *L W* 12, 120-121.

[54] *L W* 29, 117.

[55] *L W* 22, 495.

[56] *W A* 17, II, 241.

[57]*W A* 47, 86: "Und wiewol es wahr ist, das es zwej unterschiedliche dieng sien, der Schopffer und die Creatur. . . so sind si alhier vereiniget."

[58]*W A* *Tischreden* 6, 67, 69.

[59]*W A* 39, 98.

[60]*L W* 22, 493.

[61]Cited in Paul Althaus, *Theology*, 27-28.

[62]Cf. Luther's Vorlesung über den Römerbrief 1515-1516, II (Leipzig: Johannes Ficker, 1908), 172-173. Cited in E. de Negri, *La Teologia di Lutero*, 297. This particular passage (p. 172) reads: "Sed quia ex carne et spiritu idem unus homo constat totalis, ideo toti homini tribuit utraque contraria, que ex contrariis sui partibus veniunt. Sic enim fit communio ideomatum, quod idem homo est spiritualis et carnalis, iustus et peccator, bonus et malus." "But, because one and the same complete man consists of body and spirit, he attributes, for that reason, both opposites which arise from a man's opposite parts to the entire man. For thus a communication (i.e. mutual sharing) of properties comes about, namely that the same man is spiritual and carnal, righteous and sinful, good and evil."

[63]"Afflicta conscientia" is in *W A* 40, 42, translated as "afflicted conscience" in *L W* 26, 5. This latter volume notes (p. 10 n. 4): "Here, as in some other passages in Luther's writings, the Latin word *conscientia* has the meaning 'consciousness' rather than the more specific meaning 'conscience'." This is confirmed in Ph. Dietz, *Wörterbuch zu Dr. Martin Luthers Deutschen Schriften II* (Hildesheim: Georg Olms Verlagsbuchhandlung, Zweite unveranderte Auflage, 1961), 119. For *Gewissen* (*conscientia*) it indicates "dem älteren Sprachgebrauch entsprechend im simme von kenntniss, Bewusstsein." This is the sense in which Hegel takes up the term.

For *trawrigkeit des gewissens* see *W A* 41, 119. Cf. also *erschrockenen gewissen*, the terrified conscience, *W A* 36, 368 and *in istis conscientiae pavoribus*, *W A* 40, 522, translated as "in these terrors of conscience," *L W* 26, 339; *perterrefactae et desperabundae conscientiae*, the terrified and desperate conscience, and the *angustiam conscientiae*, the anguished conscience, *W A* 40, I, 483; *pusillanimis et infirma conscientia*, the timid and weak conscience, *W A* 5, 170.

For Hegel's "unhappy consciousness," cf. *Phen.*, 251; *Phan.*, 163.

[64]Cf. Paul Althaus, *Theology*, 25-34.

[65]*W A* 5, 176.

[66]*L W* 31, 224; *W A* 1, 612.

[67] L W 31, 255.

[68] L W 31, 225. Cf. also: "For in this way we conform ourselves to God, who does not regard or consider anthing in us as good. And in this way we are already good as long as we recognize nothing as good except God's good and our own good as evil. . . ." L W 25, 383.

[69] L W 31, 225.

[70] L W 31, 225; W A 1, 613.

[71] Karl Marx Frühe Schriften, ed. H. J. Li ber and P. Furth, I (Stuttgart: Cotte Verlag, 1962), 636. Further references to this edition will be given as Frühe Schriften referring to either Vol. I published in 1962 or Vol. II published in 1971.

[72] L W 25, 383; "Nec potest possideri aut attingi nisi negatis omnibus affirmativis nostris," WA 56, 393.

[73] W A 45, 222.

[74] L W 5, 227; "in illa. . . nullitate et nihilitudine Deus ostendit suam virtutem," W A 43, 585. Cf. also ". . . in deum. . . in sui nihilum," W A 5, 168; "the Lord of all who is the same as nothing, that is the lowest. . .," L W 5, 219; the latter in the original is "Dominum omnium, qui idem et nihili, id est, infimus est," W A 43, 579.

[75] Paul Althaus, Die Theologie Martin Luthers, Gütersloher Verlagshaus, Gerd Mohn, Gütersloh, 1962, 41.

[76] Phän., 152; Phen., 236.

[77] Phen., 263; Phän., 173.

[78] Phen., 225; Phän., 143. Cf. also "absolute negativity," Phen., 233, 237; "the absolute negation of this existence," Phen. 246; "absolute negation," Phen., 226.

[79] W A 17, II, 242.

[80] L W 31, 55.

[81] Rupp, 37; ut isto modo humiliati et in nihilum redacti, salvi fiant. W A 18, 633.

[82] W A 1, 29.

[83] L W 37, 95.

[84]L W 37, 135-137; W A 23, 261.

[85]Phen., 224. The upper circuit of lordship, Hegel calls "this other life" (ibid.) namely "pure self-consciousness" (Phen., 234), and Mind or Spirit (Geist), Phen., 227; Phän., 145. The characteristic movement on this latter circuit is absolute negation or total inversion. Hegel's schema of lordship and bondage unfolds in the way that it is portrayed here in our diagram but we must bypass a detailed exposition.

[86]L W 5, 220.

[87]W A 40, III, 55; cited in Paul Althaus, trans., Theology, 56, n. 38.

[88]L W 25, 382; W A 56, 392.

[89]W A 5, 168.

[90]W A 1, 269. He added as synonyms: (hat sich) gantz selber verringert, Christ diminished or reduced himself, and er hat abgelegt die gestalt Gottes, he laid aside or took off God's image.

[91]Various synonyms after 1522 included sich verzigen, (the modern German is verzichten, to renounce or waive--the synonym given in the W A for the modern Luther translation, entäussert, W A 17, II, 237, no. 1); sich enthalten, to refrain or abstain from; sich entledigen, von sich legen, or ablegen, to lay aside, to lay away from oneself, to take off. Cf. W A 17, II, 241-245.

[92]W A 17, II, 245.

[93]W A 17, II, 241.

[94]Hegel states that in Christ, "the essence of man [is] acknowledged to be Spirit, and the fact proclaimed that only by stripping himself of his finiteness and surrendering himself to pure self-consciousness, does he attain the truth" (Phil. Hist., 328). "Stripping himself of his finiteness" is in Hegel's original "sich seiner Endlichkeit entaussert" (Werke 9, 399). Luther's use of eussern for Christ's Incarnation is followed by his use of geeusert for Christ's Crucifixion and exaltation which provides the link with Hegel's usage: "und nun sich gantz geeussert und abgelegt die knechtische gestalt" (W A 17, II, 245), "[Jesus] has now completely emptied himself and laid aside his form of a servant."

For Hegel, the full ambiguity of Luther's usage was embodied in this term. Man's self-realization was through his creative activity, but this very self-embodiment was alienating; it must subsequently be relinquished through a moral or spiritual disengagement from that activity. This ambiguity was built into Helel's use of the verb Entäussern, and was a reflection in the first instance of the Incarnation, and then of the Crucifixion and Ascension as the resolution of the first act. Hegel's thesis on alienation and freedom unfold in this context. Marx's use of this term (borrowed from Hegel) is discussed below.

95 For the first meaning, "abolish," we have the example of I Cor. 15:24. The literal English translation is ". . . whenever he abolishes all rule and all authority and power." Luther renders this as "Wenn er auffheben wird alle herrschaft, und alle oberkeit und Gewalt." (Luther bible of 1546, W A 7, 131). "Abolishes" or "auffheben" is a translation of the Greek katargesei. This usage is reiterated in I Cor. 15:26, Der letzte Feind der auffgehaben wird, ist der Tod, the last enemy that is abolished is death. Cf. also the similar usage by Luther in Rom. 3:31 and Heb. 7:18.

The second sense of "raise up" or "preserve" is illustrated in Luther's translation of I Sam. 2:7,8, "der Herr. . . nidriget und erhohet, er hebt auff den dürfftigen aus dem staub und erhohet den Armen aus dem kot. . . ."--"The Lord. . . bringeth low and lifteth up. He raiseth up the poor out of the dust and lifteth the beggar from the dunghill. . . ." It can be seen that hebt. . . auff is used in apposition to erhöhet, lift up. This latter usage is particularly significant, for erhöhet is the word used by Luther in Phil. 2:9 for Jesus' exaltation after the Resurrection. This likely was at the root of Hegel's use of aufheben as illustrated in the following passage: "Weiter aber ist das sinnliche Daseyn, worin der Geist ist, nur ein vorübergehendes Moment. Christus ist gestorben; nur als gestorben ist er aufgehoben gen Himmel und sitzend zur Rechten Gottes, und nur so ist er Geist." (Werke 9, 395)--"Moreover the sensuous existence in which Spirit is embodied is only a transitional phase. Christ dies; only thus is he Spirit" (Phil. Hist., 325). A similar usage is reiterated in Werke 12, 125, 248 translated in Phil. Rel. 2, 255 and Phil. Rel. 3, 35 respectively.

In Hegelian language, Christ's finitude was both annulled and preserved after his exaltation; that is, his finitude is superseded and appears as a "moment" of God in God.

The following passage by Hegel uses aufheben in its full double meaning and shows its derivation from Christ's exaltation: "Dieser Tod ist ebenso wie die höchste Verendlichung zugleich das Aufheben der natürlichen Endlichkeit, des unmittelbaren Daseyns und der Entäusserung, die Auflösung der Schranke." (Werke 12, 302)--"This death is thus at once finitude in its most extreme form, and at the same time the abolition and absorption of natural finitude, of immediate existence and estrangement, the cancelling of limits." (Phil. Rel. 3, 93).

A striking parallel for this way of thinking is provided by the New Testament's approach to the commandments and to Mosaic law. In Heb. 7:18, the commandments are "annulled" (aufgehoben). The true meaning of this annulment becomes clear in Rom. 3:31: "Do we then make void (heben. . .auf) the law through faith? God forbid: yea, we establish the law." Matthew reiterates the same point: "Think not that I am come to destroy the law, or the prophets: I am not come to destroy but to fulfill." (Mt. 5:17).

This we believe was the religious basis of Hegel's semantics in regard to aufheben. Spirit or consciousness supersedes (i.e. annuls and preserves) finitude. Marx adopted this usage of aufheben from Hegel to refer to stages of economic development as one economic class supersedes the previous one.

A fuller treatment of the evolution of this semantic usage would include the intermediate role of erheben, to raise or lift, used in apposition to erhöhen. Luther translated Is. 52:13 as follows:

"Meinem Knecht wird's gelingen, er wird erhöht und sehr hoch erhaben sein"--"my servant shall prosper, he shall be exalted and lifted up, and shall be very high."

The Deutsches Wörterbuch by J. and W. Grimm comments as follows: "The meaning of erhöhen comes close to that of erheben, but erhöhen cannot be used concretely (in the physical sense) of lifting with hand and arm, of lifting the hand, eye, arm, wing and foot, while conversely erheben can easily be substituted for erhöhen." (J. and W. Grimm, Deutsches Wörterbuch 3 Leipzig: S. Hirzel, 1854-1960, 16 vols. in 32), 851.)

Note also the following comment: "In its meaning aufheben originally corresponds (is identical) to erheben. . . but in many cases only one of the two verbs is usual and linguistic usage has undergone diverse changes." (Alfred Götze et al., eds, Trübners Deutsches Wörterbuch 1, [Berlin: Walter de Gruyter, 1939-1957], 145.

For Hegelian usage of erheben in relation to aufheben we have the following illustration: ". . . sondern der Mensch ist nur insofern Gott, als er die Natürlichkeit und Endlichkeit seines Geistes aufhebt und sich zu Gott erhebt." (Werke 9, 394)--"Man on the contrary, is God only insofar as he annuls the merely Natural and Limited in his Spirit and elevates himself to God." (Phil. Hist., 324)

Aufheben also has a variety of other meanings beside the ones mentioned here including "stop," "arrest," "rescind," "invalidate," and "accuse."

[96] W A 41, 188.

[97] W A 34, II, 317, n.1. See for example kere ich umb and So kere ich stracks umb, W A 45, 223. Cf. also W A 9, 656; W A 8, 5 and 157; W A 6, 47.

[98] Hegel, Werke 12, 303.

[99] Schmitz, "Progres Social. . ." 424.

[100] E. de Negri, La Teologia de Lutero, 289, 290.

[101] W A 2, 127; L W 42, 77. These were frequently used Lutheran words, cf. for example, "die warheit in yhr selb besser ist. . . ." W A 7, 589, "The truth in itself is better. . . ." And "also mustu gewiss sein bei dir selbst, aussgeschlossen all menschen," W A 10, III, 260, "So you must be certain within yourself, exclusive of all others."

[102] W A 39, II, 279.

[103] Karl Marx and Frederick Engels, The German Ideology (Moscow: Progress Publishers, 1964), 275. This will be cited subsequently as G. Id.

Karl Marx, Friedrich Engels Werke 3, (Berlin: Dietz Verlag), 237. This edition of Marx's work will be cited subsequently as M E W.

[104] Karl Marx, Critique of Hegel's 'Philosophy of Right', ed. J. O'Malley (Cambridge: Cambridge University Press, 1970), 131. This

will be cited subsequently as O'Malley. *Frühe Schrifton* I, 488.

105 Karl Marx, *Capital, A Critique of Political Economy*, tras. S. Moore and E. Aveling, ed. F. Engels, (Chicago: C. H. Kerr, 1906, in three volumes, I 93, 86 respectively. This will be referred to subsequently as *Capital*.

106 Karl Marx, *Theories of Surplus-Value*, Part I(Moscow: Foreign Languages Publishing House, 377. The text translates "perversion" on p. 377 and "inversion" on p. 378 for *Verkehrung*. Cf. *M E W* 26, 365-366.Cf. also Marx's characteristic figure of speech in relation to the fetishism of commodities: "It stands on its head" (*Capital* I, 82).

107 *Capital* III, 244, italics in the text. *Es erscheint also in der Konkurrenz alles verkehrt*, M E W 25, 219.

108 Karl Marx and Frederick Engels, *Selected Works* II (Moscow: Foreign Languages Publishing House, in two volumes, 1958), 63. This edition will be cited subsequently as *Selected Works*.

109 O'Malley, 137-138. Note also Marx's and Engels' citation of some references which Hegel makes to Luther in the *History of Philosophy* and in the *Philosophy of Religion* in G. Id., 181.

110 *Karl Marx, Grundrisse, Foundations of the Critique of Political Economy*, trans. Martin Nicolaus (New York: Vontage Books, 1973), 106. The original German edition is *Grundrisse der Kritik der politischen Ökonomie* (Rohentwurf), (Berlin: Dietz Verlag, 1953).

The English edition will be cited subsequently as *Grundrisse* and the German edition as *Grundrisse* (G).

111 O'Malley, 138.

112 *G. Id.*, 161.

113 Karl Marx, Economic and Philosophic Manuscripts of 1844, ed. D. J. Struik, trans. Martin Milligan (New York: International Publishers, 1964), 128. This will be referred to subsequently as *E P M*

114 *E P M*,118; *Frühe Schriften*, I, 574.

115 *E P M*,126; *Frühe Schriften*, I, 584.

116 *E P M*, 132 *Frühe Schriften*, I, 590.

117 *E P M*, 100; *Frühe Schriften*, I, 554.

118 *E P M*, 131, 123, 126.

[119]E P M, 131, 136.

[120]Karl Marx, The Poverty of Philosophy (Moscow: Progress Publishers, 1973), 107. This will be cited as Pov. Phil.

Marx briefly reviews these two stages of economic history in the Communist Manifesto. In the feudal period, property relations were "burst asunder" by the new productive forces. In the second stage, that of "modern bourgeois society," we see "the revolt (der Empörung) of modern productive forces against modern conditions of production" that form the conditions for the rule (Herrschaft) of the bourgeoisie. (Selected Works I, 39; M E W 4, 467).

[121]Grundrisse, 501; Grundrisse (G), 400. Cf. also the scheme of economic development set out in the Grundrisse, 497-503.

[122]Capital I, 82.

[123]My translation, cf. Capital I, 91; M E W 23, 93.

[124]E P M, 132. The structure of this antithesis is repeated at greater length in The Holy Family. Marx states: "Proletariat and wealth are opposites (Gegansätze); as such they form a single whole . . . . The proletariat. . . is compelled as proletariat to abolish itself (sich selbst aufzuheben) and thereby its opposite. . . private property. This is the negative side of the contradiction (Gegensatzes) its restlessness within its very self, dissolved and self-dissolving private property."

"Within this antithesis the private owner is therefore the conservative side, the proletarian, the destructive side. From the former arises the notion of preserving the antithesis, from the latter that of annihilating it." K. Marx and F. Engels, The Holy Family or Critique of Critical Critique (Moscow: Foreign Languages Publishing House, 1956), 51. The German text in M E W 2, 37.)

See also feindlichen Gegensatz von Bourgoiesie und Proletariat, the hostile antithesis between bourgeoisie and proletariat, in the Communist Manifesto, Frühe Schriften II, 858.

[125]E P M, 168.

[126]E P M, 169; Frühe Schriften I, 635.

[127]E P M, 167.

[128]Grundrisse, 831; Grundrisse (G), 715, 716.

[129]O'Malley, 141-142; Frühe Schriften I, 503-504. The text is in italics.

[130]E P M, 118; Frühe Schriften I, 573. Italics in the original.

[131]Selected Works I, 54.

[132] *Frühe Schriften* I, 500.

[133] O'Malley, 140; *Frühe Schriften* I, 501.

[134] *Selected Works* I, 51, 53; *Frühe Schriften* II, 839, 842.

[135] *E P M*, 154.

[136] *E P M*, 134.

[137] *E P M*, 139.

[138] *Grundrisse*, 102.

[139] *G. Id.*, 44.

[140] *E P M*, 119; *Frühe Schriften* I, 574.

[141] *G. Id.*, 91-92; *M E W* 3, 74.

[142] *E P M*, 134; *Frühe Schriften* I, 593.

[143] *E P M*, 132; *Frühe Schriften* I, 590.

[144] *E P M*, 155.

[145] *G. Id.*, 47.

[146] *E P M*, 137.

[147] *E P M*, 138, 144.

[148] *Grundrisse*, 488.

[149] *E P M*, 138; *Frühe Schriften* I, 597.

[150] *Selected Works* I, 51, 53; *Frühe Schriften* II, 839, 842.

[151] O'Malley, 140; *Frühe Schriften* I, 500.

[152] *Phen.*, 256, 234.

[153] *M E W* 4, 182; my translation. The passage is from *The Poverty of Philosophy*:

In the course of its development to replace the old bourgeois society, the working class will establish an association that excludes classes and their antagonism (*Gegensatz*), and there will be no further political power as such; since it is political power that is the official expression of class antagonism within the bourgeois society.

Cf. Pov. Phil., 151. Compare also "the communist revolution abolishes the rule (Herrschaft) of all classes with the classes themselves. . . ." G. Id., 85; M E W 3, 70.

154 Selected Works I, 54. A similar passage in Engels' Socialism, Utopian and Scientific reads as follows:

The proletariat seizes political power and turns the means of production into state property.

But, in doing this, it abolishes itself as proletariat, abolishes all class distinctions and class antagonisms, abolishes also the state as state. . . . When at last it becomes the real representative of the whole of society, it renders itself unnecessary. (Selected Works II, 150)

155 Frühe Schriften II, 843.

156 W A 7, 131.

157 O'Malley, 132.

158 Selected Works I, 363.

159 Grundrisse, 463; Grundrisse (G), 366-367. "Knell to its doom" appears in English in the German text.

160 G. Id., 85.

161 G. Id., 461; M E W 3, 405.

162 G. ID., 43.

163 Selected Works I, 363.

164 O'Malley, 137.

165 O'Malley, 140.

166 W A 40, 438.

167 Christ is described by Luther as "that inexpressible union and unity of the most diverse natures"--"illam ineffabilem coniunctionem, et unitatem diversissimarum naturarum" (L W 5, 218; W A 43, 579); or "For in the same person there are things that are to the highest degree contrary"--sunt enim in eadem persona maxime contraria (W A 5, 219; W A 43, 580). Althaus points out for example, that Deus speculatus (God speculatively conceived) is matched against Deus manifestatus (God made manifest), Deus absolutus (the absolute God) is matched against Deus patrum (God of the fathers). Paul Althaus, Theology, English edition, 23-24; German edition, 34.

[168]E P M, 120; Cf. also Grundrisse, 325.

[169]Grundrisse, 159. In the Grundrisse, Marx also refers to: a "dialectic" between means of production and relations of production (109); between money and commodity "split apart" into use value versus exchange value (881); necessary labour versus surplus labour (340); machines "in antithesis to living labour. . .as power hostile to it" (832). In a different realm Marx refers to "the established contradiction of the state and civil society within the state" (O'Malley, 67).

[170]E P M, 111, 156.

[171]Grundrisse, 488; Grundrisse (G), 387. In Hegel's notion of work the individual also "sacrifices himself" (Phen., 371) but it is in Jesus' Incarnation we will recall, that He "emptied himself" and took the form of a slave, (Phil. 2:7)--a form of self-sacrifice and mortification.

[172]E P M, 126; Frühe Schriften I, 584.

[173]Grundrisse, 454; Grundrisse (G), 358. There are many variations on this theme in the Grundrisse. (The English edition will be designated here as Gr. and the German as Gr. G.) Capital as objectified labour is "the worker's non-objectivity" (Nichtgegenstandlichkeit des Arbeiters, Gr. 512; Gr. G. 412; "the real not-capital is labour," (das wirkliche Nicht-Kapital ist die Arbeit, Gr. 274; Gr. G. 185); "labour as not-capital" (Gr. 288); labour is "the negation of Capital" (Gr. 274); or is "not-property" (Nicht-Eigentum, Gr. 498; Gr. G. 398); the worker's non-being (Nicht-dem-Arbeiter, Gr. G. 716); or labour is "not value. . . as a negativity in relation to itself" (Nicht-Wert. . .sich auf sich beziehende Negativität, Gr. 296; Gr. G. 203).

[174]L W 5, 277; W A 43, 585.

[175]Grundrisse, 281; Grundrisse (G), 192; cf. also Grundrisse, 289, Grundrisse (G), 199-200.

[176]Capital I, 836-837. This last phrase, "the expropriators are expropriated," offers a rhetorical echo of a biblical passage cited by Luther: "Thou hast ascended on high, thou hast led captivity captive. . . ." (Ps. 68:18, repeated by Paul in Eph. 4:8) Luther comments: "That he ascended on high implies, of course that he first descended into hell. . ." (L W 13, 20).

[177]L W 13, 260-261, referring to Is. 54:11 and 62:4.

[178]Selected Works I, 45, 65.

[179]L W 5, 227. It is a comment on II Cor. 12:9.

[180]O'Malley, 134. _Man muss den wirklichen Druck noch drückender machen, indem man ihm das Bewusstsein des Drucks hinzufügt_. . . (_M E W_ 1, 381).

[181]O'Malley, 140.

[182]_L W_ 13, 22-23.

[183]Rupp, 138; "dum in coelum vehit, facit id ad infernum ducendo" (_W A_ 18, 633).

[184]_L W_ 14, 31f., cited in Paul Althaus, _Theology_, English edition, 30.

[185]O'Malley, 140; _Frühe Schriften_ I, 501.

[186]_L W_ 5, 227.

[187]Paul Althaus, _Theology_, English edition, 32.

[188]_E P M_, 158.

[189]_Selected Works_ I, 63; _Frühe Schriften_ II, 855.

[190]_G. Id_., 47; _M E W_ 3, 35.

[191]_Grundrisse_, 674. Cf. Martin Nicolaus' Introduction in the _Grundrisse_, 32. We do not include here the financial or accounting usage of _Umschlag_ meaning "turnover" as used in _Capital_.

[192]_M E W_ 23, 610, n. 23; _Capital_ I, 640, n. 1.

[193]_W A_ 33, 348.

[194]_Capital_ III, 966; _M E W_ 25, 838.

[195]_G. Id_., 86.

[196]O'Malley, 141.

[197]O'Malley, 142.

[198]_Capital_ I, 837.

[199]_Capital_ I, 639.

[200]_Capital_ I, 25.

[201] E P M, 119; Frühe Schriften I, 572.

[202] E P M, 134-135; Frühe Schriften I, 593.

[203] Marx refers to "a man alien to labor and standing outside it" --fremden und ausser ihr stehenden Menschen zu dieser Arbeit (E P M, 116; Frühe Schriften I, 571). Paul's alienation is rendered as "aliens from the commonwealth of Israel and strangers from the covenants of promise"--fremd und ausser der Bürgerschaft Israels und fremd von den Testamenten der Verheissung (Eph. 2:12).

This same phrase is reiterated in a close variant in Capital referring to the alienating conditions of capitalist production as Äusserlichkeit und Entfremdung translated as "alienation and expropriation" (M E W 25, 95; Capital III, 102).

[204] Grundrisse, 515; Grundrisse (G), 415.

[205] Theories of Surplus Value, Part II, (Moscow: Progress Publishers, 1968), 117-118.

[206] E P M, 181, 130.

[207] Grundrisse (G), 366 for the first usage; Frühe Schriften I, 569 and E P M, 115 for the second.

[208] Frühe Schriften I, 578, 597, 598, 600, 605, 635, 650, 659, 662. Cf. Grundrisse, 462; also 470, Grundrisse (G), 374.

[209] Frühe Schriften I, 598, 623.

[210] E P M, 181, 188; Frühe Schriften I, 651, 658.

[211] E P M, 187; Frühe Schriften I, 658. Compare the similar usage in: "The less you are, the less you express your own life (du dein Leben äusserest) the greater is your alienated life. . . (dein entäussertes Leben)" (E P M, 150; Frühe Schriften I, 612).

[212] Georg Lukacs, The Young Hegel, Studies in the Relations between Dialectics and Economics, trans. Rodney Livingstone (London: Merlin Press, 1975), 538.

The reference to the English word "alienation" is misleading since, in its early use in the economic literature, it simply meant "selling." The English political economist Sir James Steuart, whom Marx cited in regard to "alienation," used the term as a straightforward synonym for "selling." Cf. for example Grundrisse, 779; Grundrisse (G), 665.

Marx himself was careful to distinguish in the German between "selling" and the social condition of "alienation" although he linked the two issues closely. In "On the Jewish Question," Marx states that only after Christianity became a developed religion, could Judaism "make alienated man and alienated nature into *alienable*, vendible objects. . . . Selling is the practical aspect of alienation."

The editorial footnote points out the difference in the German text between Veräusserung, "selling," and Entäusserung, "alienation," (Karl Marx, Frederick Engels, Collected Works 3 [New York: International Publishers, 1975], 174. This edition will be referred to subsequently as Collected Works).

Marx's use of the term Entäusserung for the problem of alienation or estrangement under capitalism was derived from Hegel, who adapted it in turn, as I have attempted to show previously, from Luther. But Hegel's usage of the term did not derive from "selling."

[213]Marx acknowledges its Hegelian origins in the E P M: "A peculiar role, therefore, is played by the act of superseding (das Aufheben) in which denial (die Verneinung) and preservation (die Aufbewahrung)--denial and affirmation (die Bejahung)--are bound together" (E P M, 185; Frühe Schriften I, 655).

[214]E P M, 134, 136; Frühe Schriften I, 593, 595; Cf. also 556, 592.

[215]Frühe Schriften I, 590, 593.

[216]Frühe Schriften I, 645, 658, 659.

[217]E P M, 158; Frühe Schriften I, 622.

[218]Grundrisse, 450.

[219]E P M, 107; Frühe Schriften I, 561.

[220]Capital I, 128; M E W 23, 128.

[221]G. Id., 482.

[222]Grundrisse, 749-750.

[223]Collected Works 3, 152; Karl Marx, Die Frühschriften S. Landshut, ed. (Stuttgart: Alfred Kroner Verlag, 1955), 179-180.

[224]Capital III, 947.

[225]Grundrisse, 364.

[226]Capital III, 963.

[227]O'Malley, 51.

[228]E P M, 109, Frühe Schriften I, 563.

[229]W A, 43, 580.

[230] *Hist. Phil.* 3, 159.

[231] *Phil. Rel.* 3, 75, 108.

[232] *Phil. Rel.* 1, 277; *Phen.*, 231; cf. other variations in *Phen.*, 226, 229, 253.

[233] *G. Id.*, 37.

[234] *L W* 13, 22f. Cited in Paul Althaus, English edition, *Theology*, 56.

DISCUSSION

Patrick Kerans

Professor Rotstein's paper has elicited a very warm response from the conference for good reasons. It was lucidly and forthrightly argued. But an even more important reason, in my opinion, was that his chosen topic was central to the underlying theme of this conference. By "chosen topic" I mean, not Marx and Luther, but the structure of rhetoric and, more specifically, the structure of the rhetoric of transfiguration.

Rotstein seemed to apologize for stretching his argument about the relationship between Marx and Luther; there is perhaps a grain of truth in that admission. I shall return to this matter. But I do not think he need apologize for pursuing what might seem a recondite topic, for while few reflect on the relationship between the structures of the human imagination and the structures of society, it is a topical and important problem.

Rotstein is insisting that some fruitful ground common to the biblical tradition and the marxist tradition is the rhetorical structure which he dubs that of transfiguration. I pick that name rather than apocalyptic for reasons which I will develop later. For the moment I would like to elaborate on the importance of Rotstein's topic by constrasting the rhetorical structure he has explicated with the rhetorical structure of the liberal tradition which informs present day Canadian political life.

To have adopted a rhetoric of transfiguration is to have caught a vision of another social order and to have accepted it as valid grounds for a critique of the present order. This alternate vision is, I would argue, a synthesizing device and--with all the dangers involved harped on since the days of Burkhardt--a simplifying device. It enables the one who adopts it to focus sharply on the fundamental issues, to avoid the complications which, in the end, are simply distractions which occupy the time of academics.

To adopt such a synthetic, simplified vision is to court profound difficulties of communicating with those who do not share the vision. Perhaps the clearest account of these difficulties is found in Thomas Kuhn's <u>Structure of Scientific Revolutions</u>. Having developed the notion of paradigm, he asks how one paradigm topples another, and, more generally, on what grounds those who hold a new paradigm communicate with those who hold the old. His crucial contention is that they do not communicate--nor effectively argue with each other--by an appeal to "facts."

> To the historian, at least, it makes little sense to suggest that verification is establishing the agreement of fact with theory. All historically significant theories have agreed with the facts, but only more or less. (p. 146)

When does "less" become "too little"? What becomes the crux is whether those events which were not explained satisfactorily in an earlier paradigm are sufficiently important to warrant abandoning the old paradigm in favour of a new one.

On this view, brute data are not the basis of theory, nor are they the basis on which people arrive at a political consensus. The converse is the case: once people have agreed on what are the pivotal human problems, i,e, what are the important political issues, they can then work out agreement on a basic theoretical framework and, in light of that framework, find consensus concerning facts. As Kuhn puts it, any theory fits the facts, but only ". . . by transforming previously accessible information into facts that, for the preceding paradigm, had not existed at all." (p. 140) By implication, events or information about events get elevated to the status of "fact"--i.e. verification of theory or the basis of political agreement--only after they take on systematic significance within the framework of a theory.

It would be my contention that a transfiguration rhetoric, by focussing on the sharp contrast between its vision of the perfect society and the crucial defects in the present social order, is then able to highlight the salient "facts" concerning human bondage such that it can point to an appropriate political strategy. But the facts it marshals hond no meaning for those who do not share the vision, since these "facts" do not have the same systematic significance for the non-believers. Hence the difficulty of communication.

Historically this enormous difficulty of communicating across the gulf separating those with different synthetic visions paralyzed Europe in the latter sixteenth and seventeenth centuries. There had occurred a breakdown in the earlier religious consensus; in the face of the breakdown, political authorities, in the name of civil peace, saw their duty to be the persecution of dissidents and ultimately the waging of religious wars. It would be my contention that liberal political theory and its pluralist vision were divised to overcome this paralysis.

The historical achievement of the liberal tradition was to devise a new rhetoric ostensibly based on "facts." The liberal had characterized himself as being optimistic in that he has assumed human rationality and based his political structure on that assumption. I would, on the contrary, argue that his assumption of rationality is saying more about his view of social reality than it is about human reason. More exactly, he is asserting that social facts are commensurate with the human mind, such that exhaustive communicability of those facts is assured in political discourse. From my perspective, what this means is that only those social phenomena will be admissible to public discourse which fit within the liberal paradigm and hence encounter no systematic barrier to communicability.

The liberal paradigm is itself a synthetic vision. But it is not a transfigurationist vision. It has had at its heart the consensus that scarcity, as defined within the economic model, is the pivotal human problem. Its epistemological vision is that the cumulative advance of science is pragmatic; its policy approach is incremental, pragmatic. It tends to discount those who subscribe to the need for a transfiguration as idealistic or visionary at best; at worst they are characterized as dangerous because they are inclined to totalitarianism.

Because the liberal insists that the pivotal problem is scarcity, he sees no need for a transfiguration of the present system. He sees the need only for more of what we already have: more productivity, more wealth, more programs, more democracy. In other words, he insists that the only questions which can be meaningfully debated in the public realm are those technical questions which group around the fundamental problem of production. He restricts political discourse to this debate. If ethical questions regarding distribution are to be raised at all, they are subsidiary to the basic technical question of productivity; and the logic of the latter must always govern the logic of the former.

Rotstein's paper, by bringing to center stage the question of a rhetoric of transfiguration, has contributed substantially to the theme of this conference. For surely a conference on political theology is concerned with enriching our political life with the basically ethical and anthropocentric concerns which form the heart of the biblical tradition and its symbols. He has at least implicitly pointed to the fundamental problem which faces those who take seriously the biblical tradition: the very structure of their rhetoric poses a substantive communications gap relative to the mainstream of our culture. The more clearly we express ourselves, the less likely will it be that we are understood. It will be enormously difficult not to be heard as a dangerous visionary.

If Rotstein's paper has, by implication, posed the basic problem for the "political theologian" or--to call us by a better name--the "Christian socialist," does his paper also help us out of the difficulty? Here, I believe, Rotstein has been less helpful. In fact, he seems to give away most of his gains at the end of his paper with a remark like ". . . the ineluctable constraints of modern society put at risk the pristine integrity of the apocalyptic vision."

At the beginning I insisted on reading Rotstein at his best in taking him to have explored the rhetoric of transfiguration. To take his own words too literally, and to read him as really talking only of an apocalyptic vision, is to follow him into the blind alley where we find him at the end of his paper.

From a scholarly, historical point of view, one could say that Rotstein has chosen too narrow a base on which to make his stand. If the biblical tradition is indeed transfigurationist, if the good news is indeed a call to _metanoia_, an apocalyptic understanding of that transfiguration is to be seen as one extreme interpretation, at the far end of a spectrum of interpretations which have held sway during the long history of the biblical tradition. For instance H. Richard Niebuhr, in his classic _Christ and Culture_, delineates five positions a Christian can take with respect to her society. One of these, perhaps in Niebuhr's view the least satisfactory, is not a transfigurationist vision. The other four imply the need for a transfiguration of society; only one is apocalyptic. I might add that Niebuhr does not put Luther among the apocalyptics.

To have adopted an apocalyptic vision implies, I would suggest, more than simply to have a vision of the perfect community. It also implies that one takes one's vision to be a blueprint, easily read at the present moment, of what should be. In other words, the necessity of a painstaking hermeneutic of the present order and its influence on one's interpretation of the perfect order--all this is denied in an apocalyptic vision. Further, the need for strategy and the nee for energetic action towards change are also denied because the perfect order is expected to come all of a sudden in a cataclysmic break from the present order. Usually, then, apocalyptic implies either aloofness or resignation in the face of the present order, though it has on some occasions been the motive force for revolutionary fervor. If we accept this notion, which I think is fairly common coin, then I think it would be generally accepted that Luther was not apocalyptic.

Rotstein's historical, scholarly weakness has, unfortunately, strategic and political implications--which are far more serious for being real. The usual practical implication of an apocalyptic vision is that we can only wait for the Day.

One can read Marx as an apocalyptic: political and cultural arguments are but superstructure; what counts are the basic relationships to the factors of production; they will work themselves out through history until the day when capitalism will collapse, unable any longer to survive the intrinsic contradictions which wrack it; the strategy indicated is anti-reform.

But just as the Christian call for transfiguration can be read in a non-apocalyptic mode, so can the Marxist call for revolution be read in a non-apocalyptic, "reformist" mode, keeping in mind Gorz' distinction between revolutionary reform and what I might call dead-end reform. Indeed, while the apocalyptic brands of Christianity and Marxism might be at odds because they look forward to such different days of wrath, the non-apocalyptic modes are convergent.

Rotstein's paper is at this point again enormously helpful. The pivotal human problem in both visions is bondage, oppression. Each locates the source of the bondage outside of the subject: the marxist in the economic structure; the Christian in sinfulness and morality. To overcome this non-subjective element of bondage, Rotstein points out, there is a substantive inversion. But he also points to a formal inversion of bondage which implies a subjective, cultural element to the bondage. It is around this formal inversion of bondage that the ideological struggle, where the culture and the seriousness and depth of our political life are the stakes, takes place.

It would seem to me that, relative to the first struggle, the Christian needs to adopt the marxian analysis of class struggle and work through, in theological terms, a "political hermeneutic" of sinfulness. But it seems equally important to me that relative to the second, ideological struggle, the wealth of the biblical tradition, in interaction with a materialist understanding of alienation and the struggle towards liberation, can have much to offer. What is at stake is the forging of a "reformist" position--working for the betterment of people's lives, engaging in electoral politics, making no hard and fast rules about who is the true "vanguard"--which is nonetheless relentlessly revolutionary. The difficulty is deciding which issues, which problems, when pursued, open out into "transfigurationist" politics and which are merely reforms. As the most sympathetic reader will notice, everything remains to be done.

6

CHURCH AND WORKER IN QUEBEC: A CONTEXT FOR POLITICAL THEOLOGY

Guy Bourgeault

Part 1

This paper may perhaps be disappointing; it will not go very far in theological reflection. But it may also be stimulating in a certain way by presenting--as the title of the conference invites us to do--a "context" in which a certain theological reflection may be begun and pursued. Our context is Quebec.

I would like to introduce our joint statement on the _Church_ and the _workers in Quebec_ by two preliminary remarks concerning the background of a research programme in which Yves Vaillancourt and I are associated, and which concerns _The Church and the Workers' Movement in Quebec_ (project EMOQ, l'Église et le mouvement ouvrier au Québec).

1. Preliminary Remarks

My first remark concerns precisely the "context" which, in our view, made the research project urgent: The situation in which certain Christian militants find themselves when they become involved in the struggles of what we may call "the labour world."

The Church in Quebec was, and remains in large part, a national Church, even nationalist.[1] For this reason, it easily gets the image of a people's Church. The Church was in fact present, and actively present, in the collective life of the Quebec people. In this way it has done many things in the course of the years _for_ the workers. Nevertheless, the gap between the Church and labour seems to have been discovered, more than created, in recent years. In 1974, the colloquim at Cap-Rouge, Quebec, on _Christians in the Workers' World_, indicated by its very title a rupture and yet a desire to re-establish contact. This attempt by the Church to bend over in the direction of the labour movement has given it, as one of my friends suggested, a bad case of "lumbago."

I will quote here an extract from the editorial of the journal _Relations on the Workers of Quebec and the Church_, published on the occasion of this colloquim at Cap-Rouge:

The Church in Quebec can make some claim to be a national church because it has gathered into its membership nearly all the citizens in Quebec in what might appear to the outsider as a 'popular Christianity.' But perhaps this Christianity had only the appearances of being 'popular,' because its orientation is hierarchally determined. Perhaps the Church has more a superior outlook than a real grasp of the working world and its everyday reality. The 'distance' between Church and labor of which we have become conscious then seems less the result of recent breaks than the awareness of breaks that are already old.[2]

Certainly the Church has been solidly implanted in the world of the workers, and has tried to help it to structure and to organize itself. An example of this is the official action of Church leaders in the syndicated movement in the trade unions. The Church has helped the workers in certain ways to understand themselves. Perhaps this has led them or the Church to acquire a taste for freedom--with the risks and the responsibilities that must be assumed in the exercise of freedom. Let us recall the work accomplished by the various organizations of Action Catholique and by the various family associations that received Christian inspiration. These commendable actions were done <u>for</u> the workers but were not initiated <u>from</u> the workers' world. Was the whole attempt to bring a rapprochement between Church and labour really a Church-inspired attempt to regain the loyalty of the workers? The relatively recent crises of the Action Catholique movements and of the other popular organizations of Christian inspiration suggest that we should not give a categorical yes or no answer to this question.

Just balance sheets are difficult to establish; just verdicts are even more difficult to pronounce. So it is more prudent to be content with a faithful, even if painful, recognition of the present situation. Church and labour have recently discovered that they are strangers to each other.

A second issue, closely tied to the first, concerns the evolution of thinking and action that has developed amongst Christians presently active in the struggles of the workers.

Several of these Christians became more and more involved in the life and the struggles of the workers for motives which I would call ethical, or, more precisely, they were motivated by the ethical implications of the Gospel. Later, the burden and the constant tension of the two allegiances was painfully felt by several of them: allegiance to the Church on the one hand; allegiance to labour, its organizations and its struggles, on the other. This tension often left them in painful contradiction. For some, there followed a break with their Church. For others, there grew the deeply felt need for the organization of a new Christian community of prayer and sacramental celebration, joining those who have a concern in the struggle for the building of socialism. This identity makes explicit the political dimension of the Christian faith and of the Gospel. From this came the creation of the movement of Politisés Chrétiens in 1972,[3] and the Cap-Rouge meeting in 1974.

It will no doubt be useful, as a corollary to these remarks, to trace the evolution on three stages of what can be called three levels of conversion. The first, the conversion of hearts; the second, conversion of the minds; and the third, the conversion of the feet and hands. The first level of conversion has become observable as a classical liberal theology, with the social doctrine of the Church as a kind of appendix. The second became manifest in a political theology based on the awareness of the necessary political dimension of the Gospel, which involved an intellectual awareness that the Gospel as well as faith and theology are at the same time politically conditioned.[4] The third conversion was to a theology of liberation whose real, non-academic elaboration is possible only in connection with a praxis of class struggle and in solidarity with the organized workers, working for an effective political liberation and not confined to the world of spirit and ideals.

2. EMOQ: A Research Project

From this context came the research project EMOQ (l'Église et le mouvement ouvrier au Québec, Church and Workers' Movement in Quebec). This project, which is still going on, has as its object the study of "the interaction between the Church and the Workers' Movement in Quebec since the beginning of industrialization."[5]

To clarify the object of research, let us specify that by "Church" we mean principally the Catholic Church considered as an institution. That is an autonomous organization in society, with its own leaders, its own members, its means of action, its financial structure, its equipment, its property, its language, its practices, its loyalties.

By "Workers' Movement," we mean principally the organized Workers' Movement, i.e. the whole group of particular organizations which Quebec workers--especially working-class people--have created, since the beginning of industrialization, to make known their point of view, defend their interests, carry on their economic, political, and cultural struggles. This has brought them to establish workers' political parties, unions, and popular neighbourhood and regional organizations.

2.1 Why this research?

Since 1970, a number of research projects in Quebec have used the theoretical framework of class analysis in order to study such large social institutions as the State, Schools, Business, Social Service Agencies, and the Courts. The Church as an institution, however, has not yet been the object of rigorous analysis from the perspective described above.[6]

Research on the relations between the Church and the Workers' Movement, carried out from the perspective of class analysis, seems most important and useful because the Workers' Movement needs it. In fact, the Workers Movement in Quebec has been, on the level of its objectives, its practice, and its language, greatly influenced by the Church and religious ideology, even after the increasing secularization that came with 1960. Whether they are conscious of it or not, whether they admit it or not, many militants of the Workers' Movement remain influenced in their language, in their practice, in their conscience, in the choice of their strategies, and in their means of action, by the institutional Church and religious ideology. But the Workers' Movement has evolved too rapidly in recent years to allow people to imprison it in the past. Nevertheless there is a tradition of workers' struggle very much marked by a certain Christianity or by a certain "social doctrine of the Church." If it is important for the Workers' Movement to recognize its church heritage, it is also essential for Christians in the Church to understand the need for a scientific class analysis of the relations between the Church and the Workers' Movement. This will become clearer as we trace the historical stages in the relationship of the Church to the worker, particularly with the rise of a non-ecclesiastic leadership in the Workers' Movement.

3. Historical Stages in the Relationship of the Church to the Workers' Movement

3.1 Pre-Industrial Period

In the pre-Industrial period we notice that the Church in Quebec equated fidelity to our king as to our Lord: "Se conserver aussi scrupulemisement fidèle à notre Roi qu'a notre Dieu." ("You are pleasing to God only if you submit to the king in everything which is not contradictory with our religion.") During the troubles of

1837 and 1838, "Le mandement de Monseigneur Lartigue," Lartigue says (and there is a whole theology involved there, a theology where unity, peace, submission of obedience are key phrases to encourage docility),

We see everywhere brother fighting against brother, friends against friends, citizens against other citizens. (Or maybe it is better in French: "on voit partout les frères s'élever contre leur frères, les amis contre leurs amis, les citoyens contre leur concitoyens, et la discorde. . . semble avoir brisé les liens de la charité qui unissasent entre eux les members d'un même corps, les enfants d'une même Église, due catholicisme, qui est une religion d'unité.") Don't be seduced if somebody wants you to engage in rebellion against the established government, invoking the false reason that you are part of a sovereign people." "Have you reflected on the fact that almost without exception every popular revolution is not only a failure but <u>une oeuvre sanguinaire</u>, a bloody action, as experience proves."

One of our Roman Catholic friends analyzed the vocabulary of the church catechism in Quebec and noted that there were 400 obligations and different things that one must do. But only on one occasion was the word "free" included, and "freedom" never appears. There, I suggest, is a practical political theology which plays an ideological role for the dominant class.

Industrialization faced the church with the increasing alienation of labour and the need to change its identity.

3.2 <u>The Church, which was outside the Workers' Movement until World War II, infiltrated it with the appearance of the CTCC in 1921.</u>

During the "first phase of industrialization (1860-1899), the Church was exterior to the Workers' Movement and to the new proletariat which developed and deplored it. Each conflict requires penetrating analysis. When we examine the confrontation, from 1833 to 1887, between Mgr. Taschereau, Bishop of Quebec, and the Knights of Labour, we notice the Church was directly and actively implicated in a colonial type of operation while appearing to protest the exploitation inherent in industrial capitalism.

During the "second phase of industrialization (1900-1929), the Church approached the Workers' Movement and took it ideologically under its wing by its "social doctrine." About 1920, Quebec became an industrial capitalist society. In response to the need for an organization for workers to express their organizational determination within the sponsorship of the Church, the CTCC (Confédération des travailleurs catholiques du Canada, Confederation of Canadian Catholic workers) was born in 1921. This was a Catholic confederation that called for a rigorous analysis of society.

3.3 The great crisis of the 1930s led the Church to articulate and to spread the corporatist ideology, which strongly influenced the Workers' Movement at that time.

Challenged by the radicalization of the Workers' Movement in English Canada (mobilization of the Canadian Communist Party, creation of the Co-operative Commonwealth Federation--CCF--in 1932, the rise of the trade union and socialist movement in the Congres des metiers et du Travail du Canada--CMTC--etc.), the traditional petite bourgeoisie, to which the Church was bound, was afraid of losing its control over French-Canadian workers. To maintain its influence over them, it articulated and spread the corporatist ideology of the Church. For this purpose, it used the École sociale populaire, the École des Hautes Études commerciales, and the newspaper Le Devoir. Anti-communism quickly became the key element of corporatist ideology, and the Workers' Movement was influenced by this propaganda.[7]

3.4 The Church was gradually pushed outside the movement, from 1950 on, when a new petite bourgeoisie began to exercise a new leadership in Quebec society.

Little by little, in the 1940s and 1950s, a new petite bourgeoisie arose: it included Marchand, Trudeau, and Pelletier, who infiltrated the CTCC. The Church, however, remained for the most part attached to the traditional petite bourgeoisie, which continued to control hospitals, schools, and social services. Then the Workers' Movement, in the wake of the peaceful revolution of 1960 to 1965, opted for social democracy. In the period of 1966 to 1969, with some hesitation, it chose socialism. It must be recognized that there are strong economic reasons to explain this radicalization. There was a strong recession between 1966 and 1970. These three phases shook the institutional Church (especially when the modern petite bourgeoisie replaced the traditional one in the hospitals and the schools in 1966 and in the collèges classiques in 1968).[8] But small groups of Christians participated in this evolution of the Workers' Movement and took their share in shaping the transition between 1966 and 1970. When we examine this evolution more closely we see that there has been a growth into a secularized liberal society, and I think that this was the main realization of what was called the Quiet Revolution. It is a kind of French Revolution that comes too late. The Quiet Revolution was the introduction of Quebec into the world of technology and of modernity, maybe not in fact, but at least at the level of conscious thought. I don't think the Church was too much disturbed with that because during the time of the Quiet Revolution in Quebec, the Church was managing its own Quiet Revolution, the one of the Vatican II Council. There was a series of secularizations or deconfessionalizations of the schools, of hospitals, and of labour unions in Quebec, but this was accepted in a kind of unconsciousness of what was happening.

A second issue was the national question, or the question of independence. I think that during all those years the hierarchy all over Canada, and even in Quebec, had sympathies with a kind of nationalism based on equal partnership. Nevertheless, a great many of the staff people in the Church have always been on good terms with the nationalism which is found in the Parti Québecois; this means the Church in Quebec could manage quite easily with an independent Quebec.

But there is a third issue, which is the social issue, and there I think we could divide it in perhaps three periods. The first period is what I called at the beginning of our presentation a kind of new Liberalism with a social conscience. I think the Church felt at ease with this even at the level of the hierarchy. A second step in the evolution--at this level--can be called the social democrat option; there was great hesitation and there still is great hesitation about this, but I think it could be overcome. However, the problem is that a certain number of Christians now have made an option for socialism, and I think this is not at all accepted by the Church in Quebec.

Before we examine this third phase, we must consider a burning question that comes up again and in the form of an accusation. Why do Christian socialists in Quebec take up the nationalist cause instead of concentrating on social issues?

The question of separation tends to obscure other aspects of what is called the Quebec problem. For political reasons Trudeau and others want to keep the Canadian public concentrating on the question of national unity and of Quebec separatism. Within Quebec there are some who want to give priority to the national question. At the opposite end of the political spectrum within Quebec are those who call for a socialist revolution. They say the national question is only a mystification because there is no advantage to being an independent capitalist society. In my view there is a link between these two outlooks.

To help us understand this connection let us look at the fight of black people in the United States. We can't say this is a problem of black and white. It is in fact a problem of class structure and class struggle. But black people have said, "every time we have made an alliance with oppressed white people in the class struggle we have been fooled. So we want to establish our black identity." It seems to me there is an important parallel in Quebec. We want to establish our Frenchness, our Canadian French, North American personality. The oppressor or the dominant power is America; it is also Anglo-Canadian, and a small segment of this group is French-speaking.

To state the same thing in other words: there is a link between the socialist struggle and the nationalist struggle. The victory of the Parti-Québecois is ambiguous. The labour unions and other progressive movements have given their support to the Parti-Québecois, but it is what I would call a provisional support. They are saying, let us go down the road of independence with the P.Q., but let us also seek to find a more socialist group to establish our real political identity.

There is a minority of Christians for socialism, but I think the Church itself, considered as an institution, is not only out of the battle but is really fighting against socialism. Yves recalled some meetings in Rome and some actions of the Vatican against the movement of Christians for Socialism in different parts of Latin America. We could recall similar situations in Quebec or in Montreal. Maybe we could make one exception: this would be the Church of Hull in the diocese of Hull which is close to Ottawa, where the bishop is clearly, I would say, for the workers and with the workers. But in the other dioceses of Quebec this is not the case.

Among the increasingly militant Christian groups in Quebec is the Politisés Chrétiens. There is a theological job being done by them and similar groups on the basis of more and more political analysis--similar to what we have been doing at this conference. Part of this job is negative or destructive. It is a job which is necessary because the gospel and theology have been used as an ideological system for reaffirming the power of the establishment. There is a second part of the work which we try to do which is more positive: the creation of a new theology in dialogue with the theology of liberation of Latin America.

NOTES

[1]See on this subject a paper already given in another context, "L'Eglise et les nationalismes québecois" to appear soon as a post-script to a theological essay by Pieree Charritton (Basque theologian) on the right of peoples to self-determination.

[2]See Relations 34/398 (November 1974), special issue on "Les chrétiens dans le mouvement ouvrier au Québec." 290-301.

[3]See, on the evolution outlined here, the document of the P.C. network on "l'Église et les chrétiens dans l'histoire du mouvement ouvrier au Québec depuis 1960." This document was published in Relations 34/398 (November 1974), 293-297.

[4]See Église et théologie: réalités politiques," Communauté chrétienne, 65-66 (September-December 1972), 329-348.

[5]See the presentation of the EMOQ project to the Faculté de théologie de l'Université de Montréal, April 17, 1975 (a seven-page document).

[6]For various reasons, the institutional Church is the object of diatribes or of defenses. The Dumont Report (1971) is in this respect a welcome exception and the point of view of the workers leaves its mark on a few brief but remarkable passages. However, it is not at all centered on the Church-workers' world dialectic, but rather on that between the Church and the world (in Quebec).

[7]Guy Menard is now studying this anti-communist struggle carried on especially by the École sociale populaire during the 1930s.

[8]Vive Voisine, Histoire de L'Église Catholique au Québec (1608-1970), (Editions Fides, Montreal, 1971), 82-83.

7

CHURCH AND WORKER IN QUEBEC: A CONTEXT FOR POLITICAL THEOLOGY

Yves Vaillancourt

Part 2

The discussion we have initiated is divided into two parts. First we give an historical background, and from this history we point to a few hypotheses. Secondly we hope to focus on the contemporary situation and particularly the issues that have come out of the election of the Parti-Quebecois government, labour militancy, and the effect of the upheaval on the Church in Quebec. There is one further area for discussion that needs clarifying. This is to look at the methodology, particularly the vocabulary we use. In the last day and a half we have heard frequent use of the word "Marxism." If we want to use it as a tool of analysis, to identify certain events and attitudes in the political arena, we must clarify what a Marxist theory of the State looks like.

An examination of Appendix 1, "The Marxist Theory of the State and its Implications for the Churches as Institutions in our Society," helps a person build a theoretical construct to use in a concrete way in an analysis of our society. If we look at the diagram, we can see that a society may be examined as a social structure with a basement supporting other floors. The vulgar Marxist would like this approach to be understood as something which says that the infra-structure (the basement, the economic organization of production) can explain everything which is going on on the floors above, the super-structure. According to this view, the upstairs is a perfect reflection of the basement. This unfortunately is not a good analysis. I have indicated on the diagram the interaction between the infra-structure and the super-structure by showing a large and small arrow. This means that the main influence is at the bottom, the infra-structure, with the large arrow thrusting upwards. It is down below that we see what mode of production is dominant. But conversely, if you look above at the superstructure, at, for example, the schools, you will also get an indication of the basic ideological foundations of that society in the infra-structure. The arrow pointing down suggests that family, mass media, and churches are all keys to understanding the infra-structure. But if you only look at these obvious institutions in the super-structure, and imagine that they reflect what society is, and don't look at the infra-structure, i.e. the mode of production and the relation of production to goods and services, you have a very superficial explanation of society.

This might be made clearer if we look at the left and right hand sides of the super-structure in my diagram. The left I have labelled "The Political Area." Lenin concentrated on this area in his Marxist theory of the state, and he was not so concerned about the ideological or cultural area. The churches, you will notice, are well placed on the right hand side of the super-structure, the cultural or "The Ideological Area." This does not mean that the Church and all the agents in it cannot travel in other areas; they may even have some interest in the infra-structure, or they can seek to influence politics. However, the Marxist analysis concentrated on how the state served the dominant economic interests of the infra-structure (the basement).

There was no similar analysis of how the Church and other cultural institutions fitted into the schema. It was assumed that their influence was more private and more free. However, Antonio Gramsci, one of the founders of the Communist Party in Italy, gives new insight on the class analysis of religion. Gramsci was imprisoned for ten years by Mussolini and died in 1937. He was a very rare and creative Marxist. In his class analysis of society he pointed out that not only the state but other ideological institutions served the interests of the dominant class. He showed that there were obvious agencies of oppression like the government, administration, justice, and police. But if a capitalist state used only these agencies there would be no subtlety to their domination. If you move Presidential power from the tarnished Watergate villains to the smiling, converted, religious Christian, Carter, you don't have a new Mr. Clean; it just means that the forces of bourgeois and imperialist interests are served by a more subtle stooge when they are cloaked in religion. I will give another example closer to home. Let us look at the Canadian university. The university, like the Church, looks like a free ideological institution. But is it? Take this conference; to some extent it is controlled by the capitalist state. The prophets organizing the conference have to meet requirements of "academic scholarship" which are far more reflections of the ideological status quo than academic critical enquiry.

Let us consider the churches and labour unions as illustrations of institutions seeking to be free and independent in promoting worthy goals. They in fact find themselves, through compromises, in bondage to the infra-structure. The Church, in promoting evangelical enterprise, has to compromise with the capitalist organizational power. Labour unions' history is also a saga of how the state can change free organizations into prisoners serving in one way or another the capitalist interests. To say that these institutions have both a dominating and a dominated class does not mean that the suppressed cannot establish living room within their area of influence. It is important to recognize that within institutions there is first the leadership of the institution, secondly the bureaucrats of the institution, and thirdly the membership. Sometimes if you do a concrete analysis you will see that the dominant group within the institution as reflected by the leadership is split. It can be seen within the Bishops' Conference or among the bureaucrats and the membership. Sometimes you will see in some moment of history the membership or even a bishop on the side of the popular masses, but usually the leadership is on the side of the dominant block.

Let us now turn to Appendix 2, "The Pattern of Interaction between the class issue and the National Issue in Quebec Society since 1760." This diagram points to the division you find between the dominant or exploiting group and the popular masses or dominated classes. The division depends on that point of history where we stop and make our examination to determine what type of oppressor is in control. For example, in Quebec today it is important to distinguish the monopolist section of the bourgeoisie from the non-monopolist, the small enterprise, because the P.Q. government is nearer to the small enterprise and middle enterprise than to the monopolist one. If you look more closely at the diagrams, in Appendices 2, 3, 4, and 5, you will see within the circles on the right and left there are both vertical and horizontal lines. The vertical lines represent class divisions within Quebec society. The horizontal lines indicate cultural or national divisions. You will notice how frequently the class oppression and the national oppression coincide. You will notice that after the conquest the English-speaking nation in Quebec was also the dominant social class, and as you move left on the diagrams you will see that the oppressed masses nearly all belong to the French Canadian nation. In this early period the Catholic Church is on the side of the popular French Canadian masses; the leadership in the Church is partly identified with the French Canadian and partly forms an intermediate block. But the leadership of the Church has usually, particularly in moments of crisis, been on the side of the English dominant block.

One particular point of Quebec history illustrates this process: Let us look at Appendix 3, "The Interaction between the Class Issue and the National Issue in Quebec Society in 1837." I will deal with what happened in 1837 at the time of the popular struggle, what we call the revolutions of 1837 and 1838, which went on simultaneously in Lower and Upper Canada. (It would be interesting to establish comparisons with what happened in Upper Canada but my concern at this point is Quebec history.)

On the right side of the diagram is the dominant power block. In this period of the early nineteenth century there were two interacting modes of production. There were the semi-feudal and also the merchant capitalist. From the diagram it is evident that the industrial bourgeoisie was very small. There was a bourgeoisie engaged in commerce; quite often there were in the area of finance. One example is the Bank of Montreal, founded in 1818, a family enterprise with connections in other areas of commerce, but no industrial elite. At this stage in history the economy of the country was dominated by 200 families who controlled fur, wool, and commerce, with a small amount of shipbuilding and construction on the Lachine Canal. But remember, this power block of 200 families was English. You will notice I have also included in this grouping a declining social class growing steadily weaker. These were the landowners with a semi-feudal mode of production; to give them their French title, these were the "seigneurs." In 1760 they were all French; by 1837 they were half French-speaking and half English. You will also observe in this dominant block what I call the senior private managerial staff. They also belonged to the English-speaking nation; the senior public managerial were also English.

After the uprising of 1837, the economic and imperial power of Britain learned that it would be good policy to have French-speaking people serving in these managerial positions. When we look at the Intermediate Bloc on the diagram, we see that in 1837 this included four kinds of people. One of these were the soldiers; 7000 strong, all of whom spcke English, and they were the occupying forces of the Colonial power. There were also the Church clerics, who might be described as the traditional petite bourgeoisie. This group played a key role in the revolution of 1837, and it consisted of four Catholic bishops, and also a sizable group of the 400 Catholic priests of that time. But if you look more closely at this clergy group you will see that among the clergy in one church or another there were some who belonged to the popular masses; that is, they served parishes in the poor areas. Some priests serving parishes along the Richelieu River and in the St. Hyacinthe region were in the poor areas, while the richer parishes, with their upwardly mobile priests and bishops, were in the petite bourgeoisie group. The difference between the old and new petite bourgeoisie is that the old were providing a service but not on salary, while the new petite bourgeoisie, who became more and more predominant with the rise of capitalism, were all salaried. You will notice I have confined my class analysis to Roman Catholic and French-speaking clergy. I have not done studies on the Anglican or Protestant priests and ministers.

There is another social stratum that must be understood in this period: the elite of the petite bourgeoisie. These were the professionals: the doctors, the lawyers, the notaries. They were the leaders of the popular struggle of this period. The majority of these people were French-speaking, the minority, English-speaking. They were the _avante garde_ of the uprising; they formulated the reasons and provided the organization.

Further left on the diagram from the intermediate block are the popular masses. One sees that the working class, in the strict sense, is very small. Half were Irish, the workers who built the Lachine Canal in Montreal; the other half of the working class was French Canadian, but the industrial proletariat at that time did not total more than 3,000 out of a population of 600,000. The greatest part of the popular masses were the _paysans_. The equivalent in English would be peasants bonded to a landlord. But "peasant" isn't a social class in Marxist terms. You can be a proletariat peasant or you can be a petite bourgeoisie peasant (the latter would be marginal independent subsistence farmers). There were also the lower and middle sectors of the petite boureoisie--the independent loggers and the independent fur trappers. They owned their means of production, but they had to sell their produce to the merchant class at deflated prices.

What was the churches' role in this social stratification? From the diagram one sees that the exploiting classes coincided with a part of the exploiting nation, the English, who were protestant. The left side shows the exploited classes who were French and Catholic.

Following the English conquest, the French Catholic church had a difficult time, particularly for the first five years. But then its fortune changed. This is difficult to explain because one could assume that the Church of England (Anglicanism) would be favoured by the British occupying forces, particularly as the Test Act of 1673, passed in Britain, upheld the official religion of the Church of England and barred Catholics from holding any public office in Britain. This act was not repealed until 1828. Why was the situation different in Quebec? We notice that where there are three divisions of society along class lines it is very difficult for the oppressors to maintain their exploitation of the oppressed without the help of the people in between. Very quickly the British colonial power saw that it needed some help from the French-speaking elite, and this was particularly important in times of crises. This certainly was a time of crisis because the British were frightened of the same spirit of independence spreading north from the breakaway New England colonies into French and English Canada. This made the British woo the Catholic Church into a liaison where the Church would be legitimizers of English domination.

The reward for co-operation with the new masters was the assurance that the Catholic Church could build a large seminary to train clergy. They also wanted a new diocese in the expanding city of Montreal where they could name their own bishop. The Roman Catholic Church in Quebec had the very worthy motivation of finding new fields of evangelism, but the result was to make the Church a prisoner. One might say the Church was under house arrest in its own home.

An example of the compromise the Catholic church had to make is seen in the appointment of bishops. There were four bishops in Quebec. The British authorities persuaded the Church to accept Monseigneur Lartigue, who had been a bishop at Montreal since 1820, as the new bishop of Montreal in 1837. Lartigue was sympathetic to co-operation with the British. At the same time Monseigneur Bourget became auxiliary bishop of Montreal. So we see on the one hand the Colonial power making a concession in providing for a bishop of Montreal, but on the other hand making sure that the person who was appointed would support the Colonial authority.

It is important to fill in some of the details of the crisis of 1837. At this point the political organization of Quebec society was divided into four branches. Three of them were controlled by the Colonial Office in London; the fourth branch, the National Assembly, was the place where the masses could elect their representatives. The reasons for the uprising became immediately apparent when you see that for 20 years the aspirations of the popular assembly were refused--in fact they were vetoed. What added fuel to the fire was the fact that the members of the assembly were the only elected representatives, and the three colonial branches which thwarted their demands were appointed by the Colonial Office. There was also the fact that the representatives to the assembly, the deputies, were well educated.

The deputies that were elected were professionals, including lawyers who had risen out of the popular masses and from the traditional petite bourgeoisie, and who became a new petite bourgeoisie. So when we come to look at the struggle in 1837, we see that it was taking place at two levels. On the one hand, there was the struggle between the popular masses and the dominant block. Within the popular masses, the peasants were particularly suffering on the land. Their subsistence level of living was becoming lower and lower at a time that was already financially difficult. These extremes of destitution led them to revolt.

But there was a struggle going on at another level. This was the conflict between the two factions of the elite of the petite bourgeoisie. There was the clerical faction we have already described, which had mastery of the ideological persuasion within the power of the Catholic Church. But there was also the genesis of a new ideological persuasion in the new republican revolutionary outlook from France and the United States. The new secular democratic ideology insisted on the separation of Church and state. It demanded a non-confessional school system and expected more participation in public affairs.

In this struggle, the traditional petite bourgeoisie, as represented in the Church, were undoubtedly victorious. Their influence spread through the whole of the social fabric. There was a section of the Catholic Church which joined the rebellion. This division in the Church was not just within the laity, but within the clergy also.

There were clerics who were in full identity with the popular masses. But there were also loyalists among the leadership, especially the four bishops, and of that group the most fanatical loyalist was Monseigneur Lartigue. He became the epitome of the church's official support of the status quo. This loyalty to the British Crown came at a most delicate moment in the struggle.

There were three phases to the development of the crisis. The first step was parliamentary. In April 1837, the deputies who had been elected by the people found that they were vetoed every time they pushed for popular demands. The second phase, between April and October, was outside of the parliament in gaining popular support. The third step was the armed struggle which lasted through November and December of 1837.

The counter force to this popular uprising took the form of a loyalist intervention by Monseigneur Lartigue who wrote a pastoral letter to be read in all the churches on Sunday, October 24, 1837, just as the popular forces were moving from phase two to phase three. Some liberal Quebec historians excused the action of the hierarchy by saying that it was political wisdom for the leadership of the church to take this stand to safeguard French Catholic culture, as the rebellion was doomed to failure. All I can say is that it is too easy to make that excuse in light of the way things turned out. But one could easily make the counter argument that with the ideological power that was at hand in the parishes and through Sunday sermons, who knows if the hierarchy could not have given support to this popular cause. Although the leadership of the institutional church supported the dominant block, the minority of the clergy, which was nationalist and on the side of the popular masses, tried very hard to bring pressure on the bishops to change their position. They might have succeeded if Monseigneur Lartigue had not reaffirmed his loyalist position.

All this took place just a few years before the development of capitalist history, but the positions of power established in 1837 were to play a crucial role in Quebec history for more than a hundred years. It followed that the church as an institution and the clerical faction of the traditional petite bourgeoisie were on the winning side. It also meant that the petite bourgeoisie nationalists were the losers. The next 100 years assured the domination of the Catholic Church in the super-structure of Quebec society, except for the labour unions until 1920, and it was not until the Quiet Revolution of the 1960s that the professional nationalist petite bourgeoisie, who had been in a deep freeze for over a century, were able to reappear. In Latin America and Europe, the struggle between the professional elite, representing the forces of secularism, and the clerical petite bourgeoisie became more open far earlier. In Quebec, the lawyers, the notaries, and the doctors who wanted to be a part of the intellectual French-speaking elite had to follow the ideological paths and patterns defined by the Catholic Church. For example, in 1897, Felix-Gabriel Marchand, a Liberal prime minister of Quebec, tried to pass a bill setting up a department of education under a minister in the cabinet. He was strongly opposed by the leadership of the church and was forced to change his mind. But the influence of the clerical petite bourgeoisie was not confined to education--they controlled health and welfare; in fact their Catholic ideology permeated every sector of Quebec society. It would take me too long to amplify on this, but let me just say in summary that this clerical petite bourgeoisie ideology was a very important influence in the history of Quebec until the Second World War. The leadership of the church acted as a go-between. _Through their ideological control of the super-structure, they avoided a direct confrontation between the two fundamental class ideologies in the infra-structure, the dominant block and the popular masses_.

Of course, what was happening with the influence of the church in this intermediary role in society was not unique to Quebec. It would be easier in a capitalist society if we had a clear-cut battle between the proletariat ideology and the bourgeoisie ideology. Quite often what happens in the super-structure is that the in-between people interfere in the confrontation, but their work is not neutral. Their successful attempts to cool down the antagonism serves the dominant block in its continued oppression.

But let us return to the scene in Quebec. After 1840, capitalist industrialization began to develop very fast, keeping pace with Ontario and the Maritimes. However, when we say 'fast,' we do not mean overnight. It takes decades for capitalism which is taking over the infra-structure (the economic level) to become apparent in the super-structure of society. The hypothesis we have been working with in analyzing the Quebec scene is that until the Quiet Revolution of the 1960s, the dominant ideology, as represented in the French Catholic

Church, was feudalistic. There were, of course, a minority of Christians in the Catholic Church who were more advanced, but the leadership procrastinated about adjusting to the economic changes in the infra-structure. An example of this was that when the hardship of the working class became worse and worse and the exploitation of this new industrial proletariat stood at the point of erupting, the Catholic Church became aware of the importance of trade unions as an ideological tool. They saw, during the period of transition to industrial capitalism--particularly after the First World War--that the worker was not exclusively influenced through the family, the parish, and the media, but also through his union. They saw that it was far easier to influence the labourer from within the trade union movement. Early labour history, in fact the first eighty years, had virtually no influence from the church.

It is when we come to the important historical period of "The Interaction between the Class issue and the National Issue in Quebec society in 1917" (see Appendix 4) that we notice a shift. We see that the interaction between classes has changed greatly from 1837. Here the dominant power block is still predominantly in the hands of the English nation and the popular masses are still predominantly French. We also see the structure of a society in the early stages of capitalism. The most powerful group is the monopolist bourgeoisie, who are the top financiers and the heads of international companies. But there is also another group, the non-monopolist bourgeoisie, still predominantly English, who represent the large English-Canadian companies. There are also, in this power block, the people who run these companies. In the private sector, you have the high managerial staff made up almost entirely of English Canadians. But in the public sector of government, the politicians and senior civil servants (who give the English power block a good public image) are predominantly French-speaking, public staff people in higher positions.

When we look at the in-between block of this 1917 period, we notice that it is predominantly French-speaking, but that the power is shared between the traditional petite bourgeoisie (represented in the leadership of the church) and a new petite bourgeoisie of salaried people employed in the lower managerial positions of the companies. When we look at the popular masses, we see that the working class is expanding and, as we have already suggested, it took the Catholic Church some time to recognize the need to respond to this structural change. But with the persuasive ideological power of the Catholic faith and worship, and with a political crisis, it was able to retain its influence in a new way within the labour movement.

The crisis in 1917 arose out of two national issues. One was the violent opposition of French-speaking Quebecers to conscription, which became identified as a national struggle. The other was the rights for use of the French language in Ontario (Bill 17). The conscription issue particularly was viewed in Quebec as an attempt to call on their youth to spill their blood for England's embroilment in European wars. There was also another source of friction created within the working-class because of a racist outlook amongst English-speaking, working-class people. This led to a rupture amongst the workers and brought French Canadian workers to ignore the class solidarity and instead ally themselves, through their cultural link, with the traditional French petite bourgeoisie leadership. Henri Bourassa, founder of *Le Devoir*, was a good example of a leader from a different class, but the same nation. He represented the traditional petite bourgeoisie, the intellectual elite connected very closely to Catholic Church orthodoxy. This kind of petite bourgeoisie leader was in an excellent position to offer leadership to the French-speaking working-class, particularly in expressing hostility to conscription and moulding the French cultural national consciousness, and also giving advice on when it was a good time to strike.

This was the beginning of the period of yellow trade unionism in the labour history of Quebec, and it lasted until the 1940s. As we move into the 1950s, the Catholic trade unions began to take a more militant stand. First there were the Catholic action people who taught social sciences in the universities, people like George Henri Levesque who was a Dominican and who taught at Laval University. There were also the new-salaried, intellectual technocrats like Jean Marchand, Pierre Trudeau and Gerard Pelletier. Both groups offered their intellectual and technocratic help to the Catholic labour unions. This meant that the real struggle was not between the proletariat and the bourgeoisie, but between two kinds of bourgeoisie. But unlike the situation in 1837, the traditional petite bourgeoisie was losing its ideological power. It could not, any longer, resort to the anti-communist scare tactics of the 1930s.

It is interesting to observe that in Quebec in the 1930s there was an anti-communist (although not anti-capitalist) Christian tradition similar to that of the CCF in English Canada. This is not altogether surprising when we examine the nineteenth century history of immigration to Quebec. History shows that when we have been in a position to receive religious newcomers these were quite often the counter-revolutionaries of Europe and the United States. The townships of the Sherbrooke area were crowded in the nineteenth century with people coming from the United States who were against the new republic in the United States. The religious orders which came to Quebec at the end of the nineteenth century and the beginning of this century were not the most progressive Catholics in France. But there has been in our important struggle for influence, on the one side, the new petite bourgeoisie particularly based in the universities, and on the other, the traditional petite bourgeoisie in the reform movement in the Church. The forum in which the struggle took place was first the Congress of National Trade Unions and, later in the 1960s, within the Quiet Revolution in Quebec. The new petite bourgeoisie were no less committed to capitalism than the traditional group. The difference was that the new group saw ways of furthering their class interests through creating new jobs within the multinationals at the in-between level. They were technocrats who saw openings in management, research sciences, human relationships, and behaviour modification. If we tried to defend the clerical petite bourgeoisie on the grounds that they were against capitalism, in that they were anti-materialistic, we would, nevertheless, have to say that their opposition was anachronistic. They were really pre-capitalism in a socialist way.

You will notice I make some divisions within the Power Bloc. (See Appendix 5) The most powerful sector of the economy, the Monopolist Bourgeoisie, are the large multinationals; these senior executives are almost entirely English-speaking. There is also the Non-Monopolist Bourgeoisie. These are our local home-grown capitalists, and about one third of them are French-speaking. At the senior management level in the private sector this group is almost exclusively English. There is a constant debate on why there are not more French people in these senior positions in the power bloc; the rather facile answer given is that French people do not like to run businesses. In the public sector (Quebec Hydro, senior civil servants, cabinet ministers), senior management is almost entirely French-speaking.

In the intermediate bloc we see that the traditional petite bourgeoisie in the Church have been almost entirely replaced by the lower and middle strata which are secular in their orientation; they keep the ship of state on an even keel. Within the popular masses a great number of new petite bourgeoisie have dropped in status: the white collar workers on salary and the small corner-store businessmen. There are also the small independent farmers and, finally, the unorganized office people: the stenographers, clerks, and students. This group is either under-employed or unemployed. The welfare people represent 8% of the population. The Parti-Quebecois has had strong backing from these groups. These are similar to the black people in the United States and they are strong nationalists.

Although the Parti-Quebecois came to power with the support of the popular masses, this is not the group that controls the party machinery. The controlling group is the middle class of the new petite bourgeoisie. They are technocrats who are really in favour of French-speaking capitalism. So if you are a socialist in Quebec you are faced with a terrible dilemma. Is it right to support a nationalist cause and compromise you socialism? The P.Q. does have some programs that ameliorate the worst forms of oppression. They will tackle the language question. They will insist that immigrants speak French. They will improve working conditions and social welfare programs. They will improve the minimum wage. But they are not going to the roots of the national oppression when they do not take on the American multinationals. It is ridiculous to speak of an independent Quebec and be dependent on the New York financiers. Trudeau makes his reports to Washington, Rene Levesque to Wall Street.

There will be some who criticize our exposition of Quebec history by suggesting that we have been too negative about the contribution of the past. This is a fair criticism of what we have said. But if we are to rectify the situation it will be clear that in our Quebec context our problem is not the negation of history but our adoration of history at the expense of scientific analysis. Let me give you an example from the Rapport Dumont, which was published in 1971 and was an exhaustive study on the Church in Quebec. Dumont is a well known Catholic sociologist at Laval University and is considered quite progressive by many people. This Rapport Dumont could never be accused of ignoring history, in fact its major weakness is that it is obsessed with "the rich heritage" of Quebec history. The report constantly wants to show that the present church in Quebec is in historical continuity with the past. My view is that we have to overcome what has happened. Christians especially must stay alive for a new future where they stand with the oppressed people. In our context in Quebec I believe we have to be united to overcome the inertia of the past.

Appendix 1

THE MARXIST THEORY OF THE STATE AND ITS IMPLICATIONS FOR THE CHURCHES, AS INSTITUTIONS, IN A CAPITALIST SOCIETY

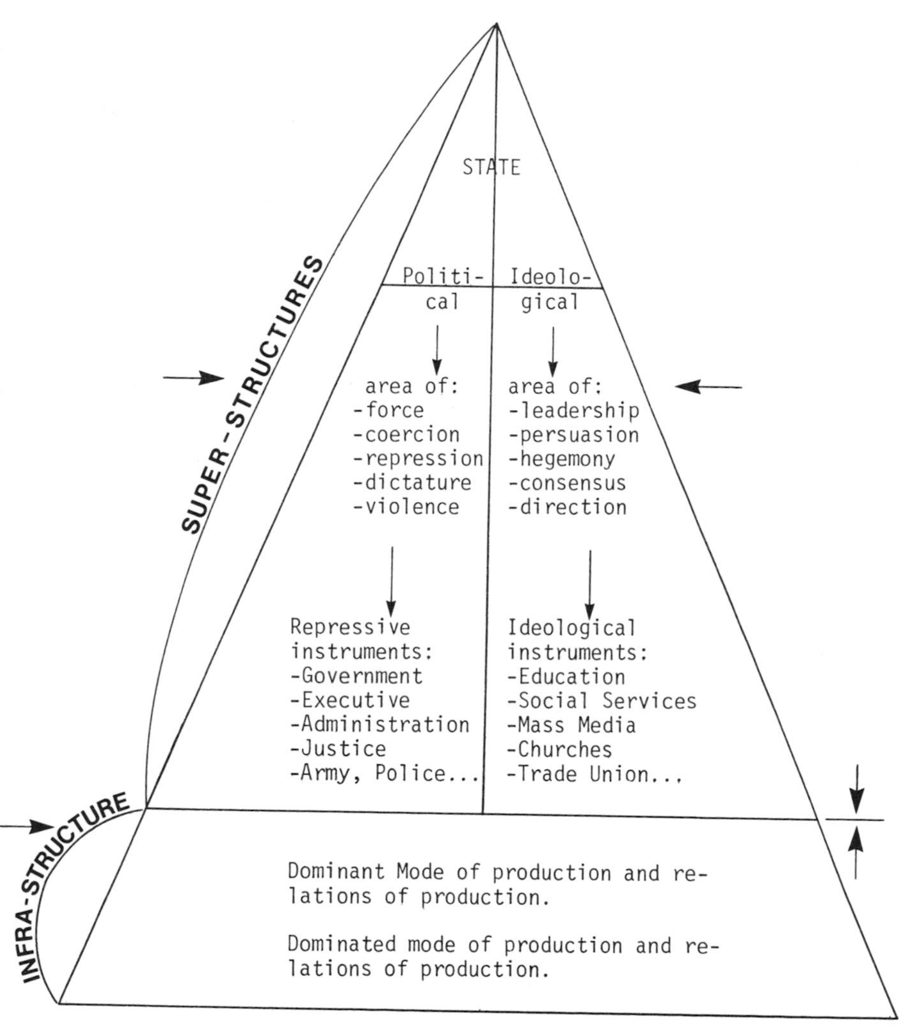

Appendix 2

LEGEND

(blank)	Francophone
(shaded)	Anglophone

THE PATTERN OF INTERACTION BETWEEN THE CLASS ISSUE AND THE NATIONAL ISSUE IN QUEBEC SOCIETY SINCE 1760.

THE "POPULAR BLOC"
↓
The side of the exploited and oppressed social classes & fractions

THE INTERMEDIARY BLOC

THE "POWER BLOC"
↓
The side of the exploiting social classes & fractions

Appendix 3

THE INTERACTION BETWEEN THE CLASS ISSUE AND THE NATIONAL ISSUE IN THE QUEBEC SOCIETY IN 1837-38

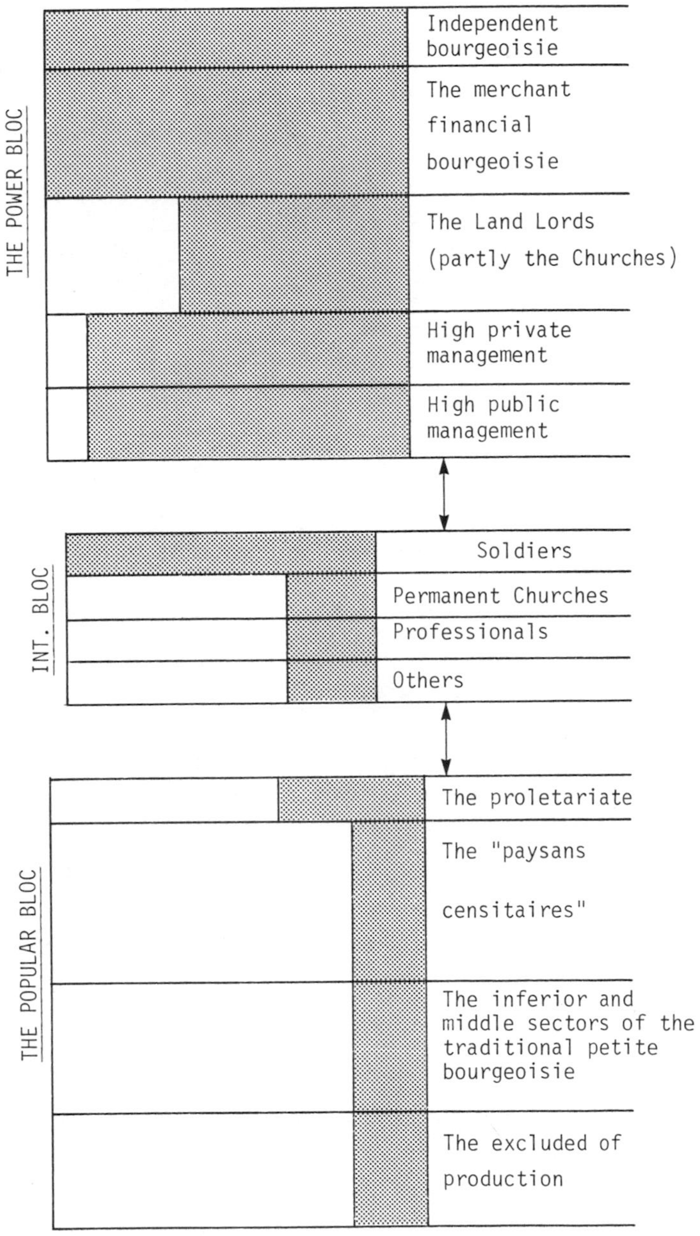

THE POWER BLOC

- Independent bourgeoisie
- The merchant financial bourgeoisie
- The Land Lords (partly the Churches)
- High private management
- High public management

INT. BLOC

- Soldiers
- Permanent Churches
- Professionals
- Others

THE POPULAR BLOC

- The proletariate
- The "paysans censitaires"
- The inferior and middle sectors of the traditional petite bourgeoisie
- The excluded of production

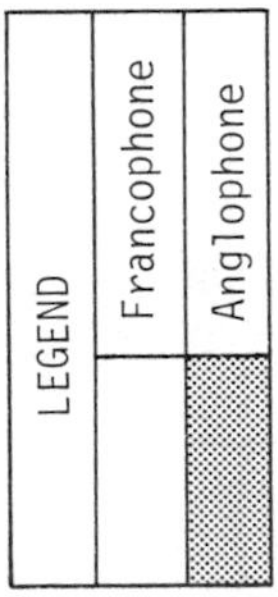

LEGEND

Francophone

Anglophone

Appendix 4

THE INTERACTION BETWEEN THE CLASS ISSUE AND THE NATIONAL ISSUE IN THE QUEBEC SOCIETY IN 1917

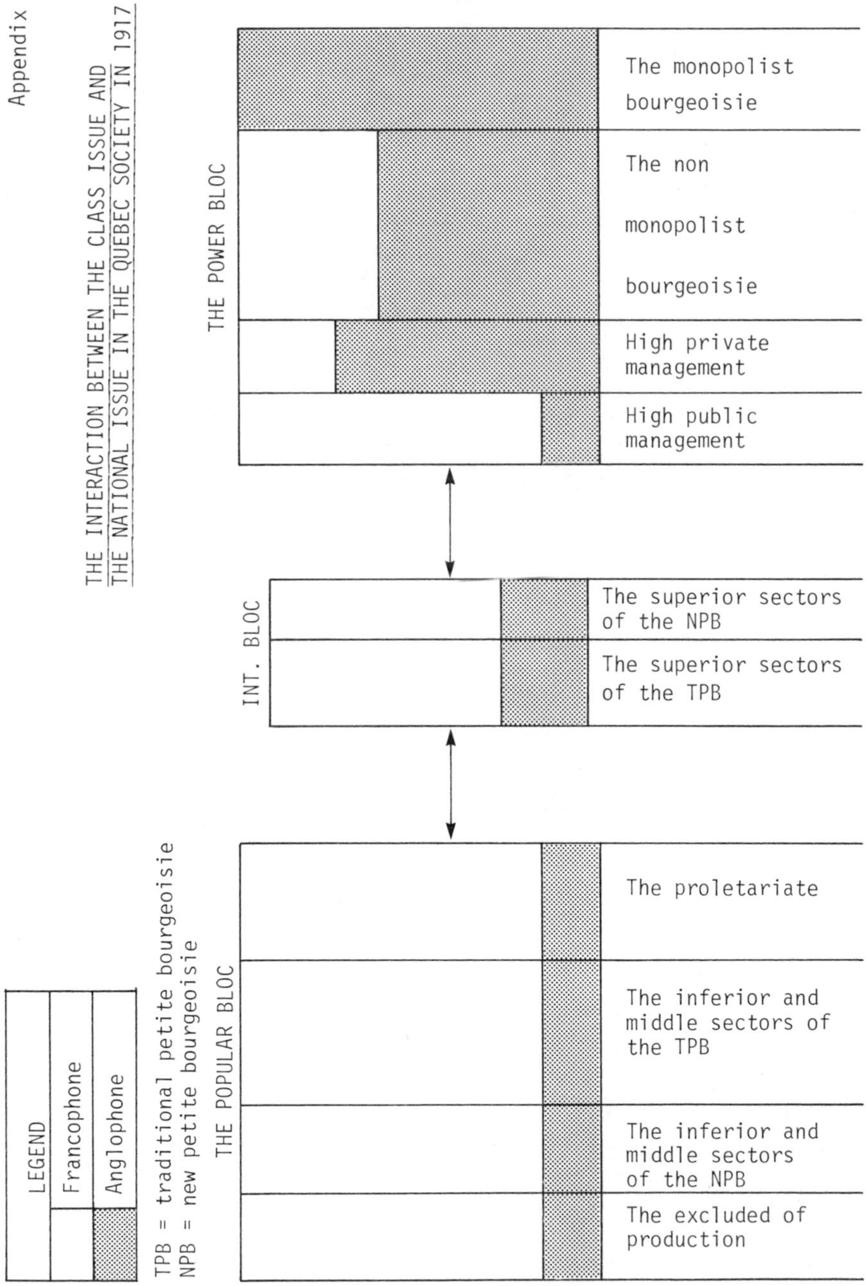

THE POWER BLOC

The monopolist bourgeoisie

The non monopolist bourgeoisie

High private management

High public management

INT. BLOC

The superior sectors of the NPB

The superior sectors of the TPB

THE POPULAR BLOC

The proletariate

The inferior and middle sectors of the TPB

The inferior and middle sectors of the NPB

The excluded of production

LEGEND

Francophone

Anglophone

TPB = traditional petite bourgeoisie
NPB = new petite bourgeoisie

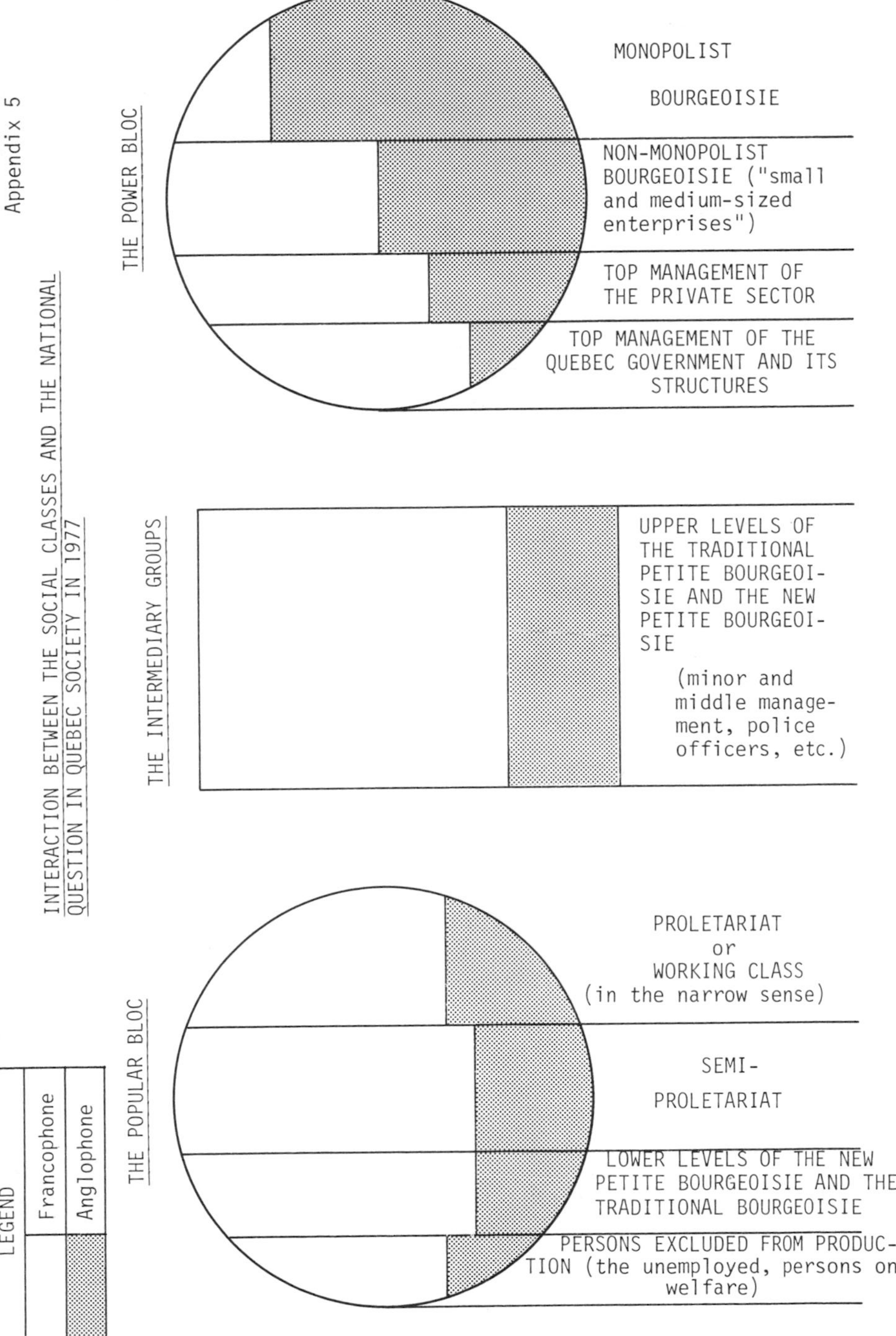
Appendix 5
INTERACTION BETWEEN THE SOCIAL CLASSES AND THE NATIONAL QUESTION IN QUEBEC SOCIETY IN 1977
THE POWER BLOC
MONOPOLIST BOURGEOISIE
NON-MONOPOLIST BOURGEOISIE ("small and medium-sized enterprises")
TOP MANAGEMENT OF THE PRIVATE SECTOR
TOP MANAGEMENT OF THE QUEBEC GOVERNMENT AND ITS STRUCTURES
THE INTERMEDIARY GROUPS
UPPER LEVELS OF THE TRADITIONAL PETITE BOURGEOISIE AND THE NEW PETITE BOURGEOISIE
(minor and middle management, police officers, etc.)
THE POPULAR BLOC
PROLETARIAT or WORKING CLASS (in the narrow sense)
SEMI-PROLETARIAT
LOWER LEVELS OF THE NEW PETITE BOURGEOISIE AND THE TRADITIONAL BOURGEOISIE
PERSONS EXCLUDED FROM PRODUCTION (the unemployed, persons on welfare)
LEGEND
Francophone
Anglophone

8

SUMMARY STATEMENT

Roger Hutchinson

I will organize my comments around four questions: "What is Political Theology?" "Why remain Christian?"; "What is the nature of our bondage?"; and, "How do we deal with the Canadian context?".

1

The answer to the first question which gradually emerged during the conference is that political theology in its most developed form is a new identity. It is a new form of piety or spirituality. That is, it is a distinctive way of bringing into focus the nature of our primary bondage and how that relates to our secondary forms of bondage.

Bill Hordern started us on the path toward this definition in his opening paper. He pointed out that political theology represented the re-engagement of Christians in the struggle to transform social structures and to overcome the individualistic piety of the 1950s. In her early remarks, Dorothee Sölle traced the development from political theology to the theology of liberation. Guy Bourgeault also drew attention to this distinction. There was a shift from dialogue between Christians and socialists to the alignment of Christians with the oppressed in the common struggle for justice.

In her essay, Dorothee Sölle pointed the way beyond liberation theology to Christians for Socialism as a new identity. The Christian and socialist aspects of this identity reciprocally reinforce and criticize one another. It is no longer a matter of taking for granted one's Christian faith and wondering whether Christians ought to support socialism. Both sides of the identity are problematic, and both sides are grounded in the same experience that mutuality is the law of life. As David Tracy argued, in his book Blessed Rage for Order, it is necessary to appropriate critically both the basis upon which we interpret our faith and the means by which we understand human existence.

I found Sölle's discussion of the Christians for Socialism identity very exciting. It is closely related to the difference in the 1930s between Reinhold Niebuhr's Fellowship of Socialist Christians in the United States and the Fellowship for a Christian Social Order in Canada. The latter group represented a foretaste of this Christian socialist identity which cuts under the old polarization between evangelism and social action. It provides the basis not merely for cultivating the will to apply one's faith to social problems, but for experiencing once more the reality of that faith that God is love. Thus it is a distinctive form of piety and not merely an ethic derived from the faith one inherited as a child or discovered in a revival tent.

Dorothee Sölle and Guy Bourgeault both made interesting comments about the stages leading up to a Christians for Socialism conversion. Guy talked about conversions of the head, heart, and feet, from knowing what to do, to feeling like doing it, to actually doing it. Dorothee discussed her work with housewives, who went from feeling that all was not well, to the awareness that the system in which they were caught destroyed their dignity, and finally to the point at which what they experienced in their own struggle for change seemed to illumine what they had always been led to believe that Christianity and socialism were all about. Mutuality is not just a value or an ideal but the most basic fact of life. Conditions which obstruct it are therefore not only wrong but sinful. The question remains, however, why retain the Christian side of one's identity once one's conversion of the feet has led one into solidarity with workers, the poor, or other oppressed groups in the struggle for justice?

2

Kai Nielsen, more persistently than anyone else, pushed the Christians at the conference to explain why they wanted to retain a label that seemed so dominated by Billy Graham piety and middle class complacency. Dorothee Sölle pointed to the advantages of being rooted in the Judaeo-Christian story which exalts the poor and places God on the side of the oppressed. Professor Nielsen countered with the claim that anyone who inherits our literature and culture has access to those stories.

Guy Bourgeault dealt with this question in his discussion of the Christians who became increasingly involved with workers. On the basis of their Christian beliefs they knew they ought to be identified with the workers' movement. As they actually became involved they began to experience tensions with the church. Some abandoned the church, or concluded that the church had abandoned them! Others found it meaningful to meet as Christians to reflect on their actions in the light of that heritage, and to pray. Similarly Dorothee Sölle told about the rediscovery of the fact that it was fun to sing hymns in the Christians for Socialism movement in her country. Although active involvement in the struggle for justice might be more important than liturgical celebrations for creating the bonds of community, the Christian stories and rituals continue for many persons to deepen that experience and to locate it in its cosmic setting.

Another aspect of the answer to the question "Why remain Christian?" has to do with how we move beyond commonsense and rationality to ground our social ethic in some grasp of what is ultimately true. The process of conversion whereby we discover that our values are rooted in reality is concrete and historical. It takes place in space and time and in the presence of other persons through symbols, stories, and rituals. There is thus a great difference between participating in the stories and ceremonies of the Christian tradition and casually observing them like a visitor at a museum. In the former case they become revelatory. They reveal the true nature of one's situation and the path one ought to be following to deal with it. For the detached observer they are a mere distraction. Or worse, by being there to be rejected they help him to evade the task of discerning the symbols and settings through which the conviction is sustained that his own values are rooted in reality.

Closely related to this claim that Christian stories and symbols disclose the true nature of reality is the further claim that they help us to maintain the vision that the future is open. We live in a time when Herman Kahn of the Hudson Institute, and others like him, are paid fancy fees to convince us that the future will be surprise free. It is much more academically sound and politically credible these days to project existing trends and conditions into the future than to envisage changes in social structures and power relationships. According to this "orthodox" view, the continued massive extraction of Northern resources to maintain southern industrial growth is "inevitable." The supermarket chains control food distribution; therefore it is "idealistic" to talk about producer and consumer cooperatives as an alternative means to ensure the use of more locally produced vegetables. But how do we sustain the vision that our future could be organized around the values of cooperation and sharing rather than competition and greed? Only the "knowledge" (revealed knowledge!) that these values are also facts, that the demand for increased mutuality in our social structures as well as in our personal relationships is not mere wishful thinking but the law of life. In so far as the Christian story continues to evoke that awareness, our concern for justice will continue to be rooted in our religious heritage, and our religious faith in turn will be rooted in reality.

There is a further dimension to the question "Why remain Christian?" We must, in one way or another, deal with the question of evil or sin, and with the fact that "the good that we would we do not." How do we locate the kinds of brokenness that keep us from being whole? How do we tap the forces in our environment which lead us toward wholeness? Obviously just to will to be whole, and to be in harmony with our selves, our neighbours and with the cosmos, is not sufficient. In the work that Patrick Kerans and I did, along with other theologians, with the Church Council of Justice and Corrections and the Federal Law Reform Commission, we discovered renewed meaning in terms like sin, reconciliation, expiation, atonement. The present system of incarceration achieves neither justice nor corrections. In part at least, this is because the theories upon which the practice is based fail to include the dimensions of reality Christians encounter through the symbols sin and reconciliation. Why remain Christian? I do not see alternative doctrines or rituals emerging in so-called secular settings which indicate to me that the fundamental level of our estrangement is being dealt with. I certainly do not see it being dealt with more adequately than in the Judaeo-Christian tradition or in the other major religious traditions.

3

To ask about the most basic forms of our estrangement is to raise the third question: "What is the nature of our bondage?" Abraham Rotstein's immense contribution to our conference was the way he provided us with a language for exploring this question. I found his analysis of the rhetorical structure of the western apocalyptic tradition, and the way he illustrated it in Luther and Marx, very interesting. I agree with Patrick Kerans, however, that the pattern Rotstein has identified is broader than which we normally think of as the apocalyptic tradition. Recognizing the distinction between the apocalyptic tradition and the more inclusive Judaeo-Christian drama of salvation will help us to clarify the recurrent tensions between those who stress fulfillment within history and those who stress the final consummation beyond history.

Rotstein's analysis, while passing over this important difference between Muentzer and Luther, clarifies the polarization between utopian and anti-utopian strands within the Christian tradition. This has been particularly important for me, because it helps me to understand Reinhold Niebuhr's criticisms of the Fellowship for Christian Social Order. It also helps me to see that the focus on liberation from oppressive social structures, on the one hand, and the preoccupation with our bondage to the sin-that-is-within-us (i.e. not just in the corrupt "system") and to death, on the other, are in principle complementary.

As Kerans pointed out in his analysis of the rhetorical structure of the domination--oppression--liberation drama of salvation Rotstein was identifying the basic features of one of the reigning paradigms of Western thought. This analysis should, therefore, help persons to locate the paradigm within which they find themselves, and to communicate with others across paradigm boundaries. It should also aid conversations within the domination--oppression paradigm between those who stress different forms of primary bondage. Barbara Bloom, for example, stressed the bondage of women to the oppressive family structure, the extent to which the victory over that particular form of oppression would liberate us all. Similarly, many Christians remain critical of Marxists who appear to neglect our bondage to personal sin and death.

If different forms of primary bondage are in fact complementary it is important that we learn to deal with them concretely in specific contexts. We must develop our senses of time and place. Sometimes it is appropriate to focus on liberation from unjust social structures; at other times one must dwell on the sin-that-is-in-me which will continue to frustrate my noblest intentions even in the cooperative commonwealth. At the death bed of a loved one, or on one's own death bed, it is timely to face the boundary question of life, and to be open to the resources in one's tradition for facing death. Thinking about a sense of place brings me to my final question: "How do we deal with the Canadian context?"

4

The dominant experience we have of the Canadian context is the extent of our regional and ethnic differences. Where we come from in Canada shapes our consciousness, our self-images, and our understanding of what we mean by Canada. One of the pitfalls of being a Canadian who has lived in different parts of the country is to assume that you know what it is like to be from another region. As an Albertan now living in Ontario I am aware of this danger. However, I think it is important to balance this sense of regional particularity with an attempt to understand the development and structure of Canadian society as a whole. The presentation by Yves Vaillancourt and Guy Bourgeault was an important step in this direction. Although it was a case study of Quebec, their categories could easily be applied in other parts of the country.

In my attempts to develop a course on the changing role of religion in Canadian society, I have used similar categories. I have, however, drawn more explicitly on the perspective on Canadian society embodied in the work of Harold Innis and S. D. Clark, than on Marxist analyses. Their perspective provides a similar basis for examining the role of different religious groups in relation to different classes, ethnic groups, etc. The Innis-Clark tradition might be as close as a democratic socialist wants to get to a Marxist analysis! On the other hand, it might mean that Marx must be rediscovered as a sociologist before he can provide a model for political organization. My point is that the categories used by Yves and Guy are both grounded in their Quebec experience and applicable to the same structural questions about the class structure, and the church's role in society in other parts of the country.

In conclusion I must confess that my trumpet does not sound a very clear call to revolutionary action. I feel both forms of bondage --the bondage to oppressive social structures and the bondage to sin-that-is-in-me and death. I thus cannot escape the ambiguities of history. I hope, however, to understand them in a way that does not undermine my conviction that our society can and must be changed. In my view, this conference has made an important contribution to this twofold task. It has helped us to face the complexity of our situation, but it has also equipped us to see the options with sufficient simplicity to act courageously. It has perhaps also made us more aware of our own conversion experiences, and more understanding of those who are at different stages on their path or on different paths. Although the final test of our faith is how we act, it is important that we continue to reflect on our actions. By talking about our differences as well as our agreements we can help one another to walk the narrow ridge between church-type accommodation to existing structures and the various forms of sectarianism which tempt us.

9

CONCLUSION: POLITICAL THEOLOGY AND POLITICAL ETHICS

Roger Hutchinson

In the "Summary Statement" which I delivered at the conference, I focused attention on some themes and neglected others. I have persuaded the editor that it would be more useful to write a new conclusion for the published proceedings than to expand or modify my earlier remarks. My present interpretation of the conference has been influenced both by hindsight and by the World Council of Churches' (W.C.C.) recently launched study of political ethics. At its 1979 Fall meeting the Central Committee of the W.C.C. initiated a study of "that political ethic which is demanded for a responsible and intelligent Christian participation in the struggle" for a just, participatory, and sustainable society. A shift in focus from political theology to political ethics brings into clearer focus the significance of some of the comments and themes I neglected in the "Summary Statement" I made at the conference.

The point of departure for political ethics is the way power is exercised in an "unjust, non-participatory, and unsustainable" society. The papers by Bourgeault and Vaillancourt, and the new introduction by Smillie, illustrate this focus of attention. A number of conference participants made it clear that the starting point for the conference should have been an analysis of concrete issues. This point was strenuously made by John Foster on the basis of his experience with inter-church coalitions such as GATT-fly and the Inter-Church Committee on Human Rights in Latin America. Since his comment from the floor has not been included in this volume, I will refer to it at some length.

In response to the uncertainty about the kind of game we should be playing at the conference, Foster pointed out that for him, "the central question that arises is how do we do political theology or reflect on our politics, or however we want to put it together." His frustration with the conference was that the Canadian context did not seem to make any difference to the way theoretical issues were being posed. He would have preferred to have started with concrete Canadian issues rather than with definitional concerns about what political theology is. A possible starting point could have been how the churches act in Canada as national institutions, and what kinds of questions they put to society. His own experiences had prompted him to conclude:

> that the questions the Canadian churches together put to the society break through the liberal framework, although perhaps unintentionally, unconsciously, or in a kind of covert way. They raise the questions that have become so central to the nature of Canada that it is impossible to pretend that they don't confront the question of transformation. And if we haven't learned that in the church, the enemy has.
>
> When the president of Canadian Arctic Gas (Pipelines Limited) comes into a meeting of the Royal Bank of Canada and says to a representative of the churches, "Oh, good afternoon, are you a Marxist like the Primate?" he has learned something about what the Anglican Church of Canada has expressed to the system in terms of its threat--a threat to the ideology of growth, a threat to the whole question of how accumulation is proceeded with in our society, whom it serves, and what services must come out of the political structure for it.

Foster suggested that, "from a kind of experiential base, a kind of fumbling around which began basically with simple guilt over the gap between rich and poor," some of the inter-church projects had "stumbled on some facts which at least lead through the nervous systems of the system to the centres of command." Through a research-action model these projects were attempting to move "toward the significant questions of our lives as Canadians." Academics could lend a hand by helping to clarify the self-understanding and class structure of the churches, and by analyzing the nature of popular religion. As Foster put it, "what is it that people really twig to in our society, why, and where is it going to lead? And what are the positive elements, the positive moments in that popular religion?"

A shift in attention from theoretical issues to practical concerns sheds new light on how the question "Why remain Christian?" was dealt with at the conference. The limited interest in either side of Kai Nielsen's theoretical case for socialism and against theology probably reflected both theoretical differences and a desire to discuss concrete issues.

The tension between establishing the normative status of Christian faith language and focusing upon the power struggles in a manner which includes Christians and non-Christians was illustrated by the exchange between Paul Newman and Gregory Baum following Kai Nielsen's address. Newman expressed the hope that someone would "talk about the way in which Jesus is normative for political theology." Baum, on the other hand, felt that an approach which "divided people into believers and atheists was an old-fashioned Christian theology." The distinction "should be between people who are with the little ones, who identify with the people to whom we do the dreadful things, and those who shrug their shoulders."

In his opening statement, and in his response to Dorothee Sölle's lecture, Gregory Baum outlined developments in Roman Catholic official social teachings which could be interpreted as a shift from theoretical statements to practical concerns. Although, as he admitted, papal documents and bishops' statements are ambiguous, they at least reflect a new openness to the left. They do not clearly promote socialism as the answer, but their focus on the way the global economic system actually works helps to strip away the aura of legitimacy which has tended to place capitalism beyond criticism in advanced industrial societies. Yves Vaillancourt's criticisms challenged Baum's optimism about the official Roman Catholic stance, and his brand of socialism, but they reaffirmed the importance of dealing concretely with the structures of Canadian society and with the question of allies and opponents in the struggle to transform those structures. Baum claimed that his aim was not to defend a conservative church, but to draw attention to the pre-liberal roots of Roman Catholic social thought for Catholics seeking support for their left-wing views and for others seeking allies in the struggle for a new society. He also implied that a firmer grounding in our traditions might help to overcome the sectarian fragmentation which plagues the left.

Preoccupation with the practical questions about allies and obstacles in the struggle to transform unjust social structures leads to increased appreciation for the theoretical contribution made by Rotstein's analysis of the rhetorical structure of the apocalyptic tradition. As Kerans points out, Rotstein's analysis helps Christians and Marxists to see how it is possible to retain a "relentlessly revolutionary" vision of a new social order without endowing the actual social movements they support with absolute rightness or pristine purity. Both groups can reject the dominant liberal view that fundamental structural change is not necessary without falling into the opposite trap of forgetting that their own strategic judgments involve interpretations of the historical situation. Since it will never be easy to determine "which issues. . . open out into 'transfigurationists' politics and which are merely reforms" (Kerans), open discourse about options can complement committed action on behalf of particular causes. Focusing on practice does not eliminate the need for theory; it forces theoretical reflection to be concretely related to particular contexts.

The way I phrased the fourth question addressed in my "Summary Statement," "How do we deal with the Canadian context?" perpetuates the misleading notion that political theology "exists" someplace and can be applied in the Canadian context. Adopting a new term such as political ethics will not in itself solve this problem. We can import a political ethic based on other people's experience as readily as we have imported theologies. The main problem, however, is not whether our methodological categories are imported or indigenous. The key question is whether the strategic moralities developed with the aid of Marxist categories or notions borrowed from European theologians are grounded in what Kerans called "a painstaking hermeneutic" of actual Canadian conditions. In his introduction to this volume, Smillie complements the contextual analyses of Bourgeault and Vaillancourt and addresses the need expressed at the conference to deal more explicitly with the Canadian context.

As long as our theoretical reflections are based on the exercise and legitimation of power in our own communities, and on the political options actually available to us, it will matter little whether the project is called political theology or political ethics. I have introduced the term political ethics as a useful way to highlight comments and themes neglected in my "Summary Statement," and to introduce a term which will become more widely used as the World Council of Churches and its member churches prepare for the Sixth Assembly to be held in Vancouver in 1983.

INDEX

SUPPLEMENTS

1. **FOOTNOTES TO A THEOLOGY**
   The Karl Barth Colloquium of 1972
   Edited and Introduced by Martin Rumscheidt
   1974 / viii + 151 pp. / $4.25 (paper)
2. **MARTIN HEIDEGGER'S PHILOSOPHY OF RELIGION**
   John R. Williams
   1977 / x + 190 pp. / $5.75 (paper)
3. **MYSTICS AND SCHOLARS**
   The Calgary Conference on Mysticism 1976
   Edited by Harold Coward and Terence Penelhum
   1977 / viii + 121 pp. / $5.00 (paper)
4. **GOD'S INTENTION FOR MAN**
   Essays in Christian Anthropology
   William O. Fennell
   1977 / xii + 56 pp. / $2.50 (paper)
5. **"LANGUAGE" IN INDIAN PHILOSOPHY AND RELIGION**
   Edited and Introduced by Harold G. Coward
   1978 / x + 98 pp. / $4.50 (paper)
6. **BEYOND MYSTICISM**
   James R. Horne
   1978 / vi + 158 pp. / $5.75 (paper)
7. **THE RELIGIOUS DIMENSION OF SOCRATES' THOUGHT**
   James Beckman
   1979 / xii + 276 pp. / $6.00 (paper)
8. **NATIVE RELIGIOUS TRADITIONS**
   Edited by Earle H. Waugh and K. Dad Prithipaul
   1979 / xii + 244 pp. / $6.00 (paper)
9. **DEVELOPMENTS IN BUDDHIST THOUGHT**
   Canadian Contributions to Buddhist Studies
   Edited by Roy C. Amore
   1979 / iv + 196 pp. / $6.00 (paper)
10. **THE BODHISATTVA DOCTRINE IN BUDDHISM**
    Edited and Introduced by Leslie S. Kawamura
    1981 / xxii + 274 pp. / $6.00 (paper)
11. **POLITICAL THEOLOGY IN THE CANADIAN CONTEXT**
    Edited by Benjamin G. Smillie
    1982 / xii + 260 pp. / $6.50 (paper)

1. **LA LANGUE DE YA'UDI**
   Description et classement de l'ancien parler de Zencirli dans le cadre des langues sémitiques du nord-ouest
   Paul-Eugène Dion, O.P.
   1974 / viii + 511 p. / $8.00 (broché)
2. **THE CONCEPTION OF PUNISHMENT IN EARLY INDIAN LITERATURE**
   Terence P. Day
   1982 / iv + 328 pp. / $6.00 (paper)

STUDIES IN CHRISTIANITY AND JUDAISM / ETUDES SUR LE CHRISTIANISME ET LE JUDAISME

1. **A STUDY IN ANTI-GNOSTIC POLEMICS: IRENAEUS, HIPPOLYTUS, AND EPIPHANIUS**
   Gérard Vallée
   1981 / xii + 114 pp. / $4.00 (paper)

Also published / Avons aussi publié

RELIGION AND CULTURE IN CANADA / RELIGION ET CULTURE AU CANADA
Edited by / sous la direction de Peter Slater
1977 / viii + 568 pp. / $8.50 (paper)

Available from / en vente chez:
WILFRID LAURIER UNIVERSITY PRESS
Wilfrid Laurier University
Waterloo, Ontario, Canada N2L 3C5

Published for the Canadian Corporation for Studies in Religion/ Corporation Canadienne des Sciences Religieuses by Wilfrid Laurier University Press